BEYOND THE BEATS:

ROCK & ROLL'S GREATEST DRUMMERS SPEAK!

BY JAKE BROWN

BEYOND THE BEATS: Rock & Roll's Greatest Drummers Speak!

Published by: Music Square Media/Bookmasters

Text Design by: Page Blaster Book Design

Cover Design by: Cesar A Torres & Jake Brown

Photo Contributions from Jason A. Miller, Zack Clifford, David Bergman, Robert Downs, Gabe L'Heureux, Andrew Lepley, Grady Clifford, Rocco Guarino

A CIP record for this book is available from the Library of Congress Cataloging-in-Publication Data

ISBN Perfect Bound: 978-0983471653
ISBN Case Bound: 978-0983471677

Distributed by: BOOKMASTERS

30 Amberwood Pkwy, Ashland, OH 44805

Printed and bound in Location by BOOKMASTERS

Table of Contents:

Dedication: This book is dedicated to my late Grandfather Armand Thieme for giving me my first make-shift drum set in 6th grade, composed of a bass drum and a snare drum from his hobby of clowning he took up after he retired. With that bass drum and snare drum, I began teaching myself to play by listening to many of the drummers in this book, and being an old-school man's man who truly marched to his own unique beat throughout his colorful life, this book is a salute to and celebration of that great spirit.

Thank You(s): I would first like to thank Chad Smith, Taylor Hawkins and Stephen Perkins (especially the brilliant "Ted" and "Three Days" descriptions) for signing on to this book concept, without their participation and in-depth interviews, the project never would have gotten off the ground; A special thanks to the legendary Joey Kramer and Danielle Friedman at HK Management for fitting us in! My childhood drum hero Tommy Lee for the privilege and for giving Motley fans another 10 years!; A special thanks to Lars Ulrich for the honor and Metallica's management at Q-Prime, specifically Justin D'Angelo, for helping make this happen; Many thanks to Wendy Brynford-Jones at Hello Wendy Publicity for arranging the interview with Doug 'Cosmo' Clifford, and to Doug for contributing the amazing conversation he did to this project; A BIG Thank You to Anthony Piedmonte and Paul Korzilius at Bon Jovi Management for bringing this project to Tico Torres' attention, and to Tico for making the time to be involved; Thank you to Matt Sorum for the great interview and Ace Harper for bringing the project to Matt's attention; a special thank you to Kenny Aronoff for allowing me to be your co-writer on "Sex, Drums & Rock & Roll" memoir and for contributing to this project as well; to Jimmy Chamberlin for such a great interview, both for the Tape Op feature w/Billy and here for fans; and finally to the great Steve Smith, welcome back to Journey and thank you for fitting us in for a conversation in these pages.

Thank you to my publisher/distributor BOOKMASTERS, and specifically Tim Leonhart for shepherding this through to retail; Anne Fontenaeu, Josh Stanton, et all at Blackstone Audio for believing in the series and all your hard work on the audio book side to bring this to retail; my longtime engineer Aaron Harmon; Larry, John et all at Tape Op Magazine; my accounting Rabbi, Alan Friedman; Hoyt and Tony at WNAH where I keep my office on Music Row; and anyone else I work with week in and out producing these projects and bringing them to market.

Personally, thank you to my patient wife, Carrie Brock-Brown, my best dog buddy Hannie, the best late-night writing companion I could ever ask for. To my wonderful parents, James Brown and Christina-Thieme Brown, and my brother Joshua T. Brown, my in-laws Bill and Susan Brock, the extended Thieme and Brown/Schweiss families, and the life-long clan of friends I've been lucky enough to keep close: Alex Schuchard, Andrew McDermott, Cris Ellauri, Sean Fillinich, Richard Kendrick, Adam Perri, Paul and Helen Watts, and anyone who has read my catalog over the past 45 books and 16 years! Visit me online at www.JakeBrownBooks.com or Twitter.com/jakebrownbooks

***"A 'Tommy Lee-type beat,'* that's the ultimate compliment right there!" - Tommy Lee**

"Percussion Hero!" - Blabbermouth.net

(photo by Jason Miller)

Chapter 1: Tommy Lee - Driven by Rhythm

Tommy Lee drums like a race horse runs - fierce, fast, and so powerfully that you feel every beat with equal thunder, no matter its tempo or rhythm. Truly the John Bonham of his generation, Tommy has been the backbone of Glam Metal founders Mötley Crüe for the past 35 years until the future Rock & Roll Hall of Fame inductees retired at the end of 2015 after giving a brand new generation of Millennials the thrill ride of a lifetime with the 10 years the band spent almost constantly on tour. Playing sold-out arenas to millions of new and lifelong fans around the world, Lee for decades stood out as a main attraction for what Rolling Stone highlighted as "gravity-defying drum solos" that became signature over the years. Long one of Rock & Roll's greatest showmen behind the kit, it was the theatrical side of playing that first captured Lee's imagination and drew him to the drum set as much as the instrument itself, blaming his first fan, father David Lee Thomas Bass, for originally putting the sticks in his hands:

> What really got me even playing drums at first wasn't even a performance, but my dad played drums in the Drum Core in school, and so I think its pretty much his fault for getting me interested. Then when I was 6 years old I got a snare drum only for Christmas and that was it man, once that happened, I was like "I gotta get a drum set!", and then I started checking out more drummers. There were two drummers who had the biggest early influence on me, first I got to see Tommy Aldridge play, and he was beyond drumming - grabbing cymbals and twirling sticks and so captivating to watch. I was like "Woah!", because I'd never seen anything like that, so between his style and then the sound and feel of John Bonham, those two guys are pretty much what got me fired up enough to take it on.

In an era where John Bonham's poster hung on the bedroom walls of millions of teenagers the same way guitar players like Jimmy Page usually dominated such idolizations, Led Zeppelin's drummer was a unique competitor as a showman and player, and a young Tommy Lee was wild to emulate his hero in every way he could - right down to his first real drum set. In a move that demonstrated just how specially Tommy stood out as a drummer, even before his teens, Lee had inspired not only his parents' support but his school music teacher's as strongly, to the extreme that by Junior High,

> when I was in the drum core in the marching band in school, we also had a Jazz band that had a full drum set and I was always eyeing that thing every day! So that was probably one of the first times playing with the Jazz band, and I remember the music teacher eventually letting me borrow and bring the drum kit home for the weekend! I was so stoked to play it because it was a gold metal -flaked Ludwig just like one of Bonham's.
>
> That's when I first got together with a friend who played guitar and having just drum and guitar jams and slowly creating our first band. I got in

> a couple different cover bands playing other people's music and playing with other musicians, that definitely went down, and I eventually mowed enough fucking lawns and painted houses with my uncle in the summer time, that I made enough money to put a down payment on a 8-piece Pearl drum set, with 5 toms, double bass and a snare drum! That was the first kit I ever bought.

A right-of-passage for any drummer that for Tommy, opened the gateway to now being able to devote that much more of his free time to drumming, he beams 40 years later reflecting back at the moment as one "of those you never forget, because you sit there and clean it every day, and that doesn't happen now, but its like getting a brand new car, where you say 'Oh my God!', and just sit there and look at it sometimes. That's the one I went crazy on!" Hearing by the sheer natural power his son hit the drums with that he needed a bigger space to practice in, the drummer jokes the move was also designed to get his set OUT of the house as Lee remembers his father once again stepping up and sacrificing to support his son's musical development:

> My father - and this is pretty awesome coming from a mechanic whose garage was his man cave - split his garage down the middle and gave up half the space and built me a sound-proofed room inside the garage! For a guy to do that, and he didn't want to hear me practicing all day and night, I think that was the inspiration, but for him to give up his space like that, he just knew it meant the world to me. That's pretty amazing.

Alongside playing live with other musicians, Tommy developed himself as a player by drumming along to his favorite Led Zeppelin records courtesy of a vinyl collection full of other influences that included alongside Tommy Aldridge drummers like Carmine Appice and Peter Criss. Its a method of practice Lee recommends to date as one that is invaluable for a drummer coming up in any era, so much so that he rates it as "totally essential man! I can't even tell you how much time I spent with headphones on just wailing through my favorite stuff, because you can sit there and take lessons all day long and get technically-schooled, but there's something really different about playing along and emulating some of your favorite stuff. Most of the things I've learned from playing drums to recording to producing to computer programming, you name it, I've learned more by listening, watching and doing than by any sort of technical lessons or instruction. I see something, I learn it, because I just jump on it and do it, so I would highly recommend for any young drummers, strap on some headphones and just play your favorite stuff."

Lee got just as high voltage a charge out of playing in front of crowds, and soon made his debut as a showman on the backyard Valley party scene where his father once again helped make his son's show an even bigger attraction when "he built me a drum riser for my first cover band, US 101, and he built some Pyrotechnics, and also lighting, it was the craziest shit man. He was a mechanic, so he could build or tear apart and put back together just about anything, so he got busy one day in the garage and I'll never forget sitting in the back yard lighting off these concussion bombs with puffs of smoke and the neighbors going 'What the hell's going on over there?!' It was so amazing, what a guy!"

Bouncing off the walls with the same energy his sticks did off the kit, as the drummer turned 16 eager to set his sights on the bright lights of the Sunset Strip club scene, Tommy Lee's Suite 19 soon took to the streets of Hollywood. Unaware that within a year he would be keeping the beat for a new generation of metal fans his very age as the 1980s prepared to explode, Mötley Crüe would soon come calling, catapulting Tommy's flashy, ferocious drum style onto MTV and making him a household name before his 18th birthday when *Too Fast For Love* dropped in November 1981. With kids soon covering his band's songs at the same backyard highschool parties he'd himself been playing only a couple years earlier, early Crue classics like *"Live Wire," "Piece of Your Action"* and the album's title track would soon bring Tommy to a cross-roads of finishing High School or signing a once-in-a-lifetime Major Label deal with Elektra Records at 17 years old. Not surprisingly, the latter choice proved an easy one for Lee, with his parents not surprisingly 100% in his corner.

Proving to be one himself behind the kit as the band dropped *"Live Wire,"* the single that launched Mötley Crüe on radio and video would debut what became a signature of Lee's playing - the drummer's dazzling double-bass action - where he remembers channeling rhythmic muses like "Tommy Aldridge, and another double-bass drummer that was influential for me was Alex Van Halen, Fuck, that was one of those times you never forget that shit when something like *'Eruption'* comes on the radio, I said 'What the fuck is this?!' I'd never heard a guitar like that, and that turned me on to Van Halen and listening to tracks like *'Runnin' With the Devil'* and *'You Really Got Me,'* all those amazing tracks they did. So Alex Van Halen was definitely another big influential double-bass guy for me."

One that would be copied by a cadre of drummers to follow over the next decade, Tommy's double-kick drum attack would dazzle Rolling Stone Magazine into correctly highlighting that "Lee's frenetic clatter helped define the glam-punk appeal of Mötley's debut *Too Fast for Love."* With a naturally-dead on compositional instinct already well developed by his first time laying beats down on tape, Tommy takes fans on a trip back into the writing of the Crue classic, recalling that

> when Mick started playing the riff to *"Live Wire"*, I was like "Oh shit, the riff is begging for that!", I think that came naturally, there wasn't alot of sitting around trying to figure it out. There was only one kind of thing you can do there, other than playing half-time or full time, and at that time, when you're 17 years old and making your first record, you have no fucking idea what you're doing, you're just doing it. All of us were so green, and we had zero experience in the studio so what you hear there is raw, green "Holy shit! Hang on" energy.

Bringing his heavy Bonham influence to powerfully bear in what became the band's break-out radio hit in 1983, *"Shout at the Devil"* landed Tommy on the covers of millions of vinyl album covers as well as feature coverage in drum magazines including DRUM!, who - along with a chorus of listening critics - were blown away by "the ear-popping force with which he walloped his snare and dug into his double bass drums practically leaped out the speakers on Mötley Crüe's 1983 commercial breakthrough." Any drummer's dream, Tommy got an even bigger thrill out of the opportunity to help introduce his hero to a new generation, revealing that

> I think in some unconscious way I'm always channeling Bonham, but I think something that would probably be noticeable would probably be *"Shout at the Devil"* with all the hi-hat pushes, that's a good one because its more on the funky Bonham side.

By 1986, a mere 5 years after co-founding Mötley Crüe, Tommy Lee was a household name courtesy of the millions of fans he played to after a high-profile 1983 stint opening for Ozzy Osbourne followed by a headlining arena turn on the *Theatre of Pain* tour. Thriving on raising the bar - both in his playing and live performances - Tommy would marry those ambitions beautifully in 1986's MTV smash hit video for the equally-as-popular rock radio single *"Wild Side."* Here, the drummer raised himself to the rank of # 1 showman of the year and inspire the Village Voice to conclude he would be "remembered as the guy who revolutionized the rotating drum cage." To imagine the coordination required to play upside down in a cage 30 feet above the arena audience each night without missing a beat is dizzying, and from Lee's arial perspective, he shares looking back that

> the first moving one we ever did was on the *Theatre of Pain* tour, where it tilted forward and I wanted to give the people in the audience sort of a bird's eye view of what was going on because I think that's where alot of people lose interest in the drum solo. Growing up, I'd sit there and watch these

> great drummers play while people were getting up to go get a beer or go to the bathroom, buy a T-shirt, and I'm looking around, going "Hold up, this guy's fucking whaling and people aren't paying attention!", and that gave me the idea: "Because they can't fucking see what he's doing!" The guitar player, you can see his hands and his fingers and the way he's picking his strings, but when a drummer's sitting behind a pile of drums, you don't see what his feet are doing, you don't see what his hands are doing, you don't see what the hi-hat's doing, you don't see any of that. So I thought "Why don't I tilt the drum set all the way forward so that they'll get a bird's eye view, and they'll see my feet and they'll see my hands, and will be like "Oh fuck, we get it!"
>
> That being said, the next step from pushing the drum set forward like that was for it to go all the way around, which we did on the *Girls, Girls, Girls* tour. That was just the next part of the evolution, "Okay, now let's spin this thing forwards, backwards, right, left," and that's how that all started really was with that first drum riser that just tilted forward.

Lee's driving drumming on the monster hit was just as thrilling to listen to as it was to watch, and *"Wild Side"* remains among Tommy's proudest performances within the Crüe catalog to date because of the way he expanded the genre's rhythmic boundaries to the cutting edge by bringing the latest technology in sampling - primarily reserved for Hip Hop production - into Hard Rock for among the first times it had been successful with fans. Rivaled arguably only by Mutt Lange and Def Leppard's competition, album producer Tom Werman confirms that "on the *Girls, Girls, Girls* LP, Tommy was doing some really great drum work then with triggers, loops, and things - he had electronic gizmos that he was getting into" - while Lee personally spotlights the song as an important point of origin in his innovative passion for pushing beat-making boundaries over the past 30+ years:

> That is when I started fucking with technology and started programming and sequencing things, and as one of the writers on that song, I play guitar also so I started taking guitar chunks and then programming them into 16th notes, and obviously building guitar sequence and then a drum sequence, and that's where that whole vibe started, and Mick my guitar player loved it, and that's when I started taking on some more production and injecting technology into Mötley.

Modern Drummer would rank Tommy Lee Best Hard Rock/Heavy Metal Drummer in their 1991 Reader's Poll based on his ground-breaking work behind the kit on the 10-million-selling *Dr. Feelgood*, where the drum icon's hometown paper the LA Weekly celebrated "a cavernous, sex-god drum pocket" that Lee co-created with super-producer Bob Rock, who proudly recalls today that "Metallica told me that they sought me out to produce the Black Album based on the drum sound I'd gotten for Tommy on *Dr. Feelgood*." Recreating the sonic laboratory that was Little Mountain Studios in Vancouver back in 1988 when they'd first begun building a temple of boom, Rock recalled making some rather unique adjustments to his usual micing architecture designed to handle the dynamics of Lee's natural thunder as a drummer:

> With Tommy's drumming back then, I think the big shocker was I had to open up the mics because he was such a loud hitter that he would actually compress the drums. He just hit so hard that the drum would almost compress itself, so I would have to back off the mics, and I remember doing that. It was really just a question of trying to tame that energy, and getting the right distance on the cymbal mics because of the size of the cymbals. I think the big thing with the sound of the drums on the album came in the mixing, and in the mixing, it was pretty much Tommy pushing me, and me kind of figuring out a way to make it happen. Tommy in terms of the drums, his whole thing was... basically, back then, it was the whole beginnings of hip hop, and I think bottom was becoming bigger and bigger.

Spotlighting Crüe's most popular anthem, *"Kickstart My Heart,"* as his favorite example of a song where his drums finally sounded as loud on record as they did when he played them live, Lee describes a layered - literally - pathway to reaching that nirvana that marked "the first time in Mötley's career where Bob had this really insane and new way of doing things for us that we'd never experienced. He built this bass drum tunnel, this long, round blanket tunnel with microphones at the end to kind of keep the bass drum isolated nicely, and we'd never done this before: we ran the drums through a huge fucking P.A. system that sat out on the loading dock in a separate room. And this loading dock was HUGE, so basically you were getting this live concert hall sound, and we didn't have to use reverbs or plates or any of that shit. It was just all natural, bombastic, drums flying out of a P.A. system in this big concrete loading docks that trucks back into, and we'd never done that and man, I got a taste of that and was like 'Oh my God!' We just crazy with it, and that's a really big part of the sound of that record."

Revolutionizing Hard Rock drumming with a sound that would in effect become the golden standard for Grunge-era heavy metal during the 1990s as Metallica embraced it throughout their decade-long collaboration with producer Rock, *"Primal Scream"* arguably marked Tommy coming full-circle in inheriting John Bonham's throne behind the kit as Rock & Roll's resident powerhouse player. Traveling back with fans once again to recount the legendary song's recording specifically from a rare look inside the headspace he was operating from during tracking, Lee reveals that while he was in the moment of playing, he purposely treated the studio like a stage as he recorded the song:

> You know what, I basically just go full out and let the engineers figure out how to gate and compress things so you're not physically distorting the microphone, so for me, I always just go for it. There is a threshold, I think, of when the drum and the microphone, that concussion that's happening after your stick smashes the snare drum, that sometimes doesn't sound good getting hit insanely hard. So lately I've switched to using wood sticks in the

> studio, because the aluminum ones I use live are just too much. Its almost like distortion, and that's cool if you're going for that effect, but there's too much concussion and sound pressure level for some microphones before they start crapping out.

The roaring lion of the album was the title cut, where Mick Mars' guitars rocketed off in the song's opening riff stabs, and Tommy rocked the pocket with what Rolling Stone Magazine registered as an "earth-shaking beat that powered *Dr. Feelgood's* title track...(to sound) as menacing and overwhelming as that song's tales of drug-fueled Eighties decadence." As Lee's exclusive producer for 7 years between 1989 and 1995, Bob Rock became an expert study of Tommy's continuing maturation as a player, watching his talent grow bored easily as the drummer pushed for higher heights to take his playing to. Proving an infectious energy within Mötley Crüe that propelled the band into some of their bravest experimental territory yet musically throughout the 1990s, it came with the producer's memory that Tommy was often a driving creative force:

> I think what Tommy always brought to Motley was pushing the muso-quality of the band. He was always trying to push, like with the different beats. For instance, with *Dr. Feelgood*, things got a little funkier. I think, in terms of the rhythms and stuff before, it had always been pretty straight-ahead. So all of a sudden with Feelgood, Tommy sort of broke away from what had been their traditional drumming sound. So Tommy was always pushing that aspect of it.

The drummer's next expansion as a player took Lee on what he - and many of the group's hardcore fans - still consider to be their boldest territory yet as Mötley sewed their full Zeppelin roots as a band the eponymous *'94* album. With Vince Neil temporarily out of the vocal fold in favor of bluesy, rootsier rocker John Corabi, Tommy listening back still holds the album high as his truest tribute to Bonham, agreeing that "I think where its really prevalent is the self-titled Motley Crue record we did when we had John Corabi singing.

That record is still today one of my favorites sonically-sounding and the best performances recorded, are on that record by far. So there's alot of channeling going on on that one."

Lee would meet his next producer-muse in Scott Humphrey during the making of Mötley's *'94* album, marking the embarking of a partnership between the drummer's desire to bring technology into his beat-making process in visionary ways and Humphrey's technical and musical know-how to pull it off as one of a small club of digitally-savvy producers already operating within the Protools realm back when it was still strictly an editing platform. Inventing a hybrid together out of their collaboration on the *Quaternary* E.P. with *"Planet Boom"* that would debut the Rock-tronica sub-genre Lee co-founded, he remains proud of the song today as an true articulation of his driving doctrine, not just as a drummer, but as a producer, songwriter, multi-instrumentalist and innovator:

> Rhythm is a language to me and I wanted to communicate that in this new form. Bob at the time knew that each guy in the band wrote music, and he heard some demos from me and some from Nikki and Mick and Corabi and was like, "I got a fucking idea! Let's put you guys all in the studio on your own with no help from me or anybody, you guys just all go off and do your thing," and there was an excellent Protools editor at the time, Scott Humphrey, and we just freaked out, I said "I wanna make a song about rhythm, and what it does to you and how it makes you feel," and that's when 'Planet Boom' came from.
>
> **Co-Producer Scott Humphrey:** We were specifically trying to do something different, that no one'd really done before, we were trying to merge together technology at the time, electronica, and mix that with heavy guitars. I think that's what Tommy and I were trying to do with the Barbed Wire soundtrack, with *"Planet Boom."* We really early on started doing that, going well 'Lets put drum loops, electronic sequencers, and heavy guitars together.' And it was like the first song- the Tommy Lee single on that

> *Barbed Wire* soundtrack, was really the first time I tried to force all those elements together, and try to make sense out of it.

Demonstrating for the first time the full, untapped dimensions of Tommy's talent as a rhythm-master regardless of its stylistic frame, *"Planet Boom"* was the drummer's big bang moment musically as his mind began racing on hyper-speed toward a new frontier he'd arguably been trying to reach for years. Finally, technology had caught up and it was here that Lee would find the true nerve center of his creative renaissance to follow, starting with his elevation to co-producer alongside Humphrey on *Generation Swine,* where their evolving Rock-tronica sound defined the album's full sonic scope as the drummer synergized his love for

> listening to alot of different styles of music, and the one music that's inspired me sonically to make things sound better is electronic music, and there's certain frequencies in electronic music that just aren't in acoustic music, its impossible, its synthesis, wave forms, and bass drums don't make sounds below 40 hertz, but electronic bass drums will go down to 30 and 20 and those move rooms! Its so low to where they're almost inaudible, where you can't hear them, you can just feel them. So I've always been searching for things that just sound incredible, and playing with synthesizers, and programming and learning what's out there: "Like, Oh my God, I didn't know you could do that, shit!", and then I'll apply it and bring that technology into Motley, so its been a constant to always try and kick things up a bit and modern-sounding, and alot of that's come from electronic music and my programming and knowledge of what's out there and what can be done and can't be done.

Taking that sound on the road would prove another challenge Lee was eager to conduct in context of the symphony of triggers, programmed and live drums he would have to hit at once as he brought the brilliant Frankenstein that was the sci-fi rhythm section of *Generation Swine* to life on stage. Alongside the technical heights he pulled off each night, Lee got his biggest kick out of the organic way the band ended each show with the biggest BALLS Rock had seen period since Eddie Vedder climbed into the rafters during the live *"Even Flow"* video when fans were invited to join Mötley onstage during the climactic performance of *"Helter Skelter."* A once-in-a-lifetime fan moment this author experienced personally climbing onto the stage of the dead-of-winter Peoria, Illinois show I'd driven 7 hours to see, as I and tens of thousands of other Crüeheads danced like banshees around the bonfire Tommy was lighting behind the kit, from the drummer's perspective looking outward, Lee describes it to date as a singular rush in his storied live career as a player:

> Man, we used to love that part of the show where we'd bring everybody up onstage, there's nothing better than that, because over the years, the stages get bigger and taller and you get further away from everybody. But there's nothing better than being face to face with somebody that's losing their fucking mind right there standing next to you where you can actually feel the power of everything when you're that close and the energy just comes flying off of everything. So yeah, that was our favorite shit ever man, I loved that - eventually we had to stop doing it for insurance purposes, BUT it was fun why it lasted! (laughs)

So was the iconic drummer's 18 year stint with Mötley Crüe when he decided to fully spread his wings creatively in 1999 to launch a solo career, the kind of gamble that 99% of drummers wouldn't have dared without keeping their signature band as a safety net of sorts. Tommy dove headfirst into the unknown with a method for the musical mayhem that would follow, producing a hybrid masterpiece that Lee candidly confirms was a "brainchild that came when I quit Mötley Crüe, because at the time I was going through some crazy shit and I wasn't happy kind of doing the same old thing, and I told the guys, 'Hey man, I gotta bail, creatively I'm fucking dying, and I understand Mötley Crüe is something everybody knows and loves,' and they're really careful about flying off in different directions, and I was like 'Creatively, as an artist, I'm slowly dying and I need to do this,' so they were like 'Totally understand, fucking go for it, good luck!', and so I bailed and was on a mission man. I was like 'I wanna create something that's an event record with a bunch of people I've always wanted to work with,' and started writing music for it, and something would come up where I'd say 'Oh, this would be perfect for Fred Durst, or George Clinton, or Lil Kim on *'Get Naked,'* or 'This would be killer for the guys in the Wu-Tang Clan,' and I had a bunch of friends who were people I always wanted to work with and this was my opportunity to basically have a full-on creative free-for-all. There were no rules, anything went, and there was never anyone who said, 'Oh, I don't know about that,' because there was just me, there was no other chefs in the kitchen. Whatever we wanted to do we did, it was fucking wild!" Elaborating on his own internally eclectic songwriting process, Lee - who famously had a habit of calling his answering machine from LA County Jail throughout the summer of 1999 to record demo ideas when they'd hit him in his cell - reveals that more generally,

> alot of times, song idea comes with just sort of noodling around on the guitar, not necessarily hearing it already, but just sitting there playing and I'll come up with something and say "Ooh shit, that's nice," and record that. Alot of times, song ideas will come from a certain beat or feel, and then I'll start figuring out what goes on top of that. Sometimes they come with a lyrical idea... They come to me in such random fucking ways man, its never really the same either, it just starts to happen, and sometimes its drums, sometimes its guitar, another time its a cool melody stuck in my head.

As Lee's co-pilot behind the console, co-producer Scott Humphrey - whose Chop Shop recording studio served as ground zero for the musical madness going down on Protools - recalled pushing the new digital recording and editing platform to its cutting edge as "I kind of took Tommy's demos and expanded from that point. We got his demos, and played over top them, and took the best of, so it was a combination of taking drum loops, electronic stuff, and then picking out a bunch of things I liked, and then he played a bunch of live passes, and then we sat down and looked at what sounded best, what was working the best. From section to section it might vary, one section might be totally programmed, and he might come in with a live fill leading into the next section with all live drums. I think I've done it both ways, where I've recorded the band live, and then later on put loops or samples over top of it. Rhythmically, he has a way of injecting his rhythm, natural rhythmic syncopation, where he could take something that's really flat sounding and turn it around and make it sound like a hook."

Lee's hometown LA Times later congratulated the drummer for taking the risk of his professional career given the celebrity capital he'd have had to spend no matter what he debuted with, celebrating his success at passing the ultimate test of trying his sound out live, where "his new band Methods of Mayhem made music that was frenetic, funky, loud and aggressively contemporary...The sound was part metal, part funk, with sudden pop flourishes, all riding a hard, relentless beat from former Jane's Addiction drummer Stephen Perkins. Even amid the storm of energy and noise, many of the songs were dramatic and melodic." Perkins spoke exclusively about the thrill of the challenge as he put Lee's collage of programmed and live drum performances side-by-side with a peer whose ability he clearly respected as a player:

> I didn't record with Tommy, but as soon as I heard the recording – which was prior to its release – and then I heard Tommy was looking for a drummer, talk about excitement for me as a drummer, I was fucking gushing because I love Tommy. How many drummers have sat next to him day after day, hour after hour, night after night playing double drummers, I'm one of maybe none.

A theme that began to emerge during the early 2000s as the reverberation of Tommy's influence as a inspiration to a younger generation of drummers was one Modern Drummer Magazine certified in 2004 when they noted that "like Ringo Starr in the '60s and Peter Criss in the '70s, Lee was a player who inspired a lot of young people to take up the drums." That clout would continue with an entirely new Millennial era of Rock & Roll fans who soon had the chance to see Tommy behind the kit where his singular sound as a player and flair as a performer would prove the main draw to what became the biggest reunion tour of the mid-Millennium. Giving fans the gift of a lifetime when Mötley Crüe took their Carnival of Sins tour on the road to $39 million in ticket sales in 2005/2006 and over a million fans world-wide, the band instantly became one of the hottest acts on the arena touring circuit for the next decade.

Dazzling millions of fans and critics alike as Lee re-established his relevance as one of Rock & Roll's most commanding showmen, Drum! Magazine 3 short years later in 2009 hailed Tommy as "the most entertaining rock drummer in the world...Supporting musicians simply disappear when they step on stage with Tommy Lee's bombastic bravado," while the New York Times in 2008 highlighted from the band's sold-out show at Madison Square Garden that "Lee brought a brute, vivid style to" his astonishing live performances. That consummate showmanship drew the awe-struck UK Daily Mail in 2012 to rave that "on stage, Tommy Lee has become famous for his drum stunts, which have included being suspended above the crowd, flying from one drum kit to another, and with the help of magician David Copperfield, making the drum kit levitate and explode while he played."

Beyond the theatrics of his nightly drum performances, Tommy got an equal kick out of the opportunity to modernize drum parts from 25 years ago and bring them current, reasoning that the re-invention was "by design, and its just by evolution because I'm constantly trying to update or modernize or make the feel better if I can, because once again, I was 17 when we recorded *'Too Fast for Love'* and it does have that wonderful, raw, adolescent energy, but over time you become a better player, and when I look back now, I'm like 'Aw man, I could have played that so much better now!' *'Shout at the Devil'* is an example of a song we remixed and re-recorded, and so I'm constantly modernizing and making it as good as I can possibly make it. "

Rhythm Magazine ranked Lee # 30 on their Top 50 Drummers of All Time list in 2010 in his late 40s, where hitting with the same power as he did as a 20-something on song after song required the kind of peak physical conditioning typically reserved for Olympian athletes. Confessing that the physical rigors of bringing the kind of sheer force of energy to the drums he did each night playing Mötley hits requires an unsexy discipline that behind the scenes defied many of the *"Sex, Drugs and Rock & Roll"* pillars of the Crüe's previous tours, Tommy argues that because

> drumming is such a fucking crazy physical sport, its really more a sport than it is musical I think, its super-physical, super-demanding, and if you're not in shape, that's not good. I was really curious one day - you'll like this story, its fucked up - and was like, "I'm going to grab one of those jogging pedometers," the ones you clip onto your tennis shoe when you're jogging and it tells you how far you've gone. Well, I clipped one on at the beginning of a show, played the show, and at the end was like, "I'm really curious..." and the thing read 12.3 miles!
>
> I'm on the skinnier side and eat like crazy, but I don't ever gain any weighty and I was always wondering, "Is there something wrong with me?", because I couldn't put on weight if I tried, and then I realized, "Dude, you're running like 12 to 15 miles every day and sweating everything out." So when I'm on tour, I don't really do any sort of exercise because I have that. When I get off tour, I get myself back in the gym and have to get it out in another way, but drumming is CRAZY physical man.

So dedicated to his job that he's even played through nights over the last 10 years Mötley Crüe toured the world where - in pushing himself to the extreme for the fans - MTV reported during the height of the Carnival of Sins tour, Lee had even begun "receiving anti-inflammatory injections to help him manage tendonitis in his right wrist," continuing such treatments into his early 50s as necessary to keep up with the demands of drumming with as much thunder through each and every show. Offering a rare look inside what that grind physically felt like from the top of a tour through the long slog to the finish line, Tommy begins with a bit of self-deprecation:

> My hands, man at the start of a tour, I call them "Girl Hands" when you don't have calluses built up, and they're all soft and nice because they haven't really done much, and then you start rehearsing for a tour and, oh man, here come the blisters, followed by the calluses, and once the hands get nice and hard, then you can fucking wail. But then what happens after that is those other problems arise where you're hurting yourself and you don't even know it every night, and Tendinitis flairs up because you're basically giving your wrists a fucking pounding! People who get that kind of stuff are roofers swinging hammers all day or someone hitting a baseball with a bat, those kind of physical either work or sports, get those kind of injuries, and so do drummers. Then I'm sitting there saying, "God dammit, why am I getting Tendinitis?", and its like "Well, because you're being a fucking maniac dude!"

When he hasn't been on stage with the Crue over their last 10 years together, often while on tour nights off, Lee has used the geographic advantage to indulge his favorite non-drumming musical past-time with DJing. Spinning alongside DJ Aero - and at times expanding their troupe to include superstars Deadmau5 and Steve Duda - before crowds at the biggest dance clubs around the country, including Belo and The Big Bang in San Diego, Crash Mansion in Los Angeles, Tentation in Orange County, the Congress Theatre, MID and Aragon Ballroom in Chicago, Pacha in New York City, Le Breton Festival Park in Ottawa, The Fillmore in Detroit, Michigan, the Palladium Ballroom in Dallas, TX, the Great Northern in San Francisco, Tommy has also visited foreign destinations like European Festivals co-headlining with Crystal Method, and even a cruise featuring the DJing elite, including Fatboy Slim, Shrillex, Diplo, and Soulwax. Hardly a token presence in the DJ booth, Tommy prides himself on treating DJing just as seriously as any other instrument he plays, while making the important distinction that

> for me is such a fucking awesome animal, its totally different than anything else I do whether its in the studio or playing drums live, its more of like just totally for fun and there's nothing more I enjoy than seeing people having fun and dancing. So whether its making some dance music or selecting stuff that I know makes me crazy and makes me move, I feel like I have a nice barometer for what moves people, just from being a drummer, and it is so fun to add electronic beats in between beats that are coming from the turn-tables, and add percussion in. Its really just a big giant tribal drum jam for me, and of course those big, sub-sonic bass lines and drums, I just lose my mind dude!

Respected across the stylistic spectrum, Tommy was tapped in 2014 by Smashing Pumpkins mastermind Billy Corgan to play drums on the band's Monuments to an Elegy album after the frontman felt he couldn't achieve the sound he was hearing in his head with any other hitter. It was a phone call that the drummer took as "a great compliment man! When I played drums on the new Smashing pumpkins record, once we started the process over here, it was really funny because Billy Corgan came over to my studio to play me the demos, and he tells me the story as they were sitting there working on these demos, Billy had looked over at his guitar player and goes, 'Fuck man, this needs that Tommy Lee groove on this shit!', and his guitar player looks at him and goes, 'Why don't you call him?' and he did!" Elaborating on what new energy and rhythmic foundational elements Lee brought into the Pumpkins' sound that satisfied what Corgan felt were missing without him, the frontman shares exclusively that

> what was exciting about bringing in Tommy Lee was there were moments on Monuments that, even though it sounds like the Smashing Pumpkins, it doesn't sound like any Smashing Pumpkins that came before, and it has everything to do with Tommy. I think it was the combination of our producer Howard Willing and space. Howard was in the modern world, I think his favorite artist is Taylor Swift, and so to Howard, production is always whatever people are listening to, and that doesn't mean he has shitty

taste. He wants the best version of that. So there was a lot of discussion of how to make Rock music but also how to make Rock music with space, and in that way, Tommy is antithetical to the way Jimmy plays. Tommy is attracted to space where Jimmy is attracted to filling up the space, but there's no loss of power.

Tommy Lee: Doing Billy's record for me was such a cool experience because stylistically, fuck man, I put on a couple different hats, because all of a sudden, I'm playing this crazy Prog Rock stuff that I don't typically play much of, and it was such a challenge for me to come up with some really cool parts and make it Smashing Pumpkins but also leave my imprint. So that was a really challenging record and I love being challenged, so I want to thank Billy for that. He's a real stickler for not editing, so we would go for the ultimate performance from top to bottom, no edits. You know what, there's nothing better than when I'm cutting drums, right, and I can see Billy through the glass, and to watch him jumping up and down dancing around like a little fucking kid when I nail a track, saying "That is fucking amazing!", it doesn't get any better than that.

Lee's recent thrill rides behind the kit included the realization of a life-long dream in 2015 to bring a real roller coaster drum set on the road with him for Mötley Crüe's final tour, which the Hollywood Reporter in animated detail described as "the much hyped 360-degree drum roller coaster that stick man Tommy Lee rides during one segment, even playing upside down as he's strapped in to the coaster, before then bringing a fan up from the audience to take a ride on his 'abusement park,' as Lee dubbed it." Admitting that taking in its actual physical size and scope blew Tommy away once he laid eyes on his invention debuting before live audiences for the first time in Rock & Roll drum history, Rolling Stone added depth to that perspective with their 2015 report that the "experience is delivered via a massive operation that travels from town to town in 12 trucks and nine buses, overseen by a crew of close to 100 people (as well as an extra hundred or so local stage hands at each stop)." A farewell fitting for the apex Lee was sitting atop at this point in his career after 35 years as one of Rock's TOP DRAW drummers, he still remembers feeling a rush of reality hit him when he laid eyes on the monster he'd created:

> The Roller Coaster drum set we finally did on the last Mötley Tour, that was one of those things where I'd been sitting there for years saying, "One day we're going to fucking do this roller coaster...", and that one day came at the top of Mötley's final tour, when I said "We GOTTA fucking do it!", and the band was like "Yep, we gotta do it!" So we started designing it, and you can imagine, when you look at a schematic or a diagram of a drawing, you'd be sitting there going, "Oh, this is going to be fucking bad ass!" Then that day comes after a couple months, the thing gets built and you walk in and see it in person for the first time and its WAY fucking bigger than you ever imagined - where you're actually shitting yourself going "What have I done? " and "Am I going to be able to pull this shit off every night?" I had that moment where I was like "Uh oh, uh oh, maybe we've gone too big dude, this is fucking nuts!"

With LA Weekly knighting him Rock & Roll Royalty in 2014 via their decree that "with the exception of maybe Keith Moon, no other drummer gives off the giddy mojo of his grooves in quite the same way, even amidst pyro, props and his bandmates' attention-whorish antics," Tommy reveals that vs. being aware of audience's "oohs" and "ahhs" throughout his routinely-sensational performances, from behind the drum kit,

> to be really honest with you, and this happens from the time the lights go out, I go to some other place, I don't even know where it is, but I really don't see people, I hear them, but I don't see them, and honestly I don't really see any of that till the very last song and things slow down for me and I look around and go "Woah, look at all these fucking people!" Its funny, I must just kind of check out because honestly, because if you're spinning round and you're focused on the crowd, you're going to get disoriented and that

> can fuck you up! Its weird, I go into some zone, put my head down and I don't really come up for air until the show's almost over.

Hailed in the band's critical coda by longtime fan Rolling Stone Magazine - who'd first recognized Lee's unique energy and sound as a drummer back in 1987 when they first starred him on one of their coveted covers alongside his Mötley Crüe bandmates - 30 years later as "one of metal's truly great showmen," in reflecting back personally on the one of a kind adventure that has been his life behind the beat, Lee does so proudly: "Its all been such an amazing roller coaster ride, the whole time with Motley's just been... I don't know anybody else whose had 35 years of so much fun, success, excess, its been fucking amazing!" Along with fulfilling his drum theme ride dream, for Tommy, the biggest thrill of the band's live swan song was sharing it with fans around the world over 164 shows in 72 markets that grossed over $100 million. It was a measure both of how many millions of multi-generational Crüeheads around the world their music had a permanent place with, but equally, how strongly that music had held up throughout the band's decades of decadence:

> This last final tour - don't get me wrong, I've loved them all - but I think on this one was really cool because everyone was just in a different mindset like, "Man, this is the last time us four guys are going to go around and play for these fans," and going around the world and playing the last night in Japan, the last night in Australia, the last night in all the different countries in Europe, it starts to hit you: "Holy shit man, this is wild to share so many years and so many experiences with four guys, and all of a sudden, its coming to an end." We got along better, because everybody knew it was coming to an end, so I think these last two years on the final tour have been enjoyable and extremely memorable. I'll never forget what we just did and what we've done.

As his beat goes on, Lee looks forward with a sense of closure toward Mötley Crüe's chapter in his musical life that has given him the freedom to "definitely have alot of fires in the oven," including producing his fiancée, German vocalist Sofi Toufa's upcoming album, and co-producing a hip, eclectic collection of singles including *"Fly Shit"* by Nick Thayer, *"Bettie"* by Violet Chachki - which reached # 5 on the iTunes U.S. Dance Chart - and *"Raw"* by The Ugly Beatroots. A passion that fuels Lee's fire to pioneer into new creative frontiers, while still allowing him the ability tap into decades of hit record-making studio experience to back it up, Tommy continues to be the captain of his own momentum, motivated at this point by the simple thrill of

> helping somebody get their visions down on tape, there's nothing better or more satisfying - especially when someone trusts you, and all of a sudden they say "Oh my God, this sounds better than I could have even imagined." I just did a remix for singer from Buckcherry and the guitar player Stevie, they're doing an electronic project, so they sent a song over to me and I whipped a remix on it, and they were like "Oh my God dude, that's how we wanted the fucking song to sound! Fuck, you nailed it!" There's nothing better than that feeling, because I'm thinking, "This is how I would make it sound, I hope you guys like it," and their reaction is "That's fucking insane!" So I definitely want to do some more of that because that was really a joy for me, I loved it, to try and take something that's already there and make it fucking killer!

These days, whenever he gets hit up by someone from his considerable social media following - which boasts over a half-million on Twitter, nearly a million on Facebook and Instagram close to 300,000 among other popular platforms - for advice on how to break into the business as a beat-maker, Tommy takes it back long before the legend to the same golden, old-school tricks with the sticks that first helped him find his own uncommon time:

> Everybody's different and inspired differently. How it was for me in the beginning, everything I could get my hands on was experience, and then all of a sudden you'll be in a situation where you're like "Oh, I got this shit,

I did this already," so experience is priceless. Another key for me as a kid to develop as a player was the fact that I was constantly trying to play with other guys, in cover bands, etc. So absolutely get involved, get your hands on anything and everything if you can, and another thing, I would say to any drummer out there: DON'T JUST BE A DRUMMER. Be an entertainer, be a songwriter, be a producer, be everything, why not? That's the way I always went to everything.

"Honestly, I can't say that *'One'* is more of a highlight than *'Fade to Black,'* most of the songs still evoke the same passion and energy up on stage." – Lars Ulrich

(photo by Jason Miller)

Chapter 2: Lars Ulrich of Metallica – Ride the Lightning

Its rare that a genre of music is defined in one of its rhythmic signatures by a single drummer's style: John Bonham did it with Led Zeppelin, Ringo Starr with the Beatles, Charlie Watts with the Rolling Stones, Neal Peart with Rush, and without a doubt, Lars Ulrich with Metallica, who pioneered the double-bass sound in metal. Modest at the mention of such comparisons, Lars is willing to give himself this much credit when it comes to maintaining the same authentic energy behind the kit that he did at 22, joking that,

> the one thing you have to remember is when you're playing these songs, it doesn't get any easier as you get older, that I can tell you. So obviously, the physical demand stays as intense as ever, but what I love about playing is this incredible, moment where you're really, really locked into what's going

> on: every beat, every cymbal hit, every nuance, every accent, every kind of moment you're locked in.
>
> To me, playing live is like Sports. When you're over 35, you move into a different league, and when you're over 45, you're a Senior. There's none of that in music, so its not like if you're over 45, you get a hall pass, and you can start playing at a different level of intensity. Especially when you have Lamb of God and Machinehead opening up for you, so you have to go out there each show and throw it down to the best of your ability, and keep it up. So at 50, 51, the physical side of it is just something that becomes more and more paramount, and it gets treated more and more with the respect it deserves. When we were 30 years old, after a show, we could drink Yagermeister till 6 in the morning, and now its like, "Okay, it's a show-day tomorrow, got to get some sleep," and we actually have 2 guys who travel with us that are literally full-time trainers, its like a sports-team backstage.
>
> We have massage tables, and nasty-smelling shit that they rub into our sore muscles, and little fucking heating pads that go on, its at that level, so the physical element of what we do, because we still play 2:15 a night generally, and to be 51 playing this stuff, it takes more concentration and more preparation, and the last hour, hour-and-a-half before showtime is nothing but stretching and warming up on the tread-mill, all that type of stuff.

Celebrated as one of metal's heaviest hitters throughout his career, from the first time his sticks struck lightning behind the kit, Ulrich has been riding a wave of his own invention, pushing the dynamics and speed of the drums in a power pocket with lead singer/rhythm guitarist James Hetfield that Billboard argued thirty years later would "change the face of music forever." Seeking to *Kill 'Em All* with a sound that, at just 19 years old, Ulrich was inventing as he went along, and he remembered feeling instinctively that he needed to head in the opposite direction of the competition on the Sunset Strip:

> One thing I think a lot of the drummers in L.A. were doing at the time – guys we would go see in the clubs, they were playing very on TOP of the beat, very lead-footed, and four-on-the-floor, that kind of Hollywood kind of drumming. But the stuff that came out of England, it had kind of a different flavor to it, different fills, different attitudes, the snare drum had a tendency to be a little bit further back behind the beat, like Phil Rudd or Charlie Watts-style. So that was kind of the thing that turned me on, was the stuff that we were more trying to emulate the first couple go-arounds.

Serving up a powerful opening ball with *"Seek and Destroy,"* the first track they recorded for their debut album, Rolling Stone Magazine would credit the band with establishing "a vital new subgenre, known as speed metal or thrash metal. As pioneered by Metallica, it was a hybrid of punk and metal, distinguished by lightning speed, manic rhythm changes." As he created from behind the kit, Ulrich remembered channeling one of the band's principle muses, Motorhead, into a forceful drive that, for the drummer,

> was at that time, with Motorhead and Phil Taylor, about playing tasty kind of things that sort of support the music, and I slowly started getting into the double-bass and sort of riding those 16th notes, but it wasn't all the stuff that like these guys in L.A. were doing twirling their sticks, and all that kind of stuff. Everything we were doing was trying to be the opposite of that. We were also listening a lot to Merciful Fate, the first year when we were writing, and certainly I think some of the slower songs we were doing like *"Seek and Destroy"* and *"The Four Horsemen"* and so on, so where the faster songs on *"Kill Em All"* came from like Motorhead, the slower songs came more from like Merciful Fate and Diamond Head and so on, and just kind of keeping a steady groove.

Taking fans further back into the belly of his roots as a child growing up where one of his first rhythmic exposures was the sound of a tennis ball bouncing off his racket, it could be argued that Ulrich's back-hand as a world-ranked child tennis star helped harness the power of his snare/tom hits. Still, as a kid, Ulrich quipped that his discovery of the instrument "wasn't this cosmic moment or anything like that." More a go-to outlet from the stresses of following in his father's footsteps playing competitive tennis, the drummer shares that

> back then, Tennis was more my primary thing where it was like carry on the family business, and music was more my hobby. So me and my friends would get together and hang out and listen to music, and pretend like kids do that we were playing band, or *playing rock group* as we called it. And I had a foosball table that was like the keyboards, and a couple tennis rackets that were guitars, and a broom shaft that was the lead vocal stand, and I always was the one that grabbed the cardboard boxes and found some paint brushes and those would be drum sticks, and then we would literally turn the heat up to 10 down in my basement on the old radiators, put Deep Purple's *Maiden Japan* on and pretend that we were Deep Purple for hours on end.
>
> There was a lot of music around me when I was growing up in Copenhagen, Denmark. My family was primarily in Tennis, but my Dad – Tennis was like his day job, his primary gig – but music was his passion. Music was his love, and he actually used to write reviews of Jazz music for Danish newspapers, so there were a lot of people coming through the house when I was around 10 years old, a lot of musicians. And we would end up in my Dad's music room upstairs on the 3rd Floor, and would listen to anything from Miles Davis to John Coltrane, to at that time Jimi Hendrix or The Doors, or The Stones, any of that kind of stuff. So there was a lot of music always around me, and I started kind of getting into some more British pop music that was on the radio when I 10, 11, like Sweet and Slade and Status Quo, and started listening to Deep Purple in 73, 74, 75.
>
> So probably around the time I was 12, after I'd taken guitar lessons for a year or two, I just started getting more and more into the drums. I remember I was hanging out with my Grandma, and I think that Grandparents, one of

> their primary functions is you can sort of beg them for anything you can't get anywhere else, so I have a pretty clear vision of being down on my knees in front of my Grandma begging her for a drum kit. And low and behold, shortly thereafter there was a drumkit that showed up, it was modeled after Ian Pace and John Coghlan, who was the drummer for Status Quo, so it was like one bass drum, one rack tom, two floor toms, and was kind of a mismatch of different things. Most of the kit had this odd, abstract crème-color to it, and I got it in probably 76 or so, and I had a music room down in my basement where it was set up along with my record player, and I would sit up and try to play along to Deep Purple and Black Sabbath records, the Uriah Heep, Sweet, stuff like that. Drumming was really my escape from Tennis back then.

Like so many children of the 70s raised on the first wave of Heavy Metal, Lars went seeking to ride one of his own in 1980 when he crossed the Atlantic, moving from Europe to America, and opening the young drummer's ears to a whole new world of possibilities where finding his true calling as a player was concerned: whether he was meant to spend his professional career using his arms to swing Tennis Rackets or Drum Sticks? Fortunately for millions of metal fans and the countless drummers he'd go on to inspire, he chose the latter, recalling a pivotal shift in focus happening at 17 right at the height of his teenage sports career:

> Fast-forwarding a couple of years to 1980, I moved to America and my object was to move to the U.S. and keep playing Tennis at a high school in Newport Beach, California. In the Spring of 1981, the try-outs for the team were going on when I was a Junior, and in Denmark, I was ranked in the Top 10 in my age-group in the country and came from a pretty prominent Tennis-playing family. But what happened at the try-outs was I actually didn't make the team, because I wasn't one of the 7 best Tennis players at that highschool. That really threw me for a fucking loop, it was like such a seminal moment where, more or less, I kind of walked away from Ten-

> nis right there and then, and drumming and music was kind of right there hovering, or bubbling under, and so I a drum kit in Newport Beach and started playing along to my Iron Maiden and Saxon and Motorhead records, and then started reaching out to other musicians and James Hetfield showed up in my life, and there you go.

Setting the pulse of a untapped fanbase off racing along with the music they made, a new style that Rolling Stone Magazine at the time called "refreshing and revelatory" was born in the creative core of Hetfield and Ulrich as a rhythm section. As they began exploring a unique metal sound that only happened when their musical forces collided playing together, Lars remembered answering what the BBC highlighted as James' mastery at "establishing; maintaining and manipulating musical tension and mood" within his riffs with as much attitude in his beats as he could throw back at Hetfield:

> When it was just James and I in the early days, James was a pretty gifted guitar and a pretty gifted piano player, he was a pretty gifted musician. I had a lot of passion and a lot of the kind of get-up-and-go energy and spark, but I wasn't particularly schooled in music, I just wanted to play and kind of enveloped myself in everything. So we were kind of Ying and Yang, and so we would sit with these records and be inspired by all these different things, and the first thing that we did was to try to emulate a lot of what really turned us on. It was all about the song, it was all about the riff, the attitude and energy, it wasn't about showmanship chops, all that stuff, it didn't interest us at all. A lot of the metal bands we were inspired by at the time, the new wave of British metal bands, they were all kind of influenced by the punk movement, which was kind of being down to earth and all that kind of dirty, punky shit.
>
> So it wasn't about "Look how good of a drummer or guitar player I am," because all the stuff that was turning us on, the attitude was: its not about ability, its not about any of that kind of stuff. Its about the attitude, its

> about being connected to the people that you were sharing the music with. It was all about the group experience, group mentality, that was the first year really when we were still writing into 1982. So the main thing was the riff, the song, all that type of stuff, so we didn't sit there and try to be all fancy or showy, none of that type stuff interested us. We were just trying to write the heaviest songs with the best riffs and the most attitude that we could at the time,

Riding the lightning that Hetfield fed him off the fret board, Lars would throw thunder back at him with beat bolts that remained as basic but still bold and powerful as possible, reinforcing the foundation they'd laid for the first time in metal history. Staying true on their sophomore album to the band's constant ambition in their early days cutting edges together behind the drums and guitars to

> just try to do different stuff and broaden our horizons, and cover different territory. That was not an easy one to track! (laughs) I think that that song is a particularly good example of to me how our songs kind of have their own life. That song, when I listen to the studio version, all the fills are different, its almost like the whole feel of the song is different, because at that time, that's kind of what we felt the song called for.
>
> *"For Whom the Bell Tolls"* stands out in particularly too because we had made *Kill Em All* and were half-way through recording *Ride the Lightning,* and when we got to *"Bell Tolls,"* it was the first song I ever played click-track to in the studio, so that was a particularly awkward studio experience. It was half-notes on the hi-hat, and a little bit slower than a lot of the other songs, so any kind of discrepancy in the tempo were obviously a lot more noticeable, and our producer Flemming Rasmussen suggested we try to record to a click, and I'm pretty sure that every drummer can tell you their first time that you experience the confinement of a click track is a particularly awkward situation.

"For Whom the Bell Tolls" became Metallica's contribution to the sports arena soundtrack, made a permanent part of the audience experience, a reflection of Ulrich's mastery at creating personalities within his beats that expertly fit the specific lyrical and musical moods of partner James Hetfield's songwriting. It's a musical personality that Lars has in fact seen grow over the years after maturing with the many generations of the band's audience,

> We tried to always let our songs breathe, and let ourselves kind of develop over the years, so 30 years later or whatever, that song's got its own thing now, a different kind of vibe and different fills and different things happening all over when I play that song. If you listen to the version in the "Through the Never" movie, its dramatically different experience than on the *Ride the Lightning* record. So I'm proud of the fact that all these songs sort of keep evolving and doing their own thing.

Chugging into the mid-1980s, the band's brand of sophisticated speed metal was continuing its journey taking the genre at large into new musical directions it hadn't yet explored before Metallica first roared onto the scene. Now with the world's full attention, the band pushed its pioneering sound toward a new nexus of innovating and influence as their revolutionary soundscapes spread out in such musical aspects as length and speed, they pushed the boundaries of the genre of speed metal itself outward. In the process, the band earned respect across the stylistic spectrum with music critics like Spin Magazine, who – importantly – recognized at the time that "few heavy-metal bands that play as intensely as Metallica are as open-minded." Traveling back in his own to the work going on behind the scenes as he and Hetfield banged away shaping this shift in the evolution of the band's sound through a tried-and-true science of jamming ideas together that Lars remembered was a daily practice where

> during the recording of both *Ride the Lightning* and *Master of Puppets*, most of those songs were written out of jams between James and I, or riffs, James would play a riff and I would kind of kick in, or I'd play a drum beat and

> James would start riffing over it. He and I used to live together in the house between all those years, 1983 to 1986, and we would just go out in the garage and start writing, and then the other guys would just sort of show up at different times, but most of the time, it always started with James and I.

Accelerating the band's musical velocity to rates that broke all previous metal sound barriers and sent a millions head banging from the opening strikes of electric energy that *"Battery"* banged out of the speakers, and a beat that Ulrich remembered some of the most challenging playing he'd pulled off in the studio up to that point in his evolution as a drummer. Deconstructing it's performance in depth for fans, Lars begins by revealing that

> at that time, it was a little bit unusual, but I used to have a hi-hat both on the left and right side of the kit. I felt for a lot of the faster songs, having a hi-hat on the right side was a little more effective, its also the weight that could be put behind the snare. So I could literally raise my left hand higher because I wasn't crossing over with my right hand, so I could play opened and play a lot. I've never been a huge ride-cymbal fan, and so I used to basically play *"Battery"* and *"Whiplash"* and *"Trapped Under Ice"* and *"Fight Fire with Fire"* over on the right-hand side with the hi-hat, and have it be opened rather than crossed.

Turning to the album's cinematic title track, a masterpiece whose musical movements span the scenery of a movie in their turns and twists, Ulrich found himself creating a canvas punctuated by precision tension within his bass-snare attacks, colorful tom crescendos and accents and a constantly-shifting journey of tempo changes that collectively painted the perfect backdrop for Hetfield's complex and constantly moving six-string storyline. The equivalent of painting Heavy Metal's Sistine Chapel within the work of art he delivered in his performance behind the kit, an ever-modest Ulrich acknowledged its greatness in terms of the music he was complimenting within his playing:

> With *"Master of Puppets,"* I was trying to play around the riffs, around the vocals, trying to find holes to put cymbal hits and accents, its trying to be completely in tune to what everybody else is doing, both in terms of playing along and then kind of locking in, and also being counter to different things. For that song, you put the fills where the fills need to roll and give the vocals some room to breathe.
>
> That song, obviously, was one of the songs where there were a bunch of different moods and different feels, kind of melodic and a little softer or mellow in the middle, and then there's that whole build-up with the double bass drums and different types of things. So obviously you could argue that Master of Puppets certainly covers all the different kinds of dynamics that Metallica embraced at that time, or would end up embracing at that time, or embracing over the years.

Hailed as a "refinement of past innovations" by Billboard, one thing that stayed the same for Ulrich and Hetfield throughout the album's recording was the singular focus the two paid to the foundations of their sound by keeping the pocket pure of any playing presence other than their own as they tracked live off the floor together in the studio:

> During recording for those albums as well, it was just James and I, neither Kirk nor Cliff were there in the studio when we were recording the drums and the rhythm guitar. So there were moments of obviously holding things down and more normal drum-bass player moments, but in the traditional kind of sense of blues rock or more rock & roll type of stuff where the drums and the bass kind of hold the pocket down, where the guitars go off into their own world, that's never been our shtick so much, and its never been the traditional set-up.

Voted the Greatest Heavy Metal Album of All Time in Rolling Stone's Readers poll upon release in March of 1986, the finished product was viewed as "fifty-four near-perfect minutes, MASTER OF PUPPETS is a genuine classic that will survive even the mortal lives of its creators," in the equally-esteemed opinion of Kerrang! Sadly, this great monument of metal would lose an important pillar when bassist Cliff Burton was killed in a tragic tour bus accident later that year in September 1986. Reflecting back on his time playing with one of the most influential neo-classical metal bass players of all time, Ulrich puts appreciation for Burton in the context of

> having played with four bass players in Metallica, and recorded with 3 of them, and obviously I can say that Burton, Newstead and Trujillo all are very, very different in their styles. Burton especially, was so unique and unpredictable and in his own world, most of the time for better, so that was a very unique type of thing. I think at that time, he was probably the most musically gifted of the four of us, and was the one who had studied music and was probably a little more enveloped in music theory and had a much broader range in terms of his influences as far as Classical music and other things, so he was very, very unique. So with Cliff, through many, many unique moments both on and off stage.
>
> The one thing you have to remember about this band, both its origins and what's kept its backbone has been the relationship between the drums and the rhythm guitar, and most of the songs have been written and given birth to between James Hetfield's rhythm guitar and the drum kit, so there's obviously a special relationship between those two instruments. And then, different bass players kind of fit their different styles and different talents within that existing dynamic.

Returning to the studio in January of 1988 after a period of mourning to record *...And Justice For All,* Lars was fired up on all creative cylinders, feeling at the top of his game as a player, confirming that "especially right around the *Justice* album, where the drums were probably the most progressive that they ever were in the Metallica catalog." Perhaps no more poignant a moment where that elevation is on display than the back half of the now-legendary *"One,"* where Ulrich became an idol, and turned his drum kit into a throne as the king of hypnotic double-bass syncopation. Causing a million non-drummers to try and pound out the pattern with their feet as eagerly as they were playing rhythm air guitars along with the air-tight pocket Hetfield and he were locked in throughout the 4-minute masterpiece, in reflecting back on the why felt it was among his finest moments as a player, Lars begins by pointing to a shift from

> *"Fade to Black"* and *"Master of Puppets,"* which was always that kind of ballady type of thing we were doing, and my recollection is they usually started off with some picking parts, and by the time we got to *"One"* a few years later, that ended up a little sparser in the front. But then where that rhythmic section in the middle where the drums mirror Hetfield's right hand, I'm not trying to steal the glory here, but a lot of that stuff was given birth to on the drums.
>
> So, for instance, the opening riff to the title track, that came straight off a drum pattern. So that was the drums opening with that pattern, and then Hetfield starting mirroring the drum pattern, so primarily on that record, a lot of those crazy, locked-in things were kind of started on the drums. That specific section in *"One"* was obviously a pretty unique moment that I'm proud of, because the back-half of that song has some pretty intense shit going on, especially the last 3 minutes of that song.

A punishing performance that has held up as challenging as ever for the drummer to this day, Lars clearly retains a healthy respect for the places he pushed himself to in the heart of the one of the most respected and revered moments in thrash metal history. Required to bring the same power and precision to parts that took every ounce of his energy to pull off back in his mid-20s when the song was first recorded, Ulrich jokes that

> its rare that I'm playing a song like *"One"* saying to myself, "Oh, look at those 7 guys down in the front row, it looks like they're having fun, I wonder if they're rocking Tequila or Jack Daniels..." That's not where I go, my head

> is in the part I'm playing, saying to myself say with that middle section of *"One,"* "Four more to go to the double, keep it up, four more to go till the vocal," I'm always thinking about right where I am in the song, or what's the next change. So I'm always focused on what the next momentum shift is, and making sure that the next change is lined up for where I need to go. So for instance, *"One"* is not one of those songs where I sit there looking at a bunch of crazy fans. There are songs like *"Enter Sandman"* that are maybe a little bit more straight-forward, *"Wherever I May Roam,"* they may be a little bit less demanding of my concentration, but for us, playing shit like *"One"* and a bunch of the stuff off Death Magnetic and when you start getting into songs like *"Fight Fire with Fire"* and crazier shit like your *"Ride the Lightning"* and *"Disposable Heroes"* and all that kind of material, you've really got to be in the pocket and in the moment.

Now the undisputed kings of thrash and every other kind of heavy metal heading into the 1990s, Metallica readied plans with the *Black Album* to take the genre at large into the musical mainstream. To accomplish this ambitious plan, the band made the decision to shift their sound sonically into new territory that producer Bob Rock would help them craft after the producer personally recalled that "Metallica told me they sought me out to produce the *Black Album* based on the drum sound I'd gotten for Tommy on *Dr. Feelgood.* The best thing I can do to describe that and then what I did on The Black Album in comparison to Tommy's drums on the *Feelgood* record was weight. I tried to give as much weight to the drums as possible. Metallica records are slightly different from Motley records in terms of the drumming. To me, Tommy as a drummer is kind of like an open nerve end, whereas Lars, to me, is probably closer to Keith Moon than anything. Tommy is a classic back-beat drummer, he is the basis, he's a rhythm kind of guy. And he does have syncopation and all the other kind of stuff, but he's a rhythm machine, whereas what makes Lars Ulrich's drumming so wonderful and so unique is that he's reactive to the music. *The Black Album* was him consciously trying to be more of a backbeat, keep-the-time kind of guy."

Elaborating on what he heard within Ulrich's playing by that point after having recorded so many world-class drummers like Tommy Lee with their own unique styles of playing, with Lars, Rock paid him the high compliment of a comparison to legendary Keith Moon, reasoning the parallel is warranted by the fact that "most of his fills and unique drumming all comes out of the fact that he plays to the riff of the music, much like with The Who. The Who and Metallica are very similar because Keith Moon played to Pete Townsend's solid rhythm playing, and Lars Ulrich has always played to James Hetfield's solid rhythms. I don't believe Lars doesn't think in the terms that most drummers do, I think he thinks in a musical world that is kind of unique. I don't really know how to describe it, other than he plays to the riff rather than trying to control the riff." For Ulrich personally, the new direction of producers was a welcome one looking back, as the drummer – warning ahead of time that "I say this with love and respect" – revealed his feeling that

> James Hetfield's rhythm guitar takes up so much of the sonic landscape that its almost like every other instrument has to kind of fit around that where there's space and where there's holes. So, for instance, the whole kind of … *And Justice For All* sound with the kick drum with the top-end and the click, the "click drum" is what we ended up calling it on that album, because in order for the kick drum to be heard, we had to put so much EQ at the top end for it to find a place where it could penetrate through Hetfield's guitar.
>
> So a lot of our sonics, up to then, was kind of dictated by the rhythm guitar. So leading into production on *the Black Album*, we started hearing albums like *Dr. Feelgood* by Motley Crue and *Sonic Temple* by The Cult and some other stuff that he'd done, and the reaction was like "Wow, there's a depth to these records that we didn't feel we had up to that point." So when we went in to work with Bob, we had to kind of start over from scratch, and reinvent our

> sonics, and we did that by sort of striking everything off and working with a lot of room, and start scooping the rhythm guitar and getting the drums more in the middle in terms of the mid-range: the snare drum and the kick drum, and Bob came in with years of expertise and put all the instruments in their own place where they could live and breathe, rather than all the instruments kind of fighting for space, and trying to take over the different sonic landscapes. It was really that, and we just spent a fuckload of time on it, I think we spent two or three weeks at One on One working on drum sounds before we even started tracking.

Making important stylistic shifts in arrangements and dynamics that retained the band's power, Ulrich felt across the album's entire spectrum of material – which launched a new generation of smash hit singles like *"Enter Sandman," "The Unforgiven," "Nothing Else Matters," "Wherever I May Roam,"* and *"Sad But True"* that still remain some of rock's most rotated on radio today – an important new balance for the band was struck within their musical spectrum between sonic and stylistic expansions:

> Obviously, the triumph of that record was the simplicity, and the fact that we were able to let the instruments breathe and be that size, and on that record, it wasn't just about what was happening but it was also about what wasn't happening because of the size of it all and the spaces in between. So on *"Enter Sandman"* and *"Sad But True"* and *"The Unforgiven"* and *"Wherever I May Roam,"* those 4 songs out of the first 5, that's a pretty good run, you know?
>
> To me, the place on the album where it opens up and is the liveliest is probably *"The God That Failed,"* the whole middle section where it really gets pretty all over the place, and there's some nice interplay between the drums and Kirk Hammett's solo guitar work. Some of the other stuff's a little more structured or contained, but in that song, the drums breath probably the most.

Taking the world by storm in 1991 as planned, Rolling Stone Magazine like many of Rock and Metal's most respected critics would conclude that Metallica was "no longer (on) the cutting edge of metal, as it was in the beginning, but… expanding its musical and expressive range on its own terms" by that point, adding in an acknowledgment of their commercial capital that "this can only be a positive step for a group that is effectively bridging the gap between commercial metal and the much harder thrash of Slayer, Anthrax and Megadeth." Feeling the band were carrying a torch of sorts that had been passed throughout important records for Rock and Metal over the years, the drummer recalled that

> at that time, you're 27, 28 years old and you have all the time in the world, you have the patience, and it also had so much to do with what everyone else was doing and what was going on musically around you, and at that time, sonics mattered. Now, its like nobody sits there and goes, "Oh, that record's really well recorded," that era came and went, and now its more about the mood and the feel, but there's a time when people would sit there and go "Fuck, *Back in Black*, the kick drum's unbelievable," and then came *Pyromania* and then came *Hysteria* and then came *Dr. Feelgood*, and then came *The Black Album.* And there was this kind of this point in the 90s of like "Where are you going to take the sonics after *The Black Album?*" It just couldn't get any bigger and couldn't get any fatter and there was nowhere else to go, other than some place different.

Co-headlining Arenas with Guns N' Roses by the summer of 1992, Metallica would go on to become the biggest Metal band of the 1990s with a formula that never lost its core synched DNA of "Lars and James kind of equally being the life blood of the band," their producer Bob Rock – who produced a decade's worth of multi-platinum albums with the band including *Load, Reload,* and *St. Anger* – recalls, adding of the drummer's lifelong musical bond with Hetfield that remains the band's creative core to date: "That is a marriage when it comes to Metallica, those two are not at all short-changing Kurt. Kurt has always been the guy who's sort of the mediator between the two, but James and Lars are kind of like—when they're both strong, they're the sound of Metallica."

Metallica would make a return to roots of sorts in 2008 when, shifting their sonic direction full circle after they recruited Jedi Master Rick Rubin to produce their first studio album in 5 years, *Death Magnetic*. With the bearded record-making wizard's decision to put the band back in a room together to write through jams, at heart, what the drummer had always loved most about being in his band after 35 years making music together:

> It's the bonding experience for me, its playing with the other 3 guys, both in the studio and live when we're connecting with the audience. I like playing, but I have a pretty short attention-span, and I get restless pretty easily, so being in Metallica now-adays pretty much stays functioning all the time, because its not like we have a year on and then a year off, we're sort of pretty much always on. We're always writing, playing festivals, working on something, and the last time I think we had a down year was in 2005, so I think we're in better shape and more connected than we used to be. For me, probably the main thing is just playing with the other guys, writing and exploring, creating, and then going out and sharing that with an audience.
>
> To me, its kind of become the "mancave" for lack of a better word, because people will say "Oh, it must be so much work to go on tour," and I go, "No, its actually the opposite. Being at home, taking care of the kids, the domestic responsibilities, all that type of stuff, that's the work. Then going out on the road and playing some gigs, that's kind of the mancave escape." We don't do anything in more than 2-week stretches, so we go out for 2 weeks, come home, go out for 2 weeks, come home, and we're lucky enough to kind of be able to afford ourselves the luxury of the 2-week run. So its like you fly off to some exotic location, you're playing gigs to 50,000, 75,000 people that are out of their minds and having the best time.

> We have a pretty deep relationship with our catalog, so probably on the Death Magnetic tour we played up to 70, 80 songs where we could rotate them throughout the shows on the tour and play lots of deeper stuff, and then we have good dinners, hang out and have a nice glass of wine and a day off in some super-exotic location. Then its off to the next show and meet-and-greets with our fans... That's not work, vs. hitting the alarm clock at 6:30 AM and battling to get 3 boys to 3 different schools, and all the rest of the responsibilities and stuff that comes with taking care of that at home. That's the "work" part of it, so I love the escapism that's associated with Metallica. Not that raising kids and whatnot is not enjoyable, but the road is where we go and enjoy ourselves.

Today, in spite of the legacy accolades he's begun to accrue, impressively including the Rock & Roll Hall of Fame-inducted drummer's well-earned rank at # 62 on Rolling Stone Magazine's 100 Greatest Drummers list, the legendary drummer remains characteristically modest in assessing his own impact as a player, arguing that no matter how big an influence he's had over shaping modern Metal drumming,

> I'm not consciously trying to do anything. I think the main thing is the band and the song and the collective, I have at different times in my career been more or less interested in where I put the drums, in terms of up front, and obviously *"Master of Puppets"* and *"...And Justice for All,"* where the drums were up front a lot in terms of coloring the sound, and obviously a lot of what we do is based around rhythmic patterns and so on, but I don't feel that there's an ego thing that drives anything in terms of "Look what I can do, look at this ability..." I've just never been interested in that.
>
> To me, its about the groove, its about the vibe, and about making the guitar riffs sing and making people kind of be able to move where it becomes kind of a physical thing. There's certain things I enjoy, like bringing in cymbal hits around the vocals and accents, and kind of playing around Hetfield's

> vocals, but to me, drums is an instrument that works the best in a collective, and I've just never been interested in them as a show-off piece. There are people who do clinics and drum magazines, and all that just really doesn't interest me, its just not my thing, I'm interested and have always been more interested in where the drums fit in a bigger picture.

Closing with the same council he gives to the countless new generations of drummers who have approached him over the years for direction about where to center their passion and focus in chasing the same dream to glory Lars did back when he was still a teenager and first linked up with James Hetfield in the Recycler, the drummer recommends a path of purity that puts front and center the importance

> I would just say of following your heart, follow your instincts, follow your gut, follow your balls. Try to not be too cerebral and over-thinking, let the music take you, and allow yourself to be sucked in to where the music is a living, breathing entity, so try and let it guide you rather than you guiding it. To me, the key thing is listening: listen to other players, listen to the people you're playing with, and listen to records. I'm not saying you shouldn't study and read, but you've got to listen and there's got to be something that kind of distinctive. You can't, like what Phil Rudd does in the *"Highway to Hell"* introduction, there's nobody else in the world that plays it like him, and it's a feel, and that's not something that you learn in a book. That's not something you learn by reading Drummer Confidential magazine, and if you can play technically that's great, but at the same time, can you play *"Highway to Hell,"* and make it swing like Phil Rudd? Because that's maybe equally as important or more important…

"I just switched over to Pearl drums, which I'm enjoying probably more than any other drums I've ever played, pleasantly to my surprise." – Joey Kramer

(photo by Zack Clifford)

Chapter 3: Joey Kramer of Aerosmith – Rockin' & Roastin'

Few drummers have held as heavy-hitting a hand in influencing the invention and shaping of a rock & roll genre as AEROSMITH's Joey Kramer has had over Hard Rock for the better part of 45 years. Whether you asked Guns N Roses in the mid-1980s who their primary descendants were derivatively, or Grunge rock titans like "Soundgarden, Nirvana, Alice in Chains and Pearl Jam," who Rolling Stone Magazine argued "all owed a serious debt to old-school Aerosmith," the story was the same. That shadow looms large over defining Millennium rockers like The Foo Fighters and Nickelback, and no doubt generations of drummers just now being inspired by the same dream themselves after seeing the band live on one of their countless world tours, often with their parents for the first time.

Critics have been equally dazzled throughout the decades: Drummer World Magazine has hailed Joey as "one of rock's greatest drummers," while the world's leading cymbals manufacturer, Zildjian, argues convincingly that Kramer throughout his career has remained "simply one of the greatest drummers of all time. Anyone involved in rock music today would be hard pressed to say they weren't, in some way, influenced by...Joey's playing." After 150 million albums sold in his career, Kramer, for his own part, still shakes his head at the wild ride he's had as one of hard rock's pioneering players behind the kit, confessing candidly that while

> first of all man, I'm honored and flattered and incredibly grateful to be even considered to be in the same genre of "greats," when it comes to my attention that other drummers have been influenced by me, I don't relate to that, I'm just another guy. I don't relate to being some super-superior drummer, I love what I do, and I think that's probably the most obvious about my playing, and what makes it as good – if you will – as it is, is because I love to do it so much that I put my heart and soul and passion into it every night, and that's what shows. So with some of these guys, it's the same thing, I can see when I watch them what they're doing and how they're doing it and how they feel about it, and the word feel is like what its all about.

Paying a nod to the players who first inspired him to pick up the sticks himself back as a kid growing up in The Bronx against the back drop of rock & roll's first generation, Kramer – like so many children of the 60s – pointed to a certain now-legendary night on the Ed Sullivan Show in 1964 that CBS recently declared "the night that changed America." For a newly teenage Joey, it wasn't the band's drummer specifically, but more generally

> the camaraderie of what those guys were doing together that I kind of zeroed in on, not so much the drums. I was 14 years old the first time I sat and watched the Beatles on Ed Sullivan with my Dad, and I remember thinking they were like a gang: they were all of the same minds and were

all going to accomplish the same dream all together. I think it was later on that the drums came, because I was never really zeroed in on Ringo on a drummer per say, although what he did in the context of the Beatles was wonderful, but the actual sitting down behind the drums I don't think really came until I got into the Young Rascals, which was Dino Danelli. Dino was definitely one of the drummers that shaped me as a kid, along with Mitch Mitchell, Clive Bunker, John Bonham, Clyde Stubblefield – who was the main drummer for James Brown for years – and another guy who played with John "Jabo" Starks.

Early on, when I was very young, I was fortunate enough to get turned on to the likes of The Temptations and the O'Jays, all that Soul/Rhythm & Blues music, and I had a pretty much instantaneous love affair with that kind of stuff. So my playing is kind of a mixture of that and the influence of the likes of Mitch Mitchell, because I liked all the licks he played, and Dino Danelli, but what its really all about for me is *feel.* If the feel is good, then its right. I'm completely self-taught, so I don't really have anything to go on by virtue of what's supposed to be right or appropriate or whatever. So those are my main influences when I was young.

Known as one of the first great "kings of swing" with hits like *"Good Lovin' "* and *"People Got to Be Free,"* Kramer was drawn as a player to the same R&B roots as Danelli had been within his own youth as a player, leading Joey to begin his performing career as a drummer not in a rock & roll band but instead

a black band called The Unique Four at the time (they eventually became Tavares), and it was 5 guys that sang out in front like The Temptations and did choreography and there was a 6-piece back-up band and I was the only white guy in the band. I joined after High School, and I remember those singers wanted me to accentuate certain moves in their choreography, so I used to go to rehearsals with just the singers, and not the rest of the band, so they could show me what they wanted. In order for me to get that, what

> they did was they brought me to the Apollo to see James Brown and the O'Jays and the Temptations, and they would tell me, "Just watch the drummer." And that's pretty much where I learned and fell in love with that sort of music. James Brown was a tremendous influence on me, and I always loved his band, and that's the story of that.

By the time blues and rock began to fuse within Kramer's playing style, he had co-founded Aerosmith with a true lightning rod of musical energy, frontman Steven Tyler, who Joey proudly credits as

> another influence on me when I was very young, because Steven was a drummer before he started singing, and then he sang lead and played drums at the same time in a lot of his old bands. So in the beginning, I sort of had the chops and the talent, but I really didn't so much have much of a direction, and he kind of steered me in to a specific direction and turned me on to things that helped me and were to my advantage. Things like not playing so much, for instance, vs. when you get a guy like Mitch Mitchell who plays a lot because he's basically in a trio and so he got the opportunity to play a lot. Whereas, in Aerosmith, what my band was looking for was more of the groove and more of the steady, keep-going kind of thing, so Steven helped me to realize that. He also pushed me to do a drum solo very early on, in 1976, where the first time I did a drum solo was live at Pontiac Stadium in Michigan in front of 80,000 people! And when I got the response that I did from that that night, that's what kept me going, doing a drum solo every night after that for 35 years.

As the band began laying the groundwork for what would become the genre of hard rock throughout the decade they dominated, starting with the band's self-titled debut LP, Joey points to one of the band's signature 70s hits, *"Mama Kin,"* as a perfect example for any young drummer on the importance of learning

> what to play, and what especially *NOT* to play. That song is pretty much straight-ahead, and it was pretty much obvious what had to be played and

> what didn't have to be played, which in that song is a lot of the verses are sang by themselves without anything. I think that less-is-more is probably, or should be, in my opinion, the golden rule for all drummers. In particular, the best example I can sight for that is John Bonham, because there were places where he didn't play, and those places that he didn't play – if you listen throughout their catalog – they really stand out, for me. Instead of what the typical drummer would do is to put something in there, wherever its at, as opposed to leaving it out and having nothing there, or a hole. I think that that's very important, and I think that a lot of drummers never realize that.

Describing his stylistic pedigree as a drummer as one where "my playing is what brings the funk and the soul and that stuff to the music, which makes it a little bit more interesting than your average rock & roll band," it was indeed Kramer's ability to authentically draw on his own roots as a constant compositional source that allowed him, in the esteemed opinion of Pearl Drums, to so expertly combine "emotional feel with technical virtuosity to convey the musical ideas of his band mates in Aerosmith." Taking fans inside the heart of that creative process from behind the set, Joey began with a cautionary note for today's generation of aspiring beat-smiths that

> I think there's too many drummers out there who don't really realize what their responsibility is. Really, what your responsibility is as a drummer is to kind of be a chameleon, so to speak. So when my guys come to me, in terms of songwriting or what they have in their heads as an idea, they usually have some sort of an idea about what they want to hear. I think that the responsibility of the drummer is to make that happen for the writer in terms what it is that he's hearing in his song. Then by virtue of doing that, at the same time, you get to put your own spin on it as well, but you have to be open to whatever it is that anyone is saying to you, especially if it's the songwriter and he has an idea in his head of what he thinks he'd like it to sound like. You can always express it the way that you want, but I think

> the most important thing is to make the song feel the way the person that is writing it sees it to begin with.
>
> For instance, I remember with *"Back in the Saddle,"* I think Joe came up with that lick, and played it on a 6-string bass, and I think it was actually Joe that suggested I ride the floor tom instead of a hi-hat or a cymbal, to give it that low, gritty texture its got to it. I think that was the right thing to do. Like I said before, by virtue of having to be a chameleon – which I think is part of a drummer's job – you have to be open to suggestions. Don't forget that all the time, no matter who you take a suggestion from, or even if its your own thing, you're the one playing it, not somebody else.
>
> Another example of that is *"Sweet Emotion,"* which pretty much dictated to me what needed to be played, it was obvious to me, because the verse part kind of goes along with the riff, and the real signature thing I think on that one is the end part, and when we do it live, its kind of a big jam at the end. That I think is more of a signature part even that the verse. With *"Walk This Way,"* it was also very obvious to me what to play, and it just kind of goes along with the main lick. I think it's probably the most sampled drum figure there is, and today, I play that pretty much completely differently live, just to keep it interesting.

When offering pointers to drummers just starting out in the studio session-gig game, Kramer begins by pointing to the importance of diversity of parts, reasoning that "one thing that I get from guys all the time is like, 'How do you remember everything that you're doing?', because sometimes they'll be 2 or 3 different drum parts within the context of one song, and I just do what feels pretty much natural to me, and the difference between a verse and a chorus is great, and it needs to be different. But a lot of times, a lot of guys will play the same thing throughout a whole song, which is not very interesting." Of equal importance, according to Kramer – who even goes as far as using himself as an example – is for young drummers to get to know and love the inevitable reality of "the click track," offering the sage advice that

> for younger studio drummers, the more you play with a click, the better your timing will become, unless your time is as perfect as it can be. I think that the only reason why certain guys may or may not like the click track, is because its one of those things that if you don't have it down and you can't do it, your ego's going to tell you, "Well, tell them: 'We don't need to do this, its just going to feel good on its own, because I'll make it feel good.' " Well, the trick to that is, to be able to play with a click, and make it feel good at the same time. I think that the main crux of playing with a click track – because when you're doing stuff up on a grid, it makes it a whole lot easier to put takes together if you're doing that – is that it gives the song a certain characteristic that you can't get if you're playing freestyle because no one's timing is that good.
>
> The first time I ever played with a click is when we did *"Permanent Vacation."* For the albums before that, I'd never played with a click track ever before in my life. When we sat down in the studio and our producer Bruce Fairbain put on the click track, I said "Wow, what's this?", and he said "It's a click, you've got to play the song to it," and I had no experience, and let me tell you, it was difficult at first. I'm not sure that I like it or dislike it, but there are definitely times where it can be a challenge. But once you get it down, once you get it mastered, it just gives it the feel that anyone needs, and any guy that's had any experience in the studio, usually has the click track down.

For a band who many times discovered and developed their greatest and most celebrated hits out of lengthy jam sessions that predated modern technology like the click track, Kramer credited the band's career-long practice of playing together ahead of studio and live performances as also being the key to securing a reputation as one of rock's greatest – and tightest- live bands to ever shake the stage, confirming that

> jamming is a big part of the band, it always has been, and that's where a lot of songs come from. We'll be jamming and something will come up, and Steven could stop us and say "Oh, what was that you played?", and we'll go over that, and come up with lines here and there, so a lot of songs come out that way. Everybody in my band all have different influences and different tastes and it's the combination of all of that that makes it as interesting as it is.
>
> We're a live band, that's what we're all about, that's what we've always been all about, and it took me a while to master playing in the studio, because playing in the studio is a completely different world from playing live. I don't mind the studio, I don't dislike it, but I certainly like playing live a whole lot more. Its just a whole lot more fun, it's a whole lot more free, there are a whole lot more things you don't have to think about, for me anyway, because my body just sort of does it automatically after all these years. So I would say live is my favorite.

For as much legendary partying as Aerosmith did on the road throughout their 40+ year career, its never been lost on Kramer that – even with as much fun as his band had on stage and off – he still had a job to do when he mounted the drum riser night after night,

> especially live, that's where the concept of "the responsibility of a drummer" rings really loud and clear with me, because – especially on stage, live, which is what we're all about – that responsibility is so there. You can't stop, you can't take a break or take a breath, and the word responsibility is really a good one.

Turning the spotlight in fuller focus to the live side of his career as a player, after over 2000 live gigs in 48 countries around the world, Kramer reveals that at age 64, his body has become conditioned to instinctively know it's a "show day," so much so that

> when I wake up in the morning, if I'm on the road and its an off day, and there's nothing in-particular – other than going to the gym – that I have planned for the day, when it's a show day, my body just kind of knows, and I prepare for that mentally for that all day. Without really concentrating on it, my body just goes into a mode where a show day is different from a regular day.

Much like a parent finding it nearly impossible to choose a favorite among the many babies that are the songs from his band's catalog to perform, Joey acknowledged that "that's really hard, because no matter what songs we play at night, I pretty much enjoy them all: none of them are really laborious for me." Where he could highlight front-runners, Kramer begins with *"Last Child,"* highlighting the Aerosmith classic as

> one of the songs that I really love playing live because its got that kind of funkiness to it, and again, there's a few different parts going on in there. Brad wrote that song, and so I got together with him, and the drum parts pretty much go along with the guitar riffs. *"Lord of the Thighs,"* that's probably my favorite song to play live, but other than that, if I had to sit down and pick one or two songs, I don't know if I could do it. I would have to say my favorite songs are all the songs.

Along with knowing it's a show day, Joey revealed that knowing his songs so well after playing them hundreds of times over the bands many tours throughout the past 4 decades, "when I'm off and I'm home, I don't really play." While a definite no-no for newer drummers missing his years of experience behind the kit, Kramer takes his physical vacations from the kit seriously, so much so that

> I can go like 3, 4, 5 months at a time without playing, and then when its time to play again, you get ready to go back out on the road. I like to get there in sort of a natural way: which is go and sit down and play because I feel like playing. That's always pretty much kept it fresh for me over the years. After all these years of doing what I do, I can honestly say to you

> that I really, really love what I do. I love playing my drums. I love being in this band. I'm very grateful for it, and its my favorite thing in the world to do. That's why its never gotten old or laborious for me.

Finding when he is out on the road that one of the favorite parts of his interactions with fans these days comes with watching the youngest faces out in the crowds of those kids being brought by their parents to see Aerosmith for the first time, the kind of traditional induction he's seen for generation after generation of new fans. A proud right of passage for one of the true patriarchs of hard rock drumming, Joey muses that

> I think now I'm kind of really tickled and thrilled that younger kids are curious about where a lot oft his stuff came from, and even though we're not the originators of what it is that we really do: you gotta remember that every kind of music that's out there is pretty much derived from the Blues. The spin that we put on it is interesting enough that it arouses their curiosity as to where it came from and what's it all about. I think we're a good example of that, but I think the definition of hard work varies from kid to kid as far as those watching who want to become drummers professionally.
>
> I would keep it very, very simple, and say that I'm obviously a perfect example of it: if you have a dream and you have a passion and you want it more than anything else in the world. I mean really want it, just go for it, and keep pounding away at it till it happens. Now, a lot of people don't realize that hard work pays off, but I think the reason they don't realize that is in today's society, I don't get that people really have a valid definition for hard work. I think that people are way more entitled today, and expect things to happen jus because, and it doesn't happen that way. You have to work really hard, and have to know what the definition of hard work really is. That's how we got to where we are.
>
> I think as far as being open minded and listening to what other people have to say, I think I would tell players just getting into the business that not only

> is that important, but it's the key. Don't forget that, when its all said and done, you're the one whose playing the part, you're the one whose putting your stamp on it. Because its you, you can't help but play it the way that you play, so even though you may be playing something that somebody else suggested, its still you playing. If you're going to allow your ego to get in the way of something that you play, even though it may be better than what you wanted to play yourself, you're kind of defeating the purpose. You're your own worst enemy.

Aerosmith continues to tour sold-out arenas and stadiums around the world, including such recent high-profile, top-grossing tours as the 2012-13 "Global Warming" tour, which grossed $31 million and took the band from North American around the globe to Asia, Australia, Central and South America, New Zealand, The Philippines, Singapore to perform before 300,000+ total fans, and 2014's "Let Rock Rule" tour, which took the band across the U.S. and 17 European countries. Still, even when Joey's not on the road, *he's still on the road,* courtesy of his burgeoning Coffee business and love for driving Lamborghinis, a hobby he recalls picking up after

> I drove Ferraris for many years, and then I had a couple fires and accidents and that convinced me I shouldn't be with them anymore, so I probably started buying Lamborghinis in 03 or 04. I find them a little bit more exciting than the Ferraris. Here's what I do: I buy them, drive them, and sell them. My favorite one right now is an Audi R8 E-10+, which I've done some modifications too, and its pushing a little over 600 horsepower, and is definitely without a doubt my most favorite car to drive, and my most favorite car that I think that I've had. We just finished a summer, 14 European tour, and while we were in Italy, I was invited to the Lamborghini factory, and I've been a fan of Lambos for many years, and I'm currently waiting on a new Huracan! I just love to drive, and the faster you go, the less time you have to think about anything else.

While fans can still count on seeing Kramer behind the kit for years to come, in recent times, he's turned his passions up to 10 over "Rockin' & Roastin' " – Joey's custom coffee company – whose brand Yahoo Finance News reported in 2014 was "set to save us from our national disgrace and the dire threat of single-serve bilge water being marketed as coffee…The drummer for the biggest rock band in American history…(is) bringing are three roasts of coffee (no blends!) being distributed through over 1,000 grocery stores in 13 states on the East Coast. Through a partnership with Comfort Foods, Rockin' & Roastin' recently shipped a massive first order to Costco." Beaming with pride and appreciation at how fast his custom coffee has taken off as a legitimate brand, Kramer returns once again to the work ethic that has driven his success over the past 40 years, pointing out first and foremost about his latest passion that

> I'm not about just putting my name on something and sitting back and trying to collect money for it: I'm about the quality of it, and how good it is and its something that I will stay on top of for the duration, because I enjoy making people happy, and coffee makes *everybody* happy! The way the whole idea started was all my years on the road, I had a very difficult time finding good coffee, so it's the age-old adage if "If you wanna get something done right, you have to do it yourself." So I'm doing it myself, its working, I'm having a good time doing it, I'm kept very, very busy by it because its a lot of work, whether I'm on the road or off the road. If I'm not on the road with the band, I'm out traveling around doing meetings and store appearances or whatever helps promote the brand, so I never stop.
>
> I'm enjoying getting an education about being a business man. I soak everything in, I love meeting and working with people, and so its working for me- I go into these companies where we have meetings with the executives, and they all come in with their suits and ties, and I come in with my guys dressed like a rock & roller, and they get the biggest kick out of it! They think it's the greatest thing on earth, and I have a good time doing it. When everybody else is off and having vacation, I'm out there working my coffee

> business. My wife Linda came up with the name of the brand, "Rockin & Roastin," and she's the one single thing that has happened to me in my life that has changed me the most and done the most for me ever, is my wife Linda. She's my favorite thing in life.

While many rockers have sunk their own money into business ventures outside the immediate arena of rock & roll over the years for the purpose of tax deductions or an interest in an investment they had no active hand in running, Joey's business is incorporated on the other end of that universe, with the drummer fulfilling another life-long dream with the company of

> always wanting to have my own business, but I just never had the time due to my career, which I'm very, very grateful for. But the last time we had some time off, we had a period of 7 months, which for us was unheard of, so I decided I was going to do my thing, so I put my team together, and I'm the C.E.O. of the company and am hands-on in every aspect, but am also very lucky I have the right people, people that I trust, and am also grateful for the way the coffee took off. So much has happened, so my advice to everyone would be: if you have a dream and you really, really want it more than anything else, GO FOR IT!

"Tico Torres has been the heart and soul of our band since we started 30 years ago." - Jon Bon Jovi, 2016

(photo by David Bergman)

Chapter 4: Tico Torres of Bon Jovi – "The Hitman"

"I always say this: *There's no bad drummers in the world.* I'll listen to anybody and learn something," legendary Bon Jovi drummer Tico Torres offers as the greatest lesson he's ever taken with him throughout his 40+ year career behind the kit. Other sage words of wisdom for keeping the rhythm of a professional career going as long as his has as a professional drummer boils down to what Torres underscores as the bedrock principle of hard work and dedication to learning the craft:

> All I did was play music, every single day, starting from when I was 12 years old, and the funny thing is, I started out as a kid playing guitar. My cousin also played guitar, and actually studied under Segovia, so he was an awesome classical guitar player, so I had a little bit of trouble keeping up with that, so I figured I'd buy a snare drum and a cymbal, those little sets, with some sticks and I'd jam along with him. I did that till I was probably 11 or 12. I was an upholsterer since I was 12, paper routes before that, and I started roofing when I was 16 as well in the summer, so I had quite a bit of

> dough, and saved up and bought two Ludwig kits and put them together. So it was 4 toms, two floors, and two bass drums, and I was off to the races.

Even though he didn't sit down behind his first full set of drums till the age of 16, Tico was a quick study because he'd always "had rhythm in me, so it was natural for me to play." Growing up against the golden age of Rock & Roll's first generation in the early 1960s around one of its true hotbeds, New York City, the young drummer remembered his listening and live exposures to many of its greatest players being immeasurable in influence:

> with music at that time in the 60s, Rock & Roll was emerging quite a bit in so many ways that it was just infectious. One of the cool things about growing up in New York and New Jersey was the Fillmore East, and all the great music came from New York. I was enamored with British music, and a lot of your British drummers were influential on me, as well as a lot of the Jazz guys, like John Heisman from Coliseum and used to play with so many other people.
>
> I first got turned on to Jazz because my stepfather used to be a Jazz drummer and introduced me to guys like Dave Burns and Morris Stanton, and then I started getting into through him guys like Elvin Jones, who was probably my big mentor in my life. I went to his studio, and I asked Elvin for lessons, and when he heard me play, he said "You don't need lessons, come and watch me play when I do gigs in the city."

An amazing acknowledgement of encouragement, Tico jumped at opportunity to become a teenage apprentice to one of the preeminent American Jazz drummers of his era. Soaking up the kind of invaluable on-the-job training on the ground floor of what would become his own "college" to come in the night clubs, Torres became Jones' shadow, in a routine where

> I would go to the Vanguard and hand him cigarettes and drinks and pretty much hawk him for months and months and months, and what he wanted

> me to do was: he wanted me to learn why he's playing what he's playing against Benny Goodman or McCoy (Piner?) – the compliment of the drums musically with the other instruments, which was key. Again, that's where you have to listen to a guitar player's melody line and the Sax player, whoever's doing the lead of that part, and not only but the head of the song and compliment it.
>
> When I first started coming up with beats, it would start with saxophone and guitar, both lead instruments, and at my young age, I was able to play with guys like Willie Bridges – who was the lead Saxophonist for King Curtis's band. I used to play at Carl's up at the corner of 124th street, and it was a regular gig, and of course you'd follow the lead guy – whoever's doing the head of the song – and these guys were 20, 30 years older than me, and Miles Davis used to come in and I met him. But these guys had an old saying, it was funny, they'd go "You ain't the most technical drummer in town, but you've got good feel," (laughs).

Sure of what he wanted to do with his life at the time when most kids his age had no clue or were just starting to try and figure it out, coming from a first-generation Cuban immigrant family where the American Dream was lived out through those immigrants' children, when Tico shared his with his mother of becoming a professional musician, he remembered the initially being met with understandably reluctant reaction typical of the average parent:

> Come 18, I was # 42 in the Viet Nam lottery, so luckily I didn't get drafted, so I won the lottery there buddy. Then my mother said "What do you want to do with your life?", and I told her, "I want to be a musician." Well, she worked for a Pharmaceutical company and got me a job interview, so I had long hair and a Fu-Manchu and I walk in there, did the interview, got the job, and said "Sir, thank you, can you write my mother a note and that says I can't accept the job because I want to be a musician?"

> So I went to my mother, said "Ma, I got the job," and she was so happy and I gave her the note and said "But I wanna be a musician." So she gave me a kiss and fully supported me, she just said, "Do me one favor: don't get any tattoos," and I said "Okay," and never got any tattoos. I was true to her in that sense, and she's supported me better since, and I couldn't ask for a more supportive person than her.

Bringing the work ethic he'd been raised with to full bear in his decision to make his living as a professional player, Torres took whatever work he could get starting out in his career, a necessity for any professional musician starting out in the business, but one that was simpler in terms of availability of opportunities to play vs. today's climate:

> I think it was a little easier when I was growing up in the 60s and the 70s because were a lot more clubs to play at, and it was before real DJs came in and started putting a lot of musicians out of work. I remember when I was growing up there were 10 clubs within a quarter mile you could play, and bands would start and creativity would start because of it. So I've got to think it's a little more difficult for guys now, I know there isn't the influx of clubs there used to be, for instance here in Miami where I live and I know in New York as well. So it's a tough gig, not in my situation now, but it is a tough gig. I'm also an artist, I'm a painter on the side, so it was either be an artist or be a musician. So the fact that I bought a car, and was able to rent my own apartment, then buy my own home through money that I made playing every night is very satisfying.

A staple on the live New York and New Jersey players' session and stage circuits in his late teens and early-mid-20s throughout the 1970s, by the early 1980s, Tico's work ethic, networking skills and consummate talent as an adaptable player to whatever was thrown at him musically had allowed him to rack up an impressive resume for anyone at that age, TWENTY SIX albums to be exact. These included stints on the road and in the studio with multi-platinum rock artists/bands like Chuck Berry, Cerisano's R-Band, Frankie and the Knockouts – whose 70s hits included the original versions of *"I've Had the Time of My Life," "Hungry Eyes,"* and the band's own Top 10 hit *"Sweetheart"* – Pat Benatar, Alice Cooper, T. Roth and Another Pretty Face, and even had enough clout in the word-of-mouth circuit to land him an audition to replace Peter Criss in KISS, all pre-dating his "Big Break" joining Bon Jovi. That moment would ironically require Torres to take a chance on the then unknown musicians considering he had a family – including a wife and young child – to support and a mortgage to pay, but was still one he felt was worth taking after

> initially, Alec Jon Such approached me and then Jon came over and played me the songs, and I'd just gotten off the road from doing my third album with Frankie and the Knock Outs, and on tour, I'd heard that Ritchie Blackmore was looking for a drummer, so I was getting ready to go back out with him. Here I am, 9 years older than the rest of those guys, married at the time, I had a house, and these guys lived at home in their parents' basement.
>
> So when I went down to check it out, I jammed with them a bit and I remember just looking at Jon and going "This kid's a star. He looks amazing, he's got the moves, good energy," so I thought it was worth a chance, and anything that musicians do, it's a gamble, and for instance, when we did the first Bon Jovi record, 7800 Fahrenheit, I wasn't making enough to pay my bills, and although we were working, we weren't making a lot of money, so I had to supplement it with a lot of studio work.
>
> So if Stevie Nicks needed somebody or Alice Cooper, Wonderbread commercials – you name it – I was doing everything to pay the bills, and it wasn't until "Slippery" hit that there actually was a payday. So it was work, and it was a gamble, but then I'd done it a million times with other bands where you do the record, you believe in it, and you work it, and some pan out and some don't. I did a record in 1975 in Sweden with a Jazz Rock band and had thought, "Woah, that's the greatest thing in the world!", and

> nobody ever heard of it past Sweden. (laughs) So joining Bon Jovi was a wonderful chance to take.

One that would make him a member of the biggest band in the world of Rock & Roll within a handful of years, over the first few he spent recording and touring with the band as they developed their sound, Torres found the road provided the band an indispensable sounding board to help hone their brand of blue collar anthem rock – both as songwriters and performers – acknowledging that even as album sales lagged, "the saving grace was the maturity of touring together." Even though Torres had played on Bon Jovi's one major hit, *"Runaway,"* and a minor follow-up with *"In and Out of Love,"* the drummer knew the band – and he personally – had a lot riding on the success or failure of their third studio album, 1986's *Slipper When Wet.* Aided by what he felt was an essential advantage to the band heading into the studio of having the "outside writing aid of Desmond Child, which brought more mature writing to the table," Tico rooted his rhythmic compliments to the band's fresh material almost entirely based around the concept of *feel* first and foremost, a specialty of his as a player that the drummer remembered being a natural fit for hits like

> *"Living on a Prayer"* for instance, which worked so well because you feel it. The key is you want to remember, "Hey, we play this live, and need to have a certain amount if feel for this," and for me, without a doubt, everything is first and foremost about feel. Without feel, people don't get it, you won't translate and you're doing the song injustice I think if you don't feel it. There's a lot of people who play and don't have feel and therefore it sounds stiff, and the song suffers for it – and I'm talking all instruments. So its important to have feel, and remember, intrinsically, you're playing something with other musicians to compliment each other, and its that beautiful magic to go in one direction. Its pretty amazing when you can find those moments. So I think feel is everything, and I've always thought you can study all you want, but if you don't feel it you're not gonna have it.

Driven as strongly in conviction by its beat as any other element of what has made the song arguably Rock & Roll's most enduring anthem across every spectrum and generation of pop culture and society over the past quarter century. From local ball games to Olympic events to fighting the wars of the 12-hour work shift and normal life's heartbreaks and glory days, the song's beat grabs ahold of the listener as powerfully as the chorus melody or lyrical theme and never let's go, starting with Tico's now-legendary opening snare count, a natural reaction the drummer remembered having as soon as

> I heard the beginning, and started counting it off and hit this roll that went into it, which is unmistakable. I always thought there was a Cha Cha feel in that with the song, and that could be my Latin roots, but it was something that felt good in that song. So that one came pretty easy.

Basing his broader beat throughout the song on a bedrock concept that any drummer is required to bring to the kit in complimenting whatever is going on within the song's melodic context, Torres has selflessly sought to always be about "complimenting the melody, that's a lot of it, not only on the guitar, but the vocal: 'Let's give it a shot, BOOM,' putting that there, it makes sense with the lyrics." Adjusting the power of his parts to match and punctuate the emotional highlights of the lyrics Jon Bon Jovi was singing throughout the song, Torres was in effect telling his own story too within the song's rhythm, a tool of his trade that Torres revealed he first picked up listening to

> music from the 50s and 60s music where the drummer would actually sometimes compliment the vocalist – what he's saying or how to bring that chorus up – and I think a lot of that came from listening to music like that. It was always about complimenting the singer and/or lead instrument was always key, and still is. Simplicity is genius sometimes.

Responding to that element he was aware was at work within the world-class songwriting team of Jon Bon Jovi, Ritchie Sambora and Desmond Child throughout much of what would become the 25-MILLION selling *Slippery When*

Wet LP, which Tico felt was an easy album to make first and foremost because "there were just a lot of good songs" to respond to with the drum parts he came up with. Working at the hungry pace of a prize fighter training for a title shot, the drummer remembered that "that album came together very quickly in a lot of ways, which is also very good, because we recorded the rhythm tracks in 3 days." Along with the preparation of being well-rehearsed heading into the studio, Tico credited the band's musical fluidity once again to the songwriting process during pre-production where open-mindedness on the part of all he and all his band mates was pivotal to their progress:

> The key in writing parts and putting songs together is *NEVER* say "No," be positive, because as soon as one negative comes out, the idea's gone. Its about throwing out as many ideas as you can. When the guys in the band come up with something, its usually acoustic, its some chords and the melody and some vocals and lyrics, and for any intents and purposes, it gives you an outline sort of for the song, but it doesn't really create itself until you get the other instruments in the room with you because now you're gonna have to massage it to make it a song that fits the genre of your band, because you can go a million different ways with it.
>
> From that point, alot of the metamorphosis comes when we're going in to do some demos, say on a Sunday for the next week, and the magic's gonna happen in the studio where you have to make it a song, because these guys write the song and might have something in their head they want to hear, so then we have to go back and forth about what works and doesn't work, and get a basis so we can grow and build it and give the song the best chance possible.

With another of the album's massive hit singles, the theme to the most popular television show ever to air on the Discovery Channel, Deadliest Catch, proving its timeless relevance decades after initially conquering the airwaves on both radio and MTV, where the song became a massive video hit as well, in divulging his secret for what makes for a great drum part within a ballad, Tico employed the classic less-is-more approach to the writing of the monster hit *"Wanted Dead or Alive."* A brilliantly and boldly written ballad put down on tape with the full confidence of rock stars well ahead of the band actually being in that position courtesy of songs like this one, Torres knew the acoustic demo was a hit as soon as his ears laid hold on it, revealing for aspiring drummers that

> I tell you how you know: if its easy to play, it's a hit (laughs). I find the best songs are the easiest, where you can go, "You know what, this song feels like red," and if you go with that and are not fighting the laws of physics, and it feels good and you go with it. That's usually how I can tell, and the best answer I can tell you is when its easy to play, its really good.
>
> With *"Wanted Dead or Alive,"* another thing I remember was we tried a couple of takes, it wasn't us, so we went out to a Sushi bar, had some drinks and food, then came back at 11:30 at night and got it in one take! It had a certain magic to it,

After blowing up into superstars with the world-wide dominance of *Slippery When Wet,* Tico and company were faced with the inevitable challenge of delivering a follow up victory in the form of the 1989 album New Jersey. It would be one the band defended handily with a collection of songs that were so universally triumphant that the LP – because of fan demand around the world – became the first by an American band of any genre to ever be released in the U.S.S.R. Arguably no greater example of what was grabbing fans by that point all over the world no matter what language they spoke was the energy of anthems like *"Lay Your Hands On Me,"* driven front and center by the arena-ready acrobatics of Tico's opening tom work that kicks off the song. Crediting the cannon-like boom of the drums in part to the sonic genius of the band's producer Bruce Fairbain and his clever choices in studio placement where the drum kit was concerned as much as he did his own powerful delivery behind the set, Tico was still willing to extend the first credit to his own natural hitting power for the end product:

> On *"Lay Your Hands On Me,"* the drums weren't dressed up with a lot of echo and stuff like that, they were more natural. For that particular record, we went to Little Mountain studio, our producer Bruce Fairbain preferred we come out and work at his studio, and they had a garage-loading bay next to the drum room, which was a substantially good-sized room. First, its all about the sound of the actual tuning of the drums and how you hit them, and then we opened up the Bay doors, put some microphones out there, and you got this natural, ambient sound, which is where that sound came from on *New Jersey*.
>
> That's what made Little Mountain such a great place to record. I think a lot of people sampled those parts as well, but that's what the room actually sounded like and that's the way the drums were tuned, so that's what made them more organic – although it sounded bombastic, because that room would give you that big sound. To me, it was like "Woah, I'm in heaven," because you sit there and hear this in your headphones, and go "Yeah, I could play this easy," it just feels so good. So it was a combination of Bruce Fairbain and his engineer and the sound that we got because of the room on the drums and the Bay. That's what made that album unique-sounding.

Traveling back to his Jazz roots in making specific drum selections for what he felt would play best throughout a song that needed to stay constantly energetic, Torres confirmed that "on that particular song, I thought I'd keep the rhythm going with the double bass on the bottom, and then be able to play the toms on the top. Remember, you grow up with Ginger Baker and a lot of guys who use the double-bass in different ways intrinsically in the music, and then I have a lot of African drums on there because I do all the percussions as well to get an effect of sound. So the whole idea is to create this feel to build the song. Now, when we do it live, I'm just doing double-bass and toms, but there are no machines giving me the other stuff unfortunately. That's the fun part about making records is you can overdub a lot of feels in there, and that just seemed like a show-opener to me, and everybody was just like "Let's build a part around that rhythm."

Turning to another of the album's massive hits, the # 1 single *"Bad Medicine,"* where Torres and Co. in the opinion of Billboard succeeded in their energetic performances with "producing an effect not unlike what these songs sounded like in the arenas and stadiums where they were most often heard." Tico remembered it as "just a good, fun, raw song," and one that he played on a Pearl kit to handle his powerful hitting, proudly endorsing the company for 25 years because

> they are always consistent with the shells, and would build kits to my specifications with thickness as well. The nice thing about being in my position and for guys in my business is if you need stuff, they give it to you, where I had to go buy stuff in the beginning (laughs).
>
> Before Bon Jovi, I started playing on Ludwigs and then when I was with the Knock Outs, I switched to DWs and when they came out I was the first guy to use them, that I know of, and I loved the drums and the shells are amazing. The problem was the hardware wouldn't hold up to roadwork, so they would break, but I found the Pearl hardware was extremely durable and very tunable, and they held up in the hot weather, cold weather, wet weather – which is key.
>
> More recently, I went back to DW because I've always loved their shells, but I had a long and very good relationship with Pearl for 28 years. But all the people I worked with there are gone and the economy of this business changed, and I thought I'd be better off working with DW again. I love the sonics behind it, and the love that they take with the shells, and I toured in 2014 with them and they were just unbelievable. They're just easy to play.

Switching speeds to the creation of the album's # 1 hit ballad, *"I'll Be There For You,"* Tico once again brought a less-is-more philosophy to his playing that drew derivatively on the fact that "I was weaned on guys like Elton John and his drummer Nigel Olsson, and when they first came to the United States, Nigel was using natural catskin heads and wooden rims and there belts on the kit, but the way he played them were bombastic in a sense, so one hit just fills up the space, and so guys like that influenced me. I think when you do a ballad, less is best. You can do one simple 2-or-3 beat roll or one hit in the right place and it just all of a sudden changes the song and makes the chorus open up, that was always key. So I think I translated that through the years and God, even Journey used to do a lot of that too."

Returning once again to the importance of feel in his performance on another of the band's most enduring ballads, *"Always,"* a Top 5 hit on the Billboard Hot 100 Singles Chart that moved fans around the world and hit # 1 on the Eurochart Hot 100, and in countries like Belgium, Ireland, and Switzerland and the Top 5 in Austria, Finland, France, Germany, The Netherlands, Norway, Sweden, the United Kingdom, New Zealand, and Canada. On the song, Torres found himself reacting once again from behind the kit to Jon Bon Jovi's emotional story telling within the song's lyric and vocal melody, approaching its rhythmic compliment it with one of the drummer's bedrock fundamentals:

> For me, its always been you've got to feel what the song feels like, in other words, I feel emotion to build that chorus. Its telling a story, but then I wanna say "Always, the sky opens up and the sun comes through," and how do you make that sound musically? How do you make that chorus open up that way?
>
> That was an interesting song because we used violins, and I use sticks in some parts and cross-sticking and then actually went into a full kit in other parts. So there was a building process without stepping on anything, and then once you were able to get in there and build that bridge, then jeez, it

> doesn't get any bigger than that. Its like you're making a statement to go "This is it," and its definite as it can be as a statement. I think personally we achieved that in the song, otherwise the song wouldn't have worked.

Exploding in to the Millennium with a new generation of hits that proved the band's staying power once and for all as a relevant vs. nostalgia-circuit band with their signature brand of uplifting rockers like *"Its My Life"* – which hit # 1 in 7 countries – and *"Have a Nice Day."* Keeping his playing behind the kit upbeat was something Torres had been a master at for decades, and in dispensing advice on how to keep performances fresh in that context after so many years in the saddle, Tico for the first time was playing in the new hybrid of live drums played over programmed beats, a reflection he remembers of

> what was going on at the time, and it's the wonderful thing about having producers. They have access to stuff like that, and there's the outer ear where you can use that as a tool as opposed to leaning on it. So it was fun to be able to do something like that, where there's a constant rhythm of percussion or a feel behind it, which enhancing the songs. In the old days, we would lay down tracks that were percussions, and we would do the track on top of that. Of course, the problem with that is you can never really translate it live, unless you hire another 2 or 3 guys to play the instruments. So it was exciting to be able to have machines do that for you.
>
> With *"Have a Nice Day,"* that one was a guitar-driven song, which was a lot of fun to do, and its bombastic drums with that triplet kind of feel. That one came together pretty easy, that was one of those songs that was like "This feels good, just bang it."

Stepping out of what was perceived to be their comfort zone in 2007 to try their hand at making a country record, *Lost Highway,* Torres actually found himself right at home musically, beginning with the band's massive cross-over hit *"Who Says You Can't Go Home,"* which reached # 1 on the Billboard US Hot Country Songs Chart in May, 2006:

Doing *"Who Says You Can't Go Home,"* we were able to mix it up a little bit with a country feel, which inertly has become, if you look at where country music's gone, the younger guys have become more rock. So it kind of worked out really good for us to do that little crossover.

The fact that we were going in to do something in Nashville was a little intense, and we used a couple of different producers, and tried our hand at country-sounding feels. Initially, I thought we were going to go in and do a really purist country record, but when we ended up recording, it really just had to sound like us, and it was fun to do because it was off the wall. I think what made it fresh was approaching songs in that sense, with some different people, some different instrumentation, some different feels, and that's really exciting when you're doing something new like that with the band that you're not used to doing.

Even with as busy as Bon Jovi has stayed throughout the years with their recording schedule, Tico has stayed even busier on the session circuit, demonstrating the kind of work ethic and love for the purity of playing that has driven him throughout his entire career. In contrasting the difference in hats he wears playing on another artist who might be stylistically foreign to a Bon Jovi album, Tico – with a deep well of influences to draw from beyond the realm of Rock & Roll – begins by explaining that

There's more leeway when we do a Bon Jovi song, because it's a band, its us, but if I'm doing something for somebody else, I'm more inclined to try to search out what the artist is looking for, what the song needs to make that song the best possible song. Of course, you don't know everybody as well when you play with new musicians sometimes, so obviously you try to gel. Most of the stuff I play is R&B, Rock, Jazz, Country, some Heavy Metal, but not much, but that covered my spectrum.

In the studio, I'm a fan of playing with a click track, and I'll tell you why: I'm really used to using it, and as I hear the click, I can bring the beat back

> behind the click or on top to push it, and that basis is always good, especially when you're doing overdubs. Because it keeps it right on and makes everybody's work a lot easier, and there's no gray area. With certain songs, if you want them to speed up, you can do it within the click, so I'm a big fan of it and think it's a great tool.

Despite a close call in 2013 when he was rushed to the hospital from a headlining gig at the Rock in Rio concert in Rio Di Janeiro to remove his gall bladder following an earlier E.R. visit where Rolling Stone Magazine reported "the band canceled their Mexico City show on September 10th and rescheduled two other dates when Torres had emergency surgery to remove his appendix." With close calls like those to help focus anyone on life's most important things, in the drumming realm, Tico offers the following advice to young players looking up to him as a resilient example of what the type of player they hope to be 30 years from now, beginning with the timeless importance of

> # 1), follow your heart, and # 2), whatever your heart desires, practice, practice, practice. Make it better, because practice doesn't make perfect, it makes you better, and 3) is Don't give up, because the darkest moment is when your probably going to be the most creative. You've read that about artists in many ways, and in essence its true because you're just opening up: there's nothing stopping you, there's no trappings of the world, and that will bring you through. So those 3 things, if you can follow those in anything you do, I think it will make you a better human being and happy.
>
> Playing with as many types of musicians as possible is important too for young drummers, because the more diverse you are, the more work you'll get, so if you can play Jazz, if you can play Latin, R&B, Rock, Heavy Metal and Country, so sometimes you want to mix it up a little bit, and the more you do the better you'll be, so don't limit yourself. So play with as many people as you can and be in as many bands as you can, and experiment, because its only gonna make you better.

Now in his fourth decade years behind the kit with Bon Jovi – a longevity unheard of both for most Rock & Roll bands and for most professional musicians to stay playing at Tico's peak level for the better part of 45 years – the drummer appreciates the constant of "the fact that I'm in a band that's been together over 30 years, it doesn't get cooler than that. Again, before that, I was in different bands, different bands – two years here, three years there – and so its nice to be able to be with the same group and create together." Bringing his story full circle with some closing reflections, the legendary drummer begins by shaking his head at how far he's taken the dream he first began chasing almost 50 years ago:

> I'm pretty amazed I did so well, although once I started making my first paycheck when I was 15, all I did was look up, because there were always places to go and things to conquer musically and to experiment with. So having that yearn as a musician, first of all, one thing that happens is you don't get old, and number two is, life flies by because you're in it. I've been making a living off it since I was a teenager, at 16 playing 3 nights a week while I was still in high school. Then when I was 18, I made a full living out of it. I decided not to go to music school and to play in the street and learn from the street guys, the Jazz guys, so I've been blessed to be able to do that all my life.
>
> Within Bon Jovi, I think something I appreciate is that the band's always had that positive attitude within the lyrics of our songs, and attitude toward the music and life, and you can always find hope in some of those stories. I think the world is hard enough on a lot of people, and we take the good with the bad, but I'd rather hear a song that's going to bring me to a better place than one that's going to bring me down to a dark place. So I gotta say that the best legacy Bon Jovi has is positive thinking, and we get a lot of that. Recently, we did a thing for the Navy Seals to raise money for them and its amazing to hear their stories, that they grew up on your songs. You get a lot of that.

I think music is the best thing that ever happened to the universe, because its not bad for you, its only good for you. It has no negative residue, it really doesn't, and that old saying, "Music makes the world go round," well that's true, period. It does, it gets people through wars and bad times, and helps them celebrate great times, so I celebrate music, because without it, I think we'd be in trouble. So I think it's a hell of a compliment that you can actually turn somebody on to something. Its nice to open a mind with your playing, and if I'm a little bit of that in somebody's playing, that's awesome. I know they're going to take from me and another 20, 30 drummers and come up with their own style, it's a beautiful thing.

"How did a knucklehead from Birmingham, Michigan ever make it to the Hall of Fame?" – Chad Smith, 2017

(photo by Jason Miller)

Chapter 5: Chad Smith of the Red Hot Chili Peppers – "Swing Batter!"

As opening balls go, *"The Power of Equality"* was the equivalent of a grand-slam hit, one where the crack of the snare equaled that of a bat echoing of a baseball stadium's walls, and the power hitter responding to lead singer Anthony Keidis' introductory invitation to "Swing batter, swing batter, swing batter batter" was answered by a true V.I.P. of the Rock drumming game, Red Hot Chili Peppers drummer Chad Smith. A literal Hall of Famer at this point his 30+ year career in the major leagues of Rock & Roll, Smith and his teammates changed the face of Alternative Rock forever with their groundbreaking fusion of Funk and Rock, and on the latter-mentioned opening track to *BloodSugarSexMagik,* their mainstream breakthrough into the big time, Smith remembered his harnessing of such explosive power within the song's drum sound was unique within its recording

> because it's the only song on the record that has two drum sets! I double-tracked it, and it was recorded in the same room as the *"Give It Away"* drums, so there were like 4 mics – kick, snare, and two mics like 4 feet away from the drums, and that's it. That's all you hear on *"Give It Away"* and on the one side of *"Power."* So Rick Rubin said, "Power's got this big, heavy thing like Give It Away, why don't you cut the drums in that room?"
>
> Because we had the luxury of having a drum kit set up in the tracking room with all the other guys, and then there was a library that had a lot of windows and real bright surfaces, and we had a drum set in there too, and again, Brendan O'Brien – who was engineer on the project – and I kind of walked around the house, and would put kick and snare in different places and he would just stand there and listen, "Okay, that sounds good, let's go somewhere else. Oh, that's too bright," so he was really cool about having these sort of options of exploring the acoustic qualities of the house we were in."
>
> We'd never done that before because we'd always been in a regular studio, so this one room was real bright and when we cut *"Power of Equality,"* we first did it in the room with 4 mics. Then I went back and listened to it, and Rick Rubin was like "You know, that was a great take, sounds good but I'm missing… You're kind of locked in to that sound because of the 4 mics and the sound of the room, he was like "I'm missing some of your grace notes and a little bit of a tighter thing, do you think you could play to the track on your regular drum out there?" And I'd never done that before, but I was like "Okay, I'll give it a shot," and so I went out there, put my headphones on, and there I am playing along to another band, except it was me! (laughs)
>
> As humbly as I can say, I played it through once and that's what you hear. There are little subtle things, like little cymbal crashes I don't do once in a

> while, but its pretty spot-on. What you do hear is all the little, subtle grace notes on the snare, and its just a little tighter sound, and when he put them together, I was like "Wow, that sounds fucking good!"

Swing has reined king throughout Smith's entire career as a drummer, dating back to his childhood growing up under the influence of the first generation of Rock & Roll drummers in the late 60s who naturally reflected it in their own playing having been universally reared on the Big Band/Jazz era of drumming superstars like Gene Krupa and Buddy Rich. By the time that had filtered into the stylistic DNA of the drummers for pioneering rock and metal bands like Deep Purple and the Jimmy Hendrix Experience that Chad was listening to growing up, the drummer recalled absorbing it as part of what he was imitating in his earliest days behind the kit learning by listening and playing along to his Rock & Roll heroes:

> I think its more because the drummers I listened to had swing, and early on, and that I'm not real taught, I'm a kind of self-taught guy, so the Ian Paces and Mitch Mitchell's and Bill Wards, they all started off as jazz drummers. Bill Ward, the heaviest hitter of all those guys, you listen to him by himself without the rest of the music, and its got all this jazz swing, and Ringo Starr, nobody swings harder than that guy. I think it an era where a lot of those guys grew up with some early Rock & Roll, but moreso, it was influenced by Jazz, and I think that element creeped into my playing without even knowing.

Drawn naturally to rhythm before he was old enough to even know what a drum set was, a young Chad's parents first recognized this interest by the sound of "me just starting to kind of bang stuff around the house, as little young people do who are prone to that." Seeking to spare their furniture and ears while still nurturing his interest to see where it might lead musically, the drummer remembered his father coming up with an inventive compromise that worked well for everyone in Smith's earliest days of rhythmic discovery:

> My parents weren't about to run out and buy little Johnny a drum set, and I don't know many parents who would say "Hey, why don't you take up the drums, that's a nice, quiet instrument." They were very supportive, but at first, they were like a little wary to see where I was gonna go with this hitting thing, so my dad went to the garbage part of the back of the local Baskin Robbins in the local town I lived in at the time, Birmingham, Michigan, and took a few thrown-out ice cream tubs and I used Lincoln log kid's toys for drum sticks.
>
> So my dad was a thief and I started out with only the finest equipment at 6, 7 years old. Then, right away, I tore through that, it was made out of cardboard, and just kind of progressed a little bit with my parents watching with the whole kind of "Is he gonna stick with this?" kind of thing, vs. a phase, and I just always loved to play and played constantly from 7 on because I loved it.

Having beaten his first kit to pulp soon enough, Chad's parents' thereafter bought him his first real drum set, a move aided in part no doubt by the generally creative atmosphere that surrounded him growing up in a musically-inclined family: "I had an older brother who played a little bit of guitar, he's 2 years older than me, and my sister – who is 5 years older than me – played piano. So my siblings were all musically inclined, and my mother played a little bit of guitar and a little piano, and my father loved music but could not carry a tune to save his life, but we always had music in the house." Influenced in his early impressions as a player no doubt by the eclectic mix of artists he heard playing throughout the house as a child, Smith remembered

> early on, my dad loved Johnny Cash and Elvis Presley and Frank Sinatra, those were his 3 favorite go-tos, I remember that music on in our house all the time as a young kid, and early on, I was like "Oh man, this is terrible music, I want Beatles music." Because this was back in the late 60s at 8 or 9 years old, and my brother Brad, being older than me, was already really into

all those hard rock blues band from England, like Led Zeppelin, Cream, The Who, Rolling Stones, Humble Pie, David Bowie, Queen, the Jimi Hendrix Experience, obviously The Beatles, Black Sabbath, Deep Purple, Mott the Hoople – all of that, some glammy, but more like the harder, heavy metal and hard rock blues bands coming out of the U.K. He just loved all that stuff, and I soaked it all up.

Ironically, I wouldn't say it was necessarily the drumming at first that grabbed my attention, per say – I'm sure subconsciously, I was listening to the drums and what they were doing and how they pertained to the music, and what the drummer was doing, because all those drummers are still some of my favorites, Ian Pace, and obviously John Bonham. But I think I just liked the attitude of the music when I was really young, I really remember coming home from school and turning on volume 4 of Black Sabbath as loud as my brother's little, crappy stereo would go, and it felt like it was my music. It wasn't my sister's Carley Simon and Carol King and Three Dog Night and Elton John and Cat Stevens – all great artists and musicians – but that was too soft for me. I was a pretty aggressive little young dude and I liked the harder stuff. What also went along with that was the love of looking at album covers and they were very dangerous and mysterious, like Led Zeppelin, and it just added the mystique, and I was very intrigued and it was very mystical, I just loved everything about it.

A world of wild wonderment for any child discovering music made just for their generation, Chad's version of this revelation was enhanced by his ability to hear what was going on within these records differently from other kids his age because of how he could translate it instrumentally. His principle tool of training as a drummer who grew up teaching himself by ear to play by drumming along to his heroes, it proved an invaluable approach to both enjoying his practice time while still challenging himself that he still recommends to this day:

> Playing along to records was something I did on a regular basis. I learned to read drum notation music from 5th grade, but mainly just the snare drum, so it wasn't a drum set, just rudiments and how its applied to concert band or symphonic band, band class in school, so I could play whatever songs we were doing. And I think that's an important thing to do, but being in a band playing Rock & Roll music, playing along to records was the best lesson, and I did it a lot. What's better than playing along to like a Led Zeppelin record or Van Halen 2 or Chicago or Black Sabbath, you're in the band! The guys that you're gonna play with aren't gonna play as good as Jimmy Page and John Paul Jones, and if you can play along to those records – first of all, I used to play really loud and still do – and the key was to get headphones and a stereo and crank it louder than I was.
>
> I think it's a wonderful lesson. You're inspired playing, and no one plays like John Bonham or Stewart Copeland, but you want to play sort of in that guy's style because you want to fit in with the band you're playing along to, and kind of swing it like they would or whatever to make it feel good. Luckily, I played along to great bands with great drummers, and I highly recommend that.

Experiencing his proverbial "Ed Sullivan" moment of discovery that he *did* want to become a Rock & Roll Star when he reached his teenage years in the early 1970s, Smith confessed that vs. the music itself, he was more enthralled by the general image of the Rocker lifestyle first painted vividly in his mind

> when I turned 13 and started reading Crème Magazine and Circus. I didn't read Rolling Stone, I would always like slum it down to these bands like Aerosmith and Kiss and Grand Funk Railroad. And I would read about these bands and they were into girls and drugs and there were always pictures of them with bottles of like Jim Beam or whatever, and I was just like "WOW! I wanna do that!"

> So through my brother's influence and his record collection, that's the music that I wanted to play, and I sort of identified with those bands and those kind of people, I just thought they were cool, and when I was 13, 14, I started playing in little bands and girls started coming into play, and smoking pot, all that teenager stuff and by the time I was 16, I stopped playing sports altogether to concentrate full-time on music, and said "This is what I wanna do, that's it."

Not having to go far to find other musicians with the same passion in mind than his own siblings, Chad started his first Garage band with his older brother Brad. When making the all important decision of what to call his first Rock & Roll group, the Smith brothers went with the catchy *"Rockin' Conspiracy,"* with the drummer shaking his head self-effacingly looking back that "we were like the Rage Against the Machine of Chicago, very controversial. This was 1973, Watergate, we were just a bunch of knuckleheads trying to fake our way through the songs of the day – *'Purple Haze,' 'Gloria,'* and *'Fire'* by Jimi Hendrix, and *'Light My Fire'* by The Doors. We had a keyboard player, and we were terrible. I was terrible, I had one beat, fast or slow, one fill, that I did every four bars. I actually heard a tape of us recently and it was pretty rough. We played like the school dance class in Junior High, in 7th grade, and we couldn't play anything they could fox trot to, and I think we got fired because the Conspiracy could not rock a fox trot (laughs). We didn't have anything in three, but maybe it was a good thing."

Making the key segway step for any journeyman musician of playing before their first live audiences no matter how badly he thought the band sounded doing so, after navigating his way through a few learning curve years, Smith found himself by his sophomore year living back in his homestate of Michigan, having apparently improved his chops enough to land a gig in a new highschool band, Northstar, where he was the group's youngest member playing with all Seniors. A significant step-up in musicianship and seriousness as a player, Chad embraced his commitment to the band so fully that

> the way I spent my sophomore year, I never made it inside the school. I would kick the bus, and end up in the parking lot in my friend's car, the singer Kevin, listening to Rush's *2112* on 8-track smoking weed, and never really made it to class and eventually got kicked out of that school. But Northstar had a gig and it was around Christmas time, so we went through our neighborhood and stole all the lights from everybody's decorations and made a light-show out of it, and the geniuses that we were, we built this big tower all rigged up with our flood lights, and we couldn't figure out how we were going to transport it anywhere. I don't even remember how we got it to the Battle of the Bands, but we did, and we played kind of the heavy rock of the day – Ted Nugent, Bad Company, Foghat – this was 77. Northstar was a little more progressive, because we were doing like Rush songs and I was really going through a real Neal Peart-phase, and I think most drummers of a certain age go through their little – its almost like a right of passage Neal Peart phase – and I had a big drum set with racks of toms and cowbells. I played all those records.
>
> Northstar broke up after 10th grade, and then I was in another band called Paradise with two guys from a different highschool. They were an established band already when I joined, and again, we did more rock stuff, and would play backyard parties and do Cream covers like *"Crossroads"* for 20 minutes, and *"Valentine"* by Deep Purple, and Mott the Hoople songs, T-Rex, that sort of thing.

As Smith continued to explore and expand his pallet of stylistic influences as a player during these formative years, side by side with Rock & Roll, Chad found himself drawn to the genre's forefather, R&B, and against the backdrop of the Motor City, he had the added benefit of being smack-dab in the genre's epicenter as a whole new era of innovators were hitting the airwaves and local live stages. Given the hybrid style of playing he would later become famous for bridging into Rock's mainstream, Smith found himself instantly drawn to Funk, a new sub-genre that had flamed up out of R&B's hotbed during its 1970s golden era:

Growing up in Detroit, I bought a lot of 45s of Motown, Rare Earth, Sly and the Family Stone, and the Temptations, Stevie Wonder, Marvin Gaye, I loved all that stuff too, but more because it was popular music. My love was that hard stuff, but I also really appreciated and enjoyed and bought those records, and tried to soak up anything I could. There was a local station out of Windsor called CKLW just across the river, and I'd listen to that all night on my headphones, this was AM, but they played a lot of really cool stuff, James Brown, and again, I *REALLY* liked Sly and the Family Stone.

I remember one 45 that I played endlessly, Side A was *"Hot Fun in the Summertime"* and the B-Side was *"Thank You For Letting Me Be Myself."* That was so unique to me, it was like nothing else I'd ever heard, and they played these short, little cool songs that were hooky and I guess Greg Errico was just playing hard 2-4 sort of 8th note pattern funk things, and that's my bread and butter to this fucking day, really. That's kind of what I do, it was really powerful to me, and its loud but musical, and I don't even know I was thinking that at the time as a player, I just knew I liked it. Something about it was great, so we'd put the needle back on and listen to it again and listen to it again, then I'd put the headphones on and play along, and it was wild.

By the time Chad graduated High School in 1980, though he'd spent years as a gigging Rock & Roll drummer on the local club circuit in and around Detroit, it wasn't until he met the musician he considers to be his greatest single musical mentor, percussionist Larry Fratangelo, that Smith truly felt be began to find his own voice as a player. The one who he credits with truly teaching Smith the dynamics required to consider himself a legitimate Funk drummer, Frantangelo's years playing as a percussionist with the legendary George Clinton and Parliament Funkadelic led up to the moment of fate where Chad at age 20 found himself suddenly sharing percussive duties with his soon-to-be mentor. An eye-and-ear opening moment of clarity for the young drummer of where he needed to head in his next evolution as a player, it was one he eagerly embraced even while feeling that

> by 1982, I had become a pretty good drummer. I could play, I'd been out of high school for two years and had been touring the tri-county area of Detroit, playing all the clubs 6 nights a week, three sets a night, and then I joined up with another band called Pharoh that featured Larry Fratangelo, who'd been a percussionist in Parliament and a big Detroit session cat. He was 10 years older than me, and I was the youngest of 8 guys in the band, and Larry – thank God, and I thank him to this day – he took me under his wing, this little 20 year old, and he really showed me the ropes.
>
> He would pick me up at my house and we'd go to rehearsal every day, and while we were driving, we'd listen to music in his station wagon, and he'd tell me, "Okay, listen to this song, this is *'What is Hip'* by Tower of Power, now listen, after the 2nd verse, Garibaldi's going to do this thing on the 1, and then he's going to lay out the snare and its not going to come back in. He's going to wait, and what that does is, that dynamic really makes the band come down. If the band can't hear you, they ain't gonna fuckin' come down," and that was like a revelation to me, because I banged the fuck out of everything! I looked up at the end of the song and was like "Woah, we made it," and I had no idea about connecting with the other musicians, playing a song, building a song, the dynamics, doing a small fill going into the first chorus and maybe a bigger one into a solo, and how to back a solo or build a solo, how to maybe go to the right on a bridge part. It sounds like Arrangement 101 shit now, but back then, man, I didn't have a fucking clue. I wasn't musical, I was a banger, and Larry taught me really how to be musical, and really how to *listen.*

A lesson that would become pivotal within Chad's future interplay with the genius of Flea and John Frusciante, a conversation of musical ideas that reflected a constant awareness of each's individual originality that as they pooled, the sound that emerged "revealed new dimensions," in the esteemed opinion of Rolling Stone, especially where "the rhythm section displayed a growing curiosity" that pushed the band into new musical boundaries unheard before they joined forces. That sense of musical curiosity within Smith while still under the wing of Larry Fratangelo was only growing exponentially as the drummer soaked up every musical lesson he could, beginning always with the fundamental importance his teacher hammed home of being a good listener.

> That's the most important thing for any musician, is: you have to be a good listener. That's it, I really think if you don't listen to what's going on when you're playing – in any musical situation – then its not going to really turn out very well, I don't think. Certainly not in any kind of music where there's any kind of dynamic. If you want to just put your head down and bang as hard as you can, that's one thing, but to be musical and to play off and with other players, a drummer has so much control over that, and Larry taught me that.
>
> Then he would play me James Brown songs, and say "See these guys, they play one groove and it never fucking changes. Chad, you and me, after rehearsal, I want you to play one groove, and I'm gonna do a bunch of shit over the percussion, and I don't want you to change the beat at all. If you can hold down the beat and play it consistently and dynamically for 6 minutes, 10 minutes, then you're a drummer. You've got to keep time, and if people are tapping their toes and singing the song, then we're going our job, because the drummer and the singer are the two most important guys in the band…" And I'm sitting there, nodding along, "Okay," but Larry was just cool, I looked up to him, he was awesome, and for a whole year we played together, and that was my school, it really was. I can never thank him, but I try to as often as possible. He still plays with Kid Rock, and I was fortunate to come upon this guy at this time in my life when I needed him like no one else, it was just a perfect storm.
>
> He was just so generous and helped me, and would say, "I can tell, you're a good player, you got it man, I just need to show you a few things," and he could see that I was like a Colt, and he turned me into a fucking race

> horse. Luckily, I was open enough to go "Yeah man, this is good, I get it, this works," and there were all these "Woah" moments of me hitting my head with the stick and going "Duh," which I never really picked up playing along to records. These great drummers would do that, but I think its different when you have to do it with somebody else, like a percussionist, and he was just really, really helpful, and I'll be forever grateful.

By the time his "Big Break" moment did arrive to audition with the Chilis several years later in 1988, Smith was armed with not only with this new arsenal of knowledge but also with the advantage of almost a decade playing on the professional gigging circuit. Following his stint with Fratangelo in Pharoh, where Smith's school of professional study as a player included recording his first studio album, 1982's *Point of Entry,* the journeyman drummer had logged time drumming and recording with the Toby Redd Band on 1986's *Into the Light* LP, but by the later 80s, had decided to pack up his kit and head West in pursuit of his break into the big time. Ironically, when that opportunity finally came knocking in 1988, where most unknown drummers would have been over the moon at getting the call to audition for an already-established band *with* a major label record contract, in Smith's case, he revealed that not only was he not a fan of the Red Hot Chili Peppers, but so much so that vs. practicing for weeks in advance becoming familiar with their back catalog,

> the funny thing was, I remember listening to their tape in the parking lot on the day of the audition! I didn't really prepare that much (laughs)." Before *Mother's Milk,* I wasn't a big fan of the Chili Peppers, and weirdly enough, the guy who first told me about the Chili Peppers was Larry – who'd played on *"Freaky Styley."* He played me like half a song in passing, and then fast forward, me going out to California and my audition was through a friend of a friend of a girlfriend – which is sort of the typical way you hear about stuff – and they had been trying to find a drummer. My friend Newt Cool – who I knew from Detroit and had also moved out to California and was dating Denise Zoom, who used to be married to Billy Zoom from X, and

had previously dated John before Newt – he says "The Chili Peppers are looking for a drummer, dude, you gotta play with these guys." He loved them and was a huge fan, and continued, "You'd be perfect for this band. They like to rock out, they can funk," and I was trying to recall them, and was like "Oh yeah, the guys with socks on their dicks! Larry talked about them years ago," and even though I wasn't a fan of them, when I heard, "They got a record deal? I'll go play with these guys!"

Because back then, I was looking for a gig, any gig, and that's how it happened – I didn't have big expectations or anything. It was like, "My friend says they're cool, and Larry played with them," and I put out the Abby Road E.P. they'd just had come out, and heard them do *"Fire"* by Jimi Hendrix, and I was like "Shit, I used to play this in Rockin Conspiracy, I know this song, they just do it fast, this sounds cool," and so I was sitting the parking lot of their rehearsal place in my little Honda Accord with my drum set, listened to the end of the tape, which had "Funky Crime" and "Fight Like a Brave," and like I said before, really just kind of winged the audition a little bit.

Confident in his ability to answer whatever they threw at him musically, Smith remembered finding immediate common ground in the comfort zone of jamming where the band's musical conversations began to click immediately in their interpretation of the Stevie Wonder classic *"Higher Ground."* Deciding almost as instantly that they'd finally found their new drummer, Chad remembered the band's producer being so blown away that

Beinhorn was in the room, and I didn't know who he was, but I remember he was laughing a lot, and as I was playing, I was thinking to myself, "Is he laughing because he's making fun of us?" It was hysterical, because we were just doing this crazy fucking jam, and John Frusciante had joined the band right prior to me and I'd spoken to him on the phone and he goes, "Buy the E.P., but we'll just jam, we like to jam, and we'll be able to tell if you're any good by jamming." I had extensive background in jamming, so I remember being like "Oh, cool!" Because that's all I used to do with a couple of my other bands, going way back to High School even, and improvising and playing off the other players and stuff, that's the same thing we do to this day. It's the same way the Chilis come up with songs 25 years later, but on the day I went in to audition, we did that and back then, everything was fast, slap-funk, and I just joined in and started playing, and that was it man: we did a little bit of *"Higher Ground"* and we kind of hit it off musically right away. The songs we were writing and the way that I played, I did have more of a rock – and still do – style!

I think they appreciated somebody that sort of took the lead. I think my aggressive drumming they enjoyed but they didn't like my look, because I had long hair and looked like I belonged on the Sunset Strip. Of course, the hair and tattoos were really important at that time, but it didn't matter, we just jammed and I liked it, and thought "This is fun, these guys are good!" They were better than I expected, the whole thing was, and I was going in with not a lot of expectation, and here we are 25+ years later. There wasn't any like "Woah, we're gonna do this kind of Funk-meets-Rock kind of thing that no one's ever done before," we just played what we wanted to play, which we always do, because it really was just about the chemistry of these 4 guys.

Rolling Stone Magazine would years later credit this as "the moment that changed (Smith's) life, re-invented his band, and ultimately made the world a little freakier," as evinced by the band's reinvention of *"Higher Ground,"* which showcased the originality they brought to the table. Stronger still was the scorching frenzy of Smith's attack in the opening moments of *"Good Time Boys"* where Billboard would find itself blown away by the "pulsating power that leapt from the blistering opener," and mound from which the drummer announced his arrival behind the kit with equal authority between both the band's funk-altrock fanbase and the hair metal crowd starting to tire of the Warrants of the world and pay attention to the band's infectious energy. Smith had credibility with these metal heads because he hit as hard and heavy as any of his competitors, channeling his Led Zeppelin hero in the album's opener:

> With *"Good Time Boys,"* drum-wise, more than anything else, that was probably me trying to do a John Bonham impersonation, so that was like very "Okay, let's think big drums." I think a lot of times with music, the chemistry of people that get together, and the timing of where stuff is at, hair metal was still going pretty strong, so early on, I remember shows that we would play, and we still got the knucklehead kind of Jock dudes, and the geeky, sort of misfits that didn't really fit in that liked us, and I guess there was kind of a more hybrid of fan, if you will, which I think is a beautiful thing.

Pulling from his entire stylistic color wheel as his sticks spun around the kit, Smith sprayed a collage of his own rhythmic influences – metal, funk, psychedelic, punk, R&B, hard rock, hip hop, thrash, and alternative - onto the band's musical canvas, venturing as well into new territory at the encouragement of producer Michael Beinhorn, who challenged the drummer on *"Subway to Venus"*

> in the chorus when he'd said, "I want you to come up with like a signature beat that you've never done on the chorus," so I had to work on that 16-th note hi-hat thing, and he helped me with that, so we figured out that chorus beat together. He didn't care about the other part of the song (laughs), but for the chorus, he wanted something very specific, but that was a fun one to play. There's a section in 5, I think it's the bridge, and when it came to the riff, that was a little tricky for me.
>
> That's like sort of a James Brown-yish thing, as far as the influence on my playing, and to be honest, on that record, Beinhorn ended up putting samples and triggers on the drums, and they were all fucked up (laughs), even though I know a lot of people love that record. But if you listen to *"Subway to Venus,"* for instance, there's no dynamics in the snare, I didn't play it like that, and *"Knock Me Down,"* all the snare sounds, it drove me crazy.

> There's real snare, but then there's also some other triggered sounds that were sampled in there that took the dynamics out of all that stuff.

Still, Smith remembered having a great time recording with his band mates live off the floor in the studio, a celebration of musical jubilation that can be heard constantly penetrating throughout the recordings that went down on tape. Kicking out an electricity captured on bottled-lightning moments like *"Stone Cold Bush,"* the drummer was inspired to "just laugh my ass off when I listen to that today because we would never, ever come up with a song like that now, but 25 years ago, it was very apropos of the Chili Peppers at that time. That was the perfect example – lyrically, musically, instrumentally, attitude-y – that was all very Chili Pepper-esque, and I had a very good time playing that music." Another musical memory that still makes the drummer smile to date came when his band mates played a bit of a songwriting trick on Smith with *"Magic Johnson,"* a track where he thought during instrumental tracking in the studio that he was paying homage to

> the Arma Mater of all 4 original Chili Peppers, because the song's opening drum cadence was the drum line cadence to the percussion section of Fairfax High, which they originally had also titled the song, and so we laid it down and they threw in that other funk section. Then I went home to Michigan after we did the tracks, came back, and they'd been working on the songs, and I couldn't wait to get back to hear that one because Anthony was like "Oh man, wait till you hear Fairfax High, we put words on it, its so fucking cool!" And this was 1989 where the Pistons and the Lakers were playing in the finals, and the Lakers beat the Pistons, and then the next year, the Pistons beat the Lakers, so we had a pretty good rivalry going because the guys in the band were all Lakers fans and me being from Detroit, my loyalties were to the Pistons. So I came back and they sat down in the studio and played me the song, and I was like "What the fuck!", and he was so happy.

Kicking their first hole in the mainstream rock door they would fully knock down with their next studio album, People Magazine would note of this transition Smith helped the band make that with *Mother's Milk,* this California quartet was anointed the standard-bearer of funk punk and hailed as the genre-bending future of rock." On the drummer's second studio outing with the band on *BloodSugarSexMagik,* the Chili Peppers stirred those elements up into a stew of musical alchemy brewed under the wizardry of new producer Rick Rubin and fittingly recorded in a 10-room haunted mansion in Laurel Canyon once owned by Harry Houdini. Dazzled more by the acoustic possibilities of the backdrop to organically improve the sonic dimensions of drum sound over the previous album, Smith found himself enchanted with

> the environment of that house, which was a little bit unique to the traditional studio, and we took advantage of that. The main tracking was done in the biggest room in the house, it was like a ballroom, and we set up a P.A. with high end, mid-range, low end speakers, like two stacks probably 15 feet away from the drums, and also had room mics, and so we'd pump the drum set through the P.A. I think the first time we did it was on *Mother's Milk,* and I'm not even sure we used it on that record, but you hear it a lot throughout *"Sex Magik."*
>
> Luckily, Brendan was an incredible engineer and musician, he played keys on *"Sir Psycho"* and mellotron on *"Breaking the Girl,"* and he has a real organic approach, real fast, so it didn't really take a lot of time to set something up, because sometimes the session can get bogged down when someone says, "Oh, I've got to try 6 different mics on this ride cymbal to see which one sounds better." That just kills the groove of the whole thing. So Brendan was just like, "Let's get it down, let's not worry about it," and he was very talented obviously and knew what he was doing, but he was just about capturing the creative moment, and we had a lot of those.

Pointing to *"Funky Monks"* as one where he felt the essence of his drum sound was fully projected and reflected from both the playing and production sides perfectly, offering his observation that "if you listen, there's a lot of space, drums in that song have a lot of sonic room, and you're getting some P.A. through that. That's pretty big, that's probably my drum sound on the record. That was one of those songs that wasn't quite finished when we went in, and we got the basic thing to it, but Anthony didn't have all the verses and the bridge section wasn't done. We kind of wrote that a little bit in the studio." Later praised by Drum Magazine for his innovative "use of open hi-hats on the offbeats, combined with a syncopated kick pattern and his patented tight snare sound," Smith remembered the song as a stand-out for the unique fact that it represented

> one of the few times we had difficulty getting a good take. With most of them, we were pretty quick at getting a good performance, but we had to labor over that one for some reason, it just wasn't feeling right. I think I had to play less, and was busier before, and then started doing this sort of disco thing with an open hi-hat and that seemed to work well. But I remember my bass drum pattern was not gelling well with what Flea was doing, and Rick told me to simplify it – which he usually does. He's really good at sort of editing, which we kind of need – or I need – because I'll play too much, and he'd be like "That's good for live, but we're making records here, so what if you do like you half of what you're doing?" (laughs) And there are times that I've fought for fills, where I'll say "I knew you were going to say that, but Rick, I'm doing this because…"
>
> Then he'll go, "That's cool, but I'm not really a drummer, just more straight ahead I think is better for the song," and he just really wants to serve the song. If something's distracting away from the essence of what the good part of the song is, he's really good at figuring that out and going, "Ehhh, its too much," or sometimes he'll say "No, can you do… it needs something to connect this part to this part, and maybe it's the drums, how about this?" So he's not a fill Nazi, but more often than not, he always encourages me

to come up with a creative, simpler way to get the point across to what I'm trying to do: to serve the song, or build the song or use dynamics. He's always up for a cool beat, but it can't be super busy, because to him, the drums are a supportive thing, and the way we play our music, I'm not the lead instrument. Phil Rudd's probably his favorite drummer, so there you go: he's a great drummer but not a lot of fills. I'll tell you something else, *"Funky Monks"* was the only song on the record that we played to a click track.

I might sound like an old fart, but I just enjoy the performance of a song. I think its important for people as a band to play it together organically, and I'm not saying what's right or wrong, this is just what works for me. This is what I like, and its what I like to hear: I like to hear people make mistakes, I like to hear people take chances. With this technology now, its so easy to fix everything, autotune everything, and it takes some of the human element out of it, and I like the human element. I like the picking up a little bit, and settling in a verse, just the human, breathing part of it connects with me, and I think it connects with a lot of people. With Rock music, that's the way I like to do it, and I'm lucky to be around other people who like that too. I work a lot with Rick Rubin, for instance, and Rick rarely ever uses click tracks, he's the same way, he wants to hear everybody playing something. People in a room, that's what I want to hear, and I think that performance connects with the listener – whether they know it or not.

Locked fully in synch with Rubin's headspace throughout the making of *BloodSugar,* Chad credits the producer with helping to elevate the Chili Peppers' musical dialogue to even greater peaks of potential than they'd reached together before as a band, first and foremost by knocking down the traditional studio walls of iso-booths, encouraging the players to be "100% about 'I want you guys to go out and play together in the room,' which was I think the first time we really captured how the band plays and how we sound together. Rick was all about that, and I think that record was the first time I really felt like 'Oh God, that sounds really like what we're doing.' Often, we'll play him the songs, and he's not emotionally or any way attached to them and just hears them for the first time. He just has such a great ear and he's such a musical guy, and we trust him."

Between he and Flea specifically, where Rolling Stone Magazine would later observe that their "rhythm section displayed a growing curiosity about studio texture and nuance," Smith felt major growth as well within their instrumental songwriting dynamism, pointing to *"My Lovely Man"* as one poignant example of such flair where

> normally, in the writing of the music, often the way that we write stuff is music comes first, and then its melody and words, but initially, I'm playing off the other two guys. Not very often, once in a while, Anthony will be there and he's coming up with ideas, but he's not the kind of guy who just jumps in and starts (scatting?) away to a jam – once in a while – but for the most part, the music comes first and that inspires him to come up with lyrics and melodies. But after that, once he has that, my part often will change to support what he's doing. *"If You Had to Ask"* came through a jam as well, there were a lot of jam-based ones.

Individually, Rolling Stone would single Smith out for his success via "the pummeling *'Give It Away'* and the incendiary *'Suck My Kiss'*" in "(establishing) a template for rock punctuated by the beatcentric relentlessness of hip-hop," Smith cited other highlights that moved at this horsepower to include *"Naked in the Rain"* where he remembered "Flea and I as a crushing bulldozer rhythm section," and *"Sir Psycho Sexy,"* where the duo delivered fans a dose of "straight up, down and dirty funk!" Still waiting out their contract with EMI when the band wrote their breakout album's title track, Chad revealed that the band used their frustration as musical fuel

> later on in the process when we were trying to get out of our deal with EMI, and they wouldn't let us out of our record deal because we didn't want to put out another record with them. We wanted to go to Warner Bros., and we had to wait out our contract, and we had to wait till the 8 years in the

> contract were up, and they weren't up yet, so we just kept writing songs, and one day, John brought in the chorus to that song and we wrote *"Blood Sugar Sex Magik!"*

Well worth the wait, the band would take over Alternative Rock in the late fall of 1991 when the album dropped like the atomic bomb that it was from the power of Smith's drumming to what a Popmatters.com critic later celebrated as "one funked-out, fucked up, diabolical swoop…(that) reconfigured my relationship to music. *Blood Sugar Sex Magik* emerged just in time to be carried along by youth culture's widespread re-fascination with the offbeat, the slacker-chic, and the underdog heroes. It was a crazy-wack-funky freakout that could keep stoners and skaters and alternateens and jocks together in the same room, treating one another civilly while getting stoopid with dance." Going on to sell 13 million albums around the world, the Red Hot Chili Peppers' influence would open a new generation's eyes and ears to stylistic fusions unheard before their amalgamation within the band's sound.

As the 1990s began to sunset, the band would book-end their defining dominance of the Alternative Rock scene with 1998's *Californication,* marking a brave and bold turn the Red Hot Chili Peppers made musically after experiencing an internal comeback of sorts when guitarist John Frusciante rejoined the band following his abrupt departure in 1993. Hungry for musical rejuvenation, the emotional range of *Californication* was panoramic and revelatory in every of its instrumental and songwriting expressions, Smith readily credits Frusciante for injecting a fresh but familiar fuel to push boundaries into the band's creative engines, including his own behind the kit:

> I would say the big, probably obviously thing was John coming back into our group, that was the biggest change and the biggest reason why we probably wrote the music that we wrote like that, because of him coming in and the chemistry of the four of us have. I don't want to discount in any way the record and the time that Dave Navarro was in the band, it was enjoyable and

> he's a great musician, and that was a different thing, but there's something special about John that the 4 of us have, and certainly when he came back in the group, it was a real sort of shock and I know we were all exciting to be making music again with him.

Pushing the Chili Peppers to a Beatles-esque level of sophistication with songwriting whose substance revealed that "overall the album has a far more meditative feel," in the esteemed opinion of the BBC, "allowing you to finally believe that they'd come to do more than just party your town dry. It was the album that confirmed them as world class. They remain such today, and it's all down to this re-birth...(where) the band's most successful album - was born." Giving Smith the opportunity to strip his playing back to the basics that great songwriting stands sturdily atop of, the drummer responding rhythmically

> to that material by was just trying to be a good listener and just trying to play what was right for the music, and if they were more straight-ahead rock songs or more melodic, I tried to reflect that in the drumming in a musical way, and I think that's what anyone should do, is just try to play what's right for the song.

Showcasing his now-innate expertise in knowing precisely what to pick as the perfect compliment to whatever Frusciante and Flew threw at him, with *"Scar Tissue"* – the Grammy-winning smash that would crack the Top 10 on Billboard's Hot 100 Singles Chart, peaking at # 9 – Smith played in the spirit of and salute to fusion forefathers, Mitch Mitchell and Ian Pace – with good old-fashioned swing. Reacting naturally to the R&B sway of the guitarist's opening riff, Chad remembered feeling

> it was just kind of a swingy kind of thing, because that's the feel of the song. It seemed like the natural thing to do. Sometimes somebody starts playing a riff and you just go with your gut feeling, like "This is what would sound good to me so I'm going to play that," and then it can evolve and often does and as the song changes dynamics, and the words and the melody will

> change it, and often it's a band or a person reference, "Hey, play it more like Devo," or "More Ringo," or I'm thinking Fugazi, any of that sort of thing. But if not, then its usually what inspires me and I just go with my gut. I don't really think about it too much.

Pointing to another of the album's pulsating pocket highlights with *"Parallel Universe,"* where Smith's syncopated lock with Frusciante's picking fury sets the pace for a freight-train of rhythm that follows throughout one of the album's most frantic performances, with Smith keeping constant control of the chaos behind the kit in a headspace where

> I was trying to be more drum machine-like, certainly in the verses with the band playing "digadigadigadiga" like that. The beat was a 16th-note hi-hat pattern, it was very straight-ahead. In the verse, we were all trying to be very metronomic, and we played to a click because we wanted it to be very staccato, so that's me doing my New Order impersonation (laughs). But when the chorus comes, then it turns into a big rock chorus, a big power chorus, and that's the cool thing of how those two parts are juxtaposed. That one came pretty quickly.

The sessions were inspired as such throughout, as Smith recalled that "we worked pretty quick, and recorded that record really fast, we were really prepared when we went in and had all those songs," with notable exception being what would become the record's title track, *"Californication."* A song as haunting for Smith's trippy ghosted snare doubles intro as it is for Frusciante's delicate and instantly infectious lead acoustic riff he was playing off of, Chad revealed that

> *"Californication"* was the only one we wrote in the studio. We had the idea for it, but just couldn't come up with the right music, and one day John came in with that riff and it took off from there. I just remember it being a really fun time and the band was just glad to be making music, and everyone was just excited to have John back among the living, let alone being in the band again. I never thought that was going to happen, and he was a

> great singer and had all these ideas for background vocals, which were even more evolved by the way, and that was the beginning of the more melodic period for the band.

Delivering the band into the Millennium with a new generation of relevance that would only grow with the renaissance of new recording achievements that followed, beginning with 2002's *"By the Way,"* with Smith once again providing the pulse for a racing rhythmic workout that proved he was still rocking as hard as ever after 15 years in the saddle. Spending 14 weeks at # 1 on the Billboard Modern Rock Tracks and 7 weeks at # 1 on the Mainstream Rock Tracks Charts, the band's title track single would prove that "the Chili Peppers have become a new breed of classic-rock band," in the estimation of Entertainment Weekly, still retaining their edge as "one whose roots lie in funk, punk, and old-school hip-hop rather than folk or blues" while still covering plenty of new musical miles Smith felt

> because that song at the time had elements of all of what you would – up to that point – think like a Chili Peppers song would have: it has a rap in the verse, there's this tribal funk thing and it opens up into really nice, melodic, powerful chorus. Writing it came out of a jam, and what happens is: sometimes we do this thing called a "Face Off." So if we have parts for a song, but we need a chorus or we need a bridge, or we feel we need another part for a song, and maybe we'd been playing one but nobody liked it enough or Anthony didn't like it, we have a face-off where the two melodic instruments – the bass and the guitar player – will go off in the corner or another part of the room or outside, and they'll both try to come up with a part to go with whatever we needed. Then they come back in the room when they're done, and we'll listen to one guy's part and then play it, then listen to the other guy's part and we'll all try it, and then figure out which one's better and hopefully one of them is good enough and that becomes the missing part of the song. Its sometimes childish (laughs) but it actually works sometimes!

By 2006, the band had exploded into the most prolific period of their second coming with John Frusciante, reflected in the ambitious *Stadium Arcadium,* a double-album dose of artistic advancement that the Rock & Roll Hall of Fame would later acknowledge as a "truly…Herculean achievement that cemented the Red Hot Chili Peppers' stature as the hardest-working and most ambitious band in popular music. The album won the group five more Grammys," including "Best Rock Album." Sharing his memory that the band was on such a fluent rapport musically by that point that

> often when we go in and rehearse, whoever's the first one to get there, just starts playing and that day, I was first one in and for whatever reason, I started playing the beat for *"Stadium Arcadium."* Then John came in and picked up his guitar, and started playing that opening riff, then Flea walked in and joins in, and I remember Anthony telling us, "I pulled up in the parking lot and hear this music, and am going 'I hope its not some other band because I really like that!' " So that's a perfect, organic example of how we make music sometimes.

With the album's biggest single, the Top 10 hit *"Dani California,"* Smith would kick the song off with the kind of instantly-anthemic power rock beats that sent Flea's bass rocketing from one side of the pocket to the other like a ball of lightning, inspiring the LA Times to note that "Flea has always been a bass virtuoso but he outdoes himself (here)…where he percolates his way through Chad Smith's churning hard-core drum blast!" Singing the praises of the player he feels he's had the privilege to hold the rhythm down with for the past quarter century, Chad begins by pointing to

> he's an incredible musician, first and foremost, and he's my good friend, he's my buddy, and for many years, having the good fortune of not having to really have much conversation about playing with each other. We talk about all kinds of music and all kinds of different things in general, but for the most part, I would say less and less as time goes on do we talk about

what we play because we just know each other so well musically and everything else. There'll just be little suggestions certainly with song ideas or feels or parts, and if anybody in the band has a specific idea, like for *"Dani California,"* John said to me, "Hey, I was listening to this Wu Tang Clan record all weekend, and it has this beat (sounds it out)," so he's singing me this sample and I turn around and play it like *"Sweet Home Alabama."* And often, when you're trying to translate and tell someone, "Hey, I hear it like this," however the guy's going to do it, its going to be how he plays, and Flea would suggest "Oh, do something on toms," which maybe wouldn't be the thing that I would go to at first, but I'm always open to trying that, especially when somebody has a piece of music that they hear something on. I owe it to them, being an open musician, to say "Well, let's try it like that," and I'm always going to do it how I do it anyway, because they're not drummers, so its gonna change, but I think through the years, Flea and I just have this musical telepathy that only comes from playing together for an extended period of time, which we've been fortunate to have that is unique.

Its funny, we were in Paris together doing an interview for Rhythm Magazine, and this woman sat down and said "So, how do you guys come up with your parts?", and we both looked at each other like, "We never talked about it, we really never did," and I'm not trying to sound like "Oh, its secret." There is no secret, but what I can say is Flea's such an always-evolving, growing, changing, challenging himself as a musician, and I have to stay on my toes to play with people like that, and that's inspiring to me. So he's always coming up with things or playing me stuff, and its more in that way than maybe "Hey, you should do two kicks there and syncopate with me on the end of one," less of that than "Hey, have you heard the new whatever band or artist, I really like this, this is really cool," or "You should check this out," that sort of thing, and visa versa. We try to play to our strengths and for whatever reason, we have this thing that we do and it sounds pretty

> good when we do it together. We just do it together, and we're lucky that we make a good racket when we come together.

With the laid-back solitude contained with *"Strip My Mind,"* Smith took an out-of-the-box route to getting a drum sound down he was happy with, showcasing the rounded expertise the drummer had racked up through his experience recording so many studio albums to know when it was worth shaking things up in pursuit of the perfect sound. Drawing comparisons critically in his performance once again with Led Zeppelin's God of Thunder, Chad humbly accepts that "its always nice to get compliments, and for anyone to compare you to someone that I think would consider the greatest Rock & Roll drummer, he's my favorite and a lot of people's favorite," and agreed looking back on the journey he took to bring the same spirit to life within its sonics:

> There's a lot of space in that song, and so the drums, I just remember thinking "Boy, that's like kind of a John Bonham wanna be," not necessarily the sound, but the funny thing about the recording was when we recorded it, it sounded good, but the drums were a little bit dry and for whatever reason, I wanted them to have more air. I wanted them to be more roomy, and when we brought up the room mics it just didn't sound right, it sounded kind of trashy.
>
> So I had done a record previously, right after Stadium Aradium, with Glenn Hughes that we recorded at my house in Hollywood, and the sound in the main room was just really great. And the engineer, Ryan Huett, who was mixing our record, and he said "Hey, what if we take the drums and play them and re-amp them, so to speak, and record the sound of your room at your house because it sounded so good?" So that's what we did! So "Strip My Mind" has ambient sound on the drums from my house, and to me, that made all the difference, especially when I heard it in the movie theatre in *"The Fighter."*

These days, Chad continues to tour sold-out arenas around the world, playing the Red Hot Chili Peppers' catalog for generations old and new, along with a healthy appetite for side projects – including Chickenfoot and The Meat Bats – to fill his tireless love of making new music, the drummer explains that he is driven by the fact that "I happen to really love what I'm doing, and there's some luck, but its a lot of hard work, I've worked really hard for a long time. I love it, and if you love something, you're gonna want to work hard at it, but in general, I just feel really lucky." A pop culture fixture with enough celebrity as a player in his own right to land him an invitation to appear on the Tonight Show with Jimmy Fallon in 2014 for a now-infamous – courtesy of its staggering 33,831, 715 Youtube views – drum off with comic superstar Will Ferrell, in addition to the pair dressing identically, they actually performed competing solos. Drumming circles around the SNL alum that would have made Gene Krupa proud, it was yet another example of the Smith's savvy for staying as relevant with the Millennials as he did with Generation X's aspiring kids just now picking up the sticks:

> If I can inspire someone to play the drums or start a band, that's awesome. I want people to have exposure to music and to play an instrument – whether its through school or with your pals or if you just pick it up because you love it. But somehow, if I can inspire someone, "Woah, I saw the Chili Peppers and Chad Smith, and he looks like he's having fun playing, I'd like to do that too…" That would be great to be in that position, I'm so lucky and fortunate that I found my passion at a young age and got to do it for my whole life – I'm not dead yet – and I'm still doing it and still love it, I've been able to experience things beyond my wildest dreams and have been so lucky.
>
> So if you stick around long enough and are lucky to find musicians that you can have the same musical goals and people like your music, and in our case, we got to travel around the world and play our music, and I've seen a lot of people happy at our concerts, that's a really lucky thing. Music is very powerful and I'm just really fortunate, so when a kid comes up to me

> and says, "Aw man, I really like your drumming, it inspired me," they have done that, and I just say, "Man, thank you so much," because you need to stay humble. If you hear people going "You're the greatest thing," you can start to believe it, and I know guys who can play circles around me.

Among the accolades he and his band have continued to receive in response to the musical karma they've put out into the universe over his 25+ years with the band, the legendary beat keeper even has his own official *Chad Smith Drum App* to keep track with fans of not only what new music he's making, but of drummers whose playing he is a fan of as well – a feature he highlights

> really my favorite thing about it, is the GPS, where the guys and girls are playing, a little bio about them, what they're doing, what they've done, and where you can go see them play. I like that, its just kind of a nice all-in-one place where there's over 100 drummers on there, and I'm always adding people, and try to keep up with their schedules as much as I can so I know what they're doing and when they're doing it. And for people who are fans and want to know what's going on and what I'm doing and what I like and other things I'm into, and other drummers and musicians, it's a good place to go.

Closing with a bit of reflection on his induction along with the rest of the Red Hot Chili Peppers into the Rock & Roll Hall of Fame in 2014 after being deemed worthy for "(creating) a synthesis of punk, funk, rock and rap to become one of the most popular and inventive groups of modern times…(selling) more than 60 million albums worldwide," Chad closes our conversation by shaking his head in surreal awe remembering the first time

> I walked in to the room where they have your names up there alongside all of people who have been inducted, and I was like "Wow," and I get down to ours, and we're right next to The Ramones the Rolling Stones. So my name is right next to Keith Richards and Charlie Watts, and I was standing there shaking my head, thinking "That's too weird. How did a knucklehead

from fucking Birmingham, Michigan ever make it to the Hall of Fame?" It's a little surreal, but I think what's nice about it is you're being honored not for like a Grammy Award – and those are great too – but the Hall of Fame induction is for your body of work, or that you've been influential, but I get just as excited about making new music.

The thing that really gets me up in the morning is I know we're going to practice from 11 to 4 and I know at 11, there's going to be not a piece of music that's written yet, and I know at 4 o'clock, more often than not, there's going to be one or two things that probably will turn into songs, or will be more furthered along in the completed-song sense, that wasn't there 3 or 4 hours ago. To me, that's just an exciting prospect of the creative process, the way that we come up with writing music.

Sometimes it sucks and we don't have a good day, but more often than not, we usually come up with music that is pretty good and we already have 20 ideas that we've demoed and everybody likes, and we're going to write some more songs and just keep making them into the best things we can do, and that's fun and creatively inspiring and everyone is on the same page and we're all happy and want to do it, so why not? I just want to keep trying to get better: as a musician, as a bandmate, and as a person.

"My motto has always been hard work fueled by passion and education." – Kenny Aronoff

(photo by Robert Downs)

Chapter 6: Kenny Aronoff of John Mellencamp/John Fogerty – The 6th Beatle

In the 1960s, a generation of kids watched Neil Armstrong take man's first step on the moon and wanted to grow up and become astronauts. Yet another saw the Beatles perform on Ed Sullivan on February 9th, 1964, and wanted to become Rock Stars. Kenny Aronoff was one of those kids, watching from his family's living room in the small town of Stockbridge, Massachusetts, his eyes wild with wonder:

> It would turn out to be the moment my life changed and my course was set forever. It was as if suddenly a tornado stopped in it's place, paused, and in that pause, I saw for the first time: The Beatles on the Ed Sullivan Show!!! BAM: "MOM, I want to be in the Beatles!"

While millions of other wanna-be Beatles focused in on their particular instrument and corresponding idol that night, some on Paul McCartney and John Lennon standing at the front of the stage singing and playing guitar and bass, while others' eyes were drawn with instant fascination to the back of the stage where Ringo Starr sat on his drum riser, head happily bouncing back and forth while he kept the beat that connected most directly to Kenny's high-wire personality:

> With my energy, playing the drums was the perfect instrument for me. My parents could see I was instantly addicted: my mom started me with piano lessons like most parents do, but I was drawn to the energy and power of the drums. One day, I decided I had enough of those piano lessons and I ripped up my piano music right in front of my mom and said, "I don't want to play the piano any more, I want to play the drums.
>
> I started using all my free spending money to buy Beatles 45's or whatever else I was digging back then. I had my ear plastered to the radio all the time and drove everyone crazy as I beat on everything and everyone like they were drums. Finally I bought a snare drum and a cymbal. I can't explain it fully, but I had a naive vision or fantasy that I would one day play with The Beatles, and I remember I was suddenly filled with a passion that hasn't left me since

Growing up on a 13-acre farm against the countryside of Stockbridge in Western Massachusetts, a young Kenny's artistic passions fit right in to a local culture of creative celebrity neighbors that included a treasured collection of the country's most celebrated painters like Norman Roçkwell, actors including Frank Langella, Richard Dryfuss, Goldie Hawn, Estelle Parsons, Eleanor Wilson, and Faye Dunaway, authors like Norman Mailer and playwrights like William Gibson, film director Arthur Penn – whose credits include "Bonnie & Clyde." Equally as cool were musician neighbors including stars like James Taylor and Arlo Guthrie, who wrote the autobiographical song *"Alice's Restaurant"* about the local diner owned by Alice Brock, which inspired a movie of the same title. For a pair of wide artistic eyes, "it was as if you took a slice of the village in New York City and brought it up into the Berkshires." With Rock & Roll playing on the radio at all times, Kenny remembered growing up as a teenager in the genre's golden era, one whose live side he took in with the fervor of a fan soaking up every great of the day:

> I grew up during an amazing time in Rock & Roll: I saw iron Butterfly when *"In A God Da Di Vida"* was a huge hit, I saw Miles Davis open up for Santana, both were at the peak of their careers, same with Joni Mitchell, James Taylor, Sly Stone, Janis Joplin, The Jefferson Airplane. I got to see The Who perform Tommy the first year they came to America. I was in the second row with my twin brother Jon and Keith Moon saw us and flipped out because he saw we were identical twins. At 14, that same year I actually got to go see the Jimi Hendrix Experience perform live one hour from Stockbridge, in Troy, New York with Noel Redding and Mitch Mitchell!
>
> Like the Beatles had been, seeing Jimi live was like a religious experience to me. When I got my first Jimi Hendrix album, *"Are You Experienced?"* for Christmas in 1967, I'll never forget it because it snowed 18 inches on Christmas Eve. On Christmas Day we got the fire place going and everyone was hanging out downstairs in the living room listening to classical and jazz music, reading their books quietly by the roar of the fire, while I was upstairs in my room, taking a couple hits off a joint, and cranking *"Are You Experienced?"* over and over again on my turntable. It was funny because my parents kept having to come upstairs every so often banging on the door for me to turn it down, but I was mesmerized. I just identified with the soul and the whole vibe of the Jimi Hendrix Experience, and specific to my instrument, I think the reason why I identified with Mitch Mitchell so much as a drummer was because I was grew up hearing Jazz on my Dad's turntable and going to jazz concerts with my parents. Mitch Mitchell was a jazz drummer improvising a lot in his playing style, so I could relate to his

style a lot. It brought both worlds – jazz and rock – together for me for the first time as a player. I got to finally meet Mitch years later.

My parents also took me as a young kid to see a lot of famous jazz musicians perform at a cool local venue called The Music Inn in Lenox, MA, where I saw all the Modern Jazz legends play live there as a child, from Dizzy Gillespie and Stan Getz to Dave Brubeck, Charles Mingus, and even Ray Charles to name a few. Outside this cool venue there was a field that sloped down to the stage and behind the stage was a huge pine forest. I saw some cool shows there: Ike and Tina Turner, Sea Level, Muddy Waters, Mahavishnu Orchestra with Billy Cobham on drums!

The presence of the world-famous Tanglewood, the neighboring town to Stockbridge where the Boston Symphony Orchestra performed during the summer months, would loom equally large as an influence in developing the classical side of Aronoff's hybrid roots as a Classical-Jazz/Rock & Roll drummer. Attracting the best Orchestral musicians in the world, as well as its finest directors like Leonard Bernstein – who Kenny would later study under as a Adult Fellowship Orchestra – the young drummer recalled striving as a player to strike a balance between the access to genius and an unbridled ambition that led Aronoff

during my Sophomore year of high school to notice my buddy Tommy Gibson was suddenly getting better on drums, and I remember asking him, "What are you doing to get better?", and he told me he'd been studying with the principle Percussionist from the Boston Symphony Orchestra, Arthur Press. During the school year, I would catch a bus from our town and go about 2 hours to Newton, just outside of Boston where Arthur lived, and take a lesson for 2 to 4 hours once a month on Orchestral snare drum, Tympani and Mallets.

Throughout the summers, when the Boston Symphony Orchestra moved to their summer location at Tanglewood 3 hours from my house, I'd have a lesson with Arthur every week at my house for one hour. He took me to a

> new place technically and mentally, even though we were studying mostly classical music. It helped me with my approach to learning new things on my drum set and in life in general. He was kicking my ass and helping me become more disciplined, more focused, practice more and practice correctly, not waste time, develop perfection skills with time and reading music, my ability to hear and execute, develop my technique and he gave me a better understanding of music. All of this helped me when I played Rock & Roll then and now. He set me on a new path.

At night, once his classical lessons were completed, Kenny would unwind, switch hats and head out to the family's locally-legendary Barn to rehearse with his Twin brother Jon, who played keys alongside Kenny behind the kit in The Missing Link. Unleashing an authentic Rock & Roll energy that would pull listeners into his world of playing from the earliest days, the drummer fondly recalls

> a cool barn we had behind our house where I would rehearse with my rock bands or practice my drums. That barn was the coolest hang for me, my brother, my sister and my friends. We would jam and rehearse with bands all year round. We tried to heat that barn with a kerosene heater to stay warm enough to rehearse in the winter. It sort of worked but we almost burnt the entire place down once with that heater, (laugh). All my friends and their friends would come to hang at our barn and watch us rehearse – it was like a private rock concert every night. From ages 16 to 18, my brother and I played in bands and would rehearse every night from 8 pm until Midnight (after we did our homework of course). On weekends, we jammed all day and into the night unless we had gigs to play.

Accepted to the University of Massachusetts's competitive music program in 1971, Kenny was already an accomplished Timpanist who had played with the Boston Symphony Orchestra, while in the same time playing in a Jazz trio 5 times a week, and a gigging Rock & Roll band on the weekend. No matter the swing he felt his style had been swung on the local live circuits, once Kenny stepped onto the major league plates

> that first year at U-Mass, which was the toughest learning curve for me because I was catching up, and I was way behind in everything, from following conductors, to reading music, my technique on all instruments, music theory, music history, ear training, piano, sight singing, conducting and playing in an orchestra. It was a slow build to success, that was just the beginning of the fuse being lit inside me, but I already had the fire, and the desire to make the most of my opportunity. I am that guy who just keeps marching, forward slow and steady, year after year after year with persistence. I practiced every chance I got.
>
> My next shot came with that Julliard-sponsored Aspen Music Program in Aspen, Colorado. Once I'd gotten ahold of the application, you could see why Julliard's reputation was written all over the instructions: 'Prepare something on 3 different percussion instruments,' and they gave you a list of 4, and rather than just picking 3, I wanted to impress the audition board so much, I picked all 4. I practiced, prepared and recorded 4 piece: one on marimba, one on tympani, one on orchestral snare drum and finally multiple percussion. I sent the tape off and never heard from anyone.
>
> I remember leaving U-Mass the last day of classes, getting about 2 miles off campus on my way back to my home town, and realized "Oops, I've forgotten my mail." Well, once I turned around to go grab it – I think there was a paycheck in my mailbox I didn't want to wait on or something – and when I opened it, no paycheck, but instead a letter telling me I'd been accepted into Julliard's summer program in Aspen! Holy Shit!!! I *couldn't* believe it. I was excited but realized I was about to face some of the best percussionists in the world who also were competitive and over achievers. Still, it was a huge boost of confidence, and it turned out to be life-changing in a nut-shell.

While studying at the Julliard summer program, Kenny would come under the wing of University of Indiana Professor George Gaber, another influential player who he credited as "a teacher who essentially influenced me to move to Indiana and that move effected the rest of my life." The type of instructor who recognized potential by squeezing the most out of it in terms of practice and an almost-militaristic expectation of dedication, Kenny remembered his instructor's regimen of discipline was good training for the thick skin the music business would require to succeed:

> George was extremely disciplined in our lessons, and taught me some very valuable lessons that will stay with me for the rest of my life. He was ruthless, and when I later studied more extensively under him at Indiana University, I actually witnessed fellow students crumble and have nervous breakdowns and leave under the pressure of studying with this guy. That's the type of professor he was, and I felt I had so much I could learn from him that I already had my mind made up that I wanted to transfer to IU. I remember bluntly telling him, "I want to go to IU, you're an amazing instructor, and I want to study under you for 4 years."
>
> Every year while I was at IU, I would audition In the spring to try and get into the Tanglewood music center fellowship program, which is the Boston Symphony Orchestra's (BSO) Summer Academy for Advanced Music Study It was made up of best students in the world, and considered the # 1 student Symphony Orchestra in the United States. One of the most exciting things for me about the prospect of getting accepted into the this distinguished orchestra was the opportunity to work with Leonard Bernstein, who was arguably among the most legendary Symphony Conductors in the world at that time – plus one of America's great living composers of musicals like West Side Story among other highlights. Besides working with Bernstein, we got to work with other master conductors who came to conduct the BSO like Aaron Copeland, Arthur Fiedler, and Seigi Ozawa.

> It took me 4 years and four auditions to finally get accepted to this program at Tanglewood, but once I did, one of the biggest highlights for me was getting to play the Timpani part in the Sibelius Fifth Symphony Orchestra with Leonard Bernstein and Seigi Ozawa conducting us on the BSO's main stage. On top of that, I got to play on the Vic Firth's Timpani, the official Timpanist of the Boston Symphony Orchestra. I still remember I almost cried my eyes out during that performance because it was such a beautiful piece and Bernstein was such a passionate, smart and brilliant conductor who knew how to get us to play at a higher level of excellence. Instead of intimidating us like some conductors would, he would make us want to play for him.

By the late 1970s, Kenny was ready to make a Pro go of his ambitions, graduating from I-U with a Bachelor's Degree in Percussion, and truly living the starving musician's lifestyle working the local club circuit with his Jazz fusion band Streamwinner. All crammed into one small band house known as "The Roach Motel," the drummer remembered that music was the literal center of their universe:

> we and had turned the small living room into a full-blown rehearsal room using part of our sound system and lights which made it possible to rehearse there any time we wanted. My daily routine was wake up, sit down at my drum set and practice all day and night unless I was playing live gigs or rehearsing with the band. I was so broke back then that I remember I used to count my quarters to see how many beers and or Space Invader games I could cover over a night at the local bars. I was truly living the starving musician lifestyle,

Vs. moving out to L.A. or back East to New York, Kenny wouldn't have to look farther than his own back yard when he wound up catching wind of the fact that John Cougar was looking for a new drummer, and through another local club circuit acquaintance, Mellencamp guitarist Mike Wanchic, landed an audition with the temperamental frontman after blowing him away with the sheer power of his playing:

> I asked John, "Well, what do you want me to play?", and he asked me if I knew anything on the album, and I said I was familiar with the songs. He said "Okay, pick one," so I did and we started playing it. I think it was *"I Need a Lover,"* and I remember I played with so much confidence, power and volume that I was probably way over the top. I was thinking stadiums and I really wanted this gig. I glanced at John at the end of the first song and it was the only time I ever saw him looking startled with his eyes and mouth wide open at the same time!

Heading out to L.A. in 1980 with his new band mates and boss to Cherokee Studios to record *Nothing Matters... And What If It Did* with legendary Booker T and the M.G.'s/Blues Brothers' guitar player/producer Steve Cropper, Kenny's Rock & Roll dream quickly got a cold bucket of water poured over it after he was woken up to the news shortly after arriving that he was being replaced by a more seasoned session drummer to make up for his inexperience in studio recording, still a new world to Aronoff. Vs. protesting, the young drummer swallowed his pride and took the opportunity to turn the defeat into a learning experience akin to getting cut from the first string but still remaining on the team:

> I made him the best offer I could come up with, and said "Look, if I'm still the drummer in your band, you don't have to pay me anything. I'll sleep on the floor, and I'll go to the studio every day and watch what the session drummers play and I'll learn from them, and benefit from that. And then you're going to benefit from that because I'm going to get better, and I'm your drummer."
>
> I can say looking back it was honestly one of the most humbling moments of my life. I had to take a step back from my excitement and realize that, in a way, this was like being back at auditions again where even though I'd made the squad, I still had A LOT to learn. So I became a student again,

> and I think my passion and commitment convinced John to let me stay part of the band, even though I had been serious demoted from my previous spot sitting behind the drum kit for the moment.

Once he landed back in Indiana, Kenny began the kind of grueling training regimen reserved for athletes ahead of Olympic try-outs, applying his Herculean work ethic to the goal of readying himself for his first shot at redemption when the band hit the road to support the material on *Nothing Matters… And What If It Did.* This meant listening to and learning the very beats that he was replaced on the record by session drummers to play, a humbling experience that a hungry Aronoff nonetheless embraced and used as fuel, reasoning that

> this was real life and definitely not the Rock & Roll fantasy land you might expect it to be. John was my boss, and was paying me to give him everything I had, so working these songs from the ground up in rehearsals day in and out was pretty stressful. We'd usually start at 11, work till 5, take a 2 hour dinner break, and then come back and work from 7 till 11, 5 days a week.

Mounting a successful comeback from behind the drum set throughout the tour that followed, Kenny's next shot at truly cementing the notion that he had "made it" – which the drummer knew meant actually playing on a John Mellencamp album and hit – came in 1981 when the band re-grouped to begin writing and recording what would become one of the cornerstones of Heartland Rock, *American Fool,* Aronoff and Mellencamp both had everything riding on the line, and for Kenny, he had a mindset going into the sessions was militant in his resolve: "I'd vowed to myself at the outset of *'American Fool'* that no matter how much shit I had to go through, you're gonna get on this record."

Mellencamp needed hits to avoid being dropped from his record contract, and he was counting on everyone in the band to help create them around his acoustic songwriting demos. Kenny's moment would shine would arrive when the band was struggling to make rhythmic sense of one what would become one of the album's – and artist's – biggest hits, *"Jack and Diane,"* and one of Kenny's most recognizable and imitated air-drum parts, an inspiration that came to him when

> I was under a serious gun to come up with parts for his songs that suited his style of playing, he needed that from me, that's what he was paying me to do: in fact, the beat for *"Jack and Diane"* saved the song from being kicked off the record. The truth is: that song was off the record before I got my hands on it, GONE, because they couldn't figure out what to do with it until our producer, Don Gehman, walked in one day with a Linn 1 drum machine.
>
> In my competitive way, I grabbed that thing and said "Let me have a shot at it," still wanting to inject my live energy into the performance and programmed that beat, which was basically the beat I'd been playing on the kick drum. But instead of using a kick drum, I used a floor tom and Linn 1 drum machine, and instead of the hi-hat, I used the tambourine. Even after that, they still got to the part of the song where the big famous drum fill comes in, that was the point where they felt there was still something missing that needed to happen, and called on me. So I had to create that drum break on the spot!

The knockout moment of triumph for Aronoff would arrive when he was tasked to open a song Mellencamp had written at the last minute, and delivered a beat that would become one of Rock & Roll's most recognizable, *"Hurts So Good,"* Kenny's first number one hit on the Billboard Hot 100 Singles chart that has dominated dance floors and radio for decades ever since. Taking fans back into the memory of the signature beat's creation, the drummer began with his recollection that

> when he wrote *"Hurts So Good,"* John stripped the band down to just me, himself and the two guitar players Mike and Larry, and he'd said "Its just going to be the four of us, no bass, no keys," and so after all that, once again, we headed back to work. It was ironic to me that we started up that second set of recording sessions for 'American Fool' Part II in 1981 at the same studio

> where I'd been fired on the previous album. Cherokee Studios was where I redeemed myself by coming up with that beat you hear on *"Hurts so Good."*
>
> That beat first came to me while I was practicing left-handed, and I had gotten so bored with playing simple that I'd started practicing with all my drum books backwards, with my left hand leading on the hi-hat and my right hand on the snare. That's how I came up with the whole feel and the sound for the song. Again, simple, simple beat, but because I was leading with my left hand on the hi-hat and my right hand on the snare drum- that was an ambidextrous move- now I was basically like a right-handed batter batting left-handed, which gave the beat a different feel, and that feel was the fuel John was looking for. His goal with that song was to create a hit where no song that came on the radio before or after it could stand up to our song, so he wanted to make sure that any single that followed us was dwarfed, and any song that we followed got trampled, and we definitely pulled that off because once we had fleshed out the keeper beat and got to the studio at Cherokee to record it, you hear that intensity and energy and the attitude coming through in my playing that "I'm going to score a touch-down, and no one's going to get in my way." That's the way I played that song.
>
> In the Mellencamp band, I began for the first time to appreciate the concept of less-is-more, which was the opposite approach from the fusion stuff I'd been playing in my college band Streamwinner. I began to realize I could feel the music, and I think you could hear that in the beats of songs like *'Hurts So Good'* and *'Authority Song'* and so many others.

Exploding onto MTV in the early 1980s courtesy of those hits, Kenny became one of this new era in Rock & Roll's most recognizable drummers overnight, based on a combination of the heavy rotation the smash singles he played on received on both FM radio and over and over again in music videos where fans could watch and listen to Aronoff create his beatscapes, amplifying his celebrity as a player in the process. By the time *Uh Huh* was released in 1983, Kenny's exposure would only expand after the band shot a new round of videos to monster hits from the new album that all featured as a stand-out more of Kenny's instantly memorable drum beats, including the aforementioned *"Authority Song," "Crumblin' Down,"* and what would become one of John "Cougar" Mellencamp's biggest career hits, *"Pink Houses (Ain't That America),"* which Kenny still regards as

> one of the best songs I had ever recorded with him. I still remember that moment vividly when he played me *"Pink Houses"* for the first time. It was a rare moment when it was just the two of us hanging out and John said "Hey Aronoff, come in here, I wanna play you something." I could picture everything he was singing and then he hit the chorus, "Oh but Ain't that America, for you and me, Ain't that America, Something to see, baby, Ain't that America, home of the free, yeah, little Pink Houses for you and me, oooh yeah, for you and me." As soon as I heard it, I immediately thought, "Wow, that's a hit," and the first thing that came out of my mouth was, "This is going to be fucking huge John!" . He always had the pulse of the people, whether in his live performances or in his songwriting, which always felt like you could instantly relate to the people he was talking about – let alone playing for. That connection was always ever-present in John as a songwriter, and it was very inspiring to me as a drummer to try to compliment that with my drum parts. I eventually tapped into that same heartbeat of Middle America that John was speaking about and representing at that time in our music.

When he remembers what he was tapping along to muse-wise for one of his most exciting drum performances from the Mellencamp catalog on *"Authority Song,"* which featured one of Kenny's famously energetic, eye-and-ear catching tom workouts during the breakdown, the drummer reveals that he was channeling two odd bookends in

> Charlie Watts from the Rolling Stones meets Stewart Copeland from The Police, and with Charlie, whenever he played a fast beat, he lifts his hi-hat

> when he hits the snare drum on beats 2 and 4, he's famous for that, so I did that, but I was also trying to do some fills and some of the other subtle type of things that Stewart Copeland would do when he played, and the combination really worked in conjunction with having the Aronoff edge to it. The whole guitar introduction to *"Authority Song"* John came up just as we were about to record the song, and if you listen, there were shots to the snare drum with these tom-toms, and the snare drums came quicker and quicker and quicker, which was my way of creating tension and excitement as we built toward the full band launching into the song full-on. By *'Uh Huh,'* I'd come into what became my signature drumkit sound: which was a Ludwig 1962 Supraphonic 400 snare drum. I went to a 5-inch, and that became my sound from then on.

With *"Crumbling Down,"* another of the album's Top 10 hits at Radio (# 8) and on MTV's Top 10 Countdown, Kenny pointed to the song as a great example of the inspirational interplay between the band's members as they jammed up song ideas during rehearsals, sharing from behind the kit that in reacting to a riff his bandmate Larry Crane came up with on the spot, the beat was born after

> I started to mimic the guitar part that Larry was playing, which was a pumping 8th note kind of rhythm, so I started pumping my kick drum with it. Then, with my fingers, I began playing softly on my snare drum – instead of with sticks- and when the guitar would do this little rhythm thing, there was a hole where I put a little hit on a hi-hat. I used that also in the vocal, because it fit perfectly in the space, "Some people are no damn good," then a space where I would hit a little "chick" on the hi-hat right in the hole. That was a beat I'd never done up to that point, and had never done since, and it was perfect for that song.

By 1985, Kenny was riding high at the top of the Charts and ready to ascend even higher after the band graduated into sold-out Arenas based on the run of hits up the charts and miles on the road they'd racked up weaving their sound out across the country playing for an ever-expanding fan base. Having successfully "consolidated the band's rugged, roots-rock thrash" into a focused sound, Rolling Stone Magazine highlighted the important sonic note that *Scarecrow* was "recorded at Mellencamp's own Belmont Mall studio…(its sound) intentionally low tech, built around Kenny Aronoff's enormous snare-drum beat. The sinewy mix is all drums and guitar, with Toby Myers' bass and John Cascella's keyboards emphasized sparingly and strategically." A salute in many ways musically to John Mellencamp's childhood love of 1960s American Rock & Roll, Kenny began to wrap his mind stylistically around the concept

> one day when John walked into the studio with a box of records from the 60s and 70s. He had this brilliant plan, and said "I want you to listen to these records and learn all these great songs note for note. Kenny, I want you to know the drum parts, Mike and Larry the guitar parts, and I want learn these songs and figure out what made these songs so great." That's when I came up with what I called "The Book of Beats," so let's say we were listening to a song by The Young Rascals or Simon & Garfunkel, and I'd write all the drum parts out, to all the different songs, and what happened was it did give us some ideas. We did that for a month or two, and then whenever John started coming in with a new song, I would look through my book of beats to see if there was something I could use, even if it was part of the beat."

Spotlighting the album's biggest hit, *"Smalltown,"* as an example of that concept in action, Kenny tapped once again into his Charlie Watts influence, recalling that "with that song, like so many others, John always said 'Rolling Stones, simple, Rolling Stones man, Rolling Stones.' So the beauty of that song, again, lied in the simplicity of it, and it opens that way with just John, a guitar, and the drum for the first verse before, BAM, the whole band kicked in!" Calling on Kenny specifically within his drum beat to compliment the song's simplicity without losing any punch in the process, the drummer confessed that

> when we started working on *"Smalltown,"* the first time I heard him play it for the band on acoustic guitar, to myself, I was thinking "God damn... How am I going to make this special?", because it was such a simple song that almost seemed perfect as an acoustic ballad, but I knew John wanted the band to electrify it – literally – with amplifiers. Larry and Mike also were great at helping come up with intros, like the one that opens *"Smalltown,"* because John's original demo went right into the first verse. I started the beat off for that song simply, so that it left me somewhere to go, which was a common strategy I brought to bear with Mellencamp song beats compositionally. I used to see John in the studio when we were developing the arrangements for these songs as a band, keeping the backbeat with his both his hands, like up and down, and for that song, it made sense to follow with the kick drum and the snare, and we built it up.

Bringing their tribute to 60s rock into full visualization in the hit music video for another of the album's biggest hits, Kenny and company were required to raid the era stylistically for the characters they would be playing on MTV in the filmed performance: "The video we shot for the song demonstrated that louder than anything else, because we went for the total black and white 1960s American Bandstand TV show concept. When we shot the video, I even dressed up in a beret looking like kind of New York beatnik drummer." In selecting his costume for the part, the combination of the authenticity within Kenny's performance itself and his fashion decision to wear a beret would later become the muse for Tom Hanks' in writing his 1996 film, "That Thing You Do," which Aronoff would ironically play the drums too. Dialing back a decade earlier to the song's creation, the drummer grouped the song into last-minute club, sharing that

> when we finally got around to recording what became one of the album's biggest hits – and a live favorite – *"R.O.C.K. in the U.S.A.,"* it was one of the last songs we recorded for the album, and wasn't one of John's favorite because with his songwriting on this newest album, he was looking for

> credibility. So he knew it was a hit, but the truth is: *he wasn't there in the studio when we recorded it.* You can actually hear me goofing around with a cowbell at the beginning of the song, and as the song built, I was again trying to start it off very simply and get the same kind of vibe as those old 60s hits John had had us study so hard on before we'd begun recording the record.

By the mid-1980s, Aronoff had become one of the most popular and acclaimed drummers working in Rock & Roll, evident in his growing profile on the critic circuit, including being named Drummer of the Year by Rolling Stone Magazine in 1987. Grateful for this phenomenon in his career, it soon took on a life of its own in terms of demand for Kenny on the drum clinic tour, where the focus was solely on his performances within the hits, an up close and personal opportunity for him to meet fans in the form of a generation of young drummers who now idolized him as their hero behind the kit:

> In the drum world I had become one of the new guys on the scene: I had already been featured as an up and coming drummer in Modern Drummer Magazine back in 1982 and in 1986 I got my first of three covers in Modern Drummer Magazine. I started winning or placing in the top five in drum magazine polls and that's been going on non stop for 28 years. At one point I had won Best Pop/Rock drummer five years in a row in Modern Drummer, and after that they decided to not let me be in that category anymore (laughs).

With the release of 1987's *The Lonesome Jubilee,* Aronoff would be heard at the top of his game, not only holding down the roots-rock end of Mellencamp's Heartland brand of Rock but also expanding it into new stylistic territory that put praise for his playing front in center in the broader critical acclaim the album was showered with, including People Magazine's declaration that "this may well be the rock album of the year. The music is charged up, rollicking, and Drummer Kenny Aronoff keeps things thumping right along," while Entertainment Weekly correctly congratulated the band for "hitting a creative plateau with the exhilarating double whammy of Scarecrow and The Lonesome Jubilee."

A new twist in Americana the band was pioneering with a unique Accordion-Violin blend that Kenny's ever-steady drumming was the perfect dance partner for. As the band evolved together, the drummer remembered within his playing throughout the album feeling that

> '*The Lonesome Jubilee*' was an even more mature effort for John as a songwriter than 'Scarecrow' had been, from *"Paper in Fire"* to *"Cherry Bomb"* and *"Check it Out"* an on and on. The recording of the latter single *"Check it Out,"* was a great example of a pretty ground-breaking exercise that John had given us in pre-production for the album where he'd said to everybody in the band, "I want you all to learn instruments that you can't play." So I learned how to play the hammered dulcimer, which I played on *"Check it Out."*

Launching the album's "artful instrumentation," as the New York Times would later muse, was another of Kenny's electric, eclectic drum introductions that drew listeners instantly inside his cross-sticking fireworks, demonstrative of the drummer's gift for conjuring up catchy parts with cutting edge techniques, often unheard to the rock ear before Aronoff introduced them on one of his hits:

> With *"Paper in Fire,"* I wanted a beat that would drive that song. That meant the kick-drum playing four-to-the-floor, which is like an accented beat in 4/4 time where the kick drum plays 1-2-3-4, because the song had a very suspenseful opening. We were trying to build to a chorus, because the chorus was the most important thing, it's the big payola for a song. So I turned it back out and simplified it going into that chorus, because it was the peak of the song, so with the intro, it was the tempo and the cross-stick which drove that. At that point, I was also very influenced by Stewart Copeland of The Police, and that song was something of a quiet salute to him.
>
> The song's beat was designed to create urgency and excitement, but in a way that wasn't loud because I was playing it on a cross-stick. There was also this strong foundation with the pulse of that kick drum I was beating with my foot, and when I would break away from the cross-stick, I would

answer the lyrics and respond to different melodic ideas the guitar parts and the harpsichord and fiddle were doing. It was like a bomb getting ready to go off, where you hear the ticker counting down, we were creating more tension until the chorus exploded! It is by far still one of my favorite songs in the Mellencamp catalog,

Demonstrating his flair for capturing a nostalgic mood within his rhythm when called for, on arguably the album's most soulful performance on the Top 10 hit, *"Cherry Bomb,"* creating what iTunes years later would celebrate as "the infectious and utterly irrepressible…nostalgic paean to the innocence and folly of youth, its squeezebox and fiddle shuffling along on top of Kenny Aronoff's clipped, crisp snare is pure finger-popping joy." Drawing directly from his authentic background as a Jazz fusion drummer in the brilliant way he swept couples around the dance floor with his swing, Kenny remembered that

when we were recording *"Cherry Bomb,"* I remember I was thinking Motown, so I had an R&B swing vibe going, but as always, when John had first presented it to us, it was in acoustic form so it was then up to the band to help flesh out the songs. Being really into Mitch Mitchell and Jazz natively as a player and listener, I was always trying to introduce more and more of that into our sound when I could. John had been living in Hilton Head, and explained that he'd seen this whole new kind of dance vibe going on down there among the islanders in the clubs that he wanted to capture that soul in the swing of the song. He even showed it to us, and the way that song's drumbeat sounds is the way I was feeling it, it was cool, like James Brown, but in the cool, relaxed way.

In the late 80s, Kenny would start a second career as a session drummer, quickly growing over the next few years into one of the most in-demand in the business. Now that word was out on the street that "Mellencamp's secret weapon" was available for hire, the calls came pouring in. Following producer Rick Nowels' ringing Kenny up in 1987 to play drums on his first non-Mellencamp # 1,

Belinda Carlisle's *"Heaven On Earth,"* super-producer Don Was reached out to Kenny in what would become a kindred collaboration that immediately elevated Kenny to the elite of playing with legends like Bob Dylan, Iggy Pop, and Elton John, explaining that "with Kenny, I wanted him to take as much license as possible. During those years we worked together in the late 80s and early 90s, I used Kenny on every record, and that only changed when Mellencamp went out on tour, but I'd book him whenever I could." Kenny has similarly-fond memories of working in the studio with Was, recalling an intuitive trust that developed almost instantly between the two, who often kept the beat together as a pocket with Don accompanying Aronoff on bass:

> Don was cool as shit, he always let me do whatever I wanted. Every so often he might say, "Hey, let's use brushes on this one," but most of the time, he let me do what I wanted, unless I asked him for direction on something. He's very good at hiring people purposely because he liked what they did, there was more freedom with parts. The thing about Don was, as a producer, he had incredible instincts, both in how to make decisions quickly and direct things, and he's never longed for an answer, he always comes up with something that keeps a session going right.

When the phone call came in 1990 from Jon Bon Jovi to record the biggest hit of the summer of 1990, *"Blaze of Glory,"* Aronoff's profile would rise right to # 1, capping of a run of recognition over the past 5 years that had included being voted BEST DRUMMER in Rolling Stone Magazine, and # 2 Pop/Mainstream Rock Drummer three years in a row by Modern Drummer Magazine, and a continually-distinguished list of session-and-touring superstars he was playing with that included Bob Seger, The Indigo Girls, Hall and Oats, Bonnie Raitt, B.B. King, and Neil Diamond. Getting the call from Jon Bon Jovi to play on the *"Blaze of Glory"* soundtrack to the motion picture Young Guns II, Aronoff – who after so many years as a hitmaker knew exactly what to bring to his beats to make chart-toppers out of the songs he was playing on – recalled feeling something special

> when I heard *"Blaze of Glory"* for the first time, I knew instantly this was going to be a huge hit. It sounded like a complete story or movie all in itself. It was a signature Bon Jovi-type song but different in a cool way. I was very concerned about how I could help make this a hit. The song has so many dynamics and emotions in it, and it opens with a very mysterious heavy intro vibe, and then into a more developed 2nd verse, back to a break-down before finally exploding into that huge, powerful chorus! Then another intro that goes into a third driving verse that slams right into a powerful second chorus, back down again for a short break down section that helps set up Jeff Beck's guitar solo. The song then breaks down one more time for a 3rd verse where I wrote and played an orchestral cadence on 4 different size snare drums to create a military-type vibe. This sets up what became a signature drum fill that I came up with on the spot which leads into two huge choruses and out.

Kenny's critical accolades by 1991 reflected his successful transition into the studio world after Modern Drummer Magazine's readers' voted him # 3 Studio Drummer in the business, moving up to # 2 on that list in 1992 and to the top of the list as the magazine's # 1 Pop/Mainstream Rock Drummer, a position born out by his continued relevance across multiple music charts. In 1993, Kenny would get a call from legendary songwriter/producer Jim Steinman to play on Meat Loaf's comeback smash, *"I Would Do Anything for Love (But I Won't Do That),"* joking in hindsight that in spite of what the world-wide hit the song would become, charting at # 1 in 28 countries, at the time he was recording its majestic beatscape,

> I thought we were wasting our time because it was 10 and a half minutes long. I remember saying "There's no way radio will play a song that is 10 ½ minutes long." A year after I'd recorded the album, shortly before it was about to be released to radio, I got another call from Meatloaf's people and they say, "Kenny, Jim wants you to fly back to New York, they want to put an intro on Anything for Love," and I said "Are you kidding me? The song

> is already 9 ½ minutes long and you're going to add an intro to it. You're wasting your money and time, no one is ever going to play a song that is that long," and I really thought nobody on the radio would play it. Boy was I wrong, because it went to # 1 in 15 countries *in the same fucking week* and relaunched his career.

By the mid-1990s, Kenny had connected with another kindred spirit in Melissa Etheridge, beginning a decade-long collaboration in the studio and on stage that produced hits like *"I Want to Come Over,"* another classic Aronoff power-driver that dominated pop radio alongside what would be his final radio smash with John Mellencamp after almost 15 years behind the kit with the # 3 smash on the Billboard Hot 100 Singles Chart, *"Wild Nights,"* a Van Morrison cover reinvented almost entirely by Aronoff's urban-flavored drum acrobatics, its an achievement he stills regards as

> another of my prouder examples of helping to write a hit with John by coming up with the beat that drove that song right there in the studio. I had just finished playing on a Waylon Jennings album *Waymore's Blues (Part II)* in L.A. and I used some of the creative ideas I had just come up with for Waylon's record in John's session. John is always looking for new ideas so he was happy with some of mine, I used some of these ideas on John's next record "Dance Naked," which we started recording a month later. The song that I was able to apply some of these new sounds and ideas was on a Van Morrison song we covered called *"Wild Nights."* Me'Shell NDegeo-cello played an amazing bass line and John and Me'Shell snag the song as a duet. I played a unique-sounding funky beat. My right hand played an Englehart metal crasher with a Vic Firth dreadlock and my left hand used a plastic Meinl Guord with beads on a 12" piccolo wood snare. My kick drum was small and I a D-Drum trigger on it. That song went to # 3 on the Billboard Hot 100 Singles chart.

When I started working with Melissa Etheridge, right from the first rehearsal, I loved playing with Melissa because I felt like we both had the same energy. When I recorded with her, that was the first song we cut, and I immediately went "Holy shit, wow!" It was the most powerful thing I'd ever been around and I was blown away because she was singing the way I play drums, and I was playing the drums the way she sang, it was so matched. Not only that, but she allowed me to stretch out and play the parts I wanted on the record,

Melissa Etheridge: The way he hit the snare drum was above and beyond anyone else who was playing drums at that time. You can tell, there's not many drummers where you can listen to a recording, and go "Oh, that's Kenny," just because of the way the snare drum sounds. It was the sound of the late 80s and 90s, that was Kenny, he was a force to play with, to harness, and the first time I ever played with him, I turned around, looked at him, and said "Woah, you gotta be my drummer!" He was amazing. He was a beautiful drummer with an amazing feel, and he used to come in with just walls of snare drums, including one called The Black Beauty we would always end up using, but we would try many others, and when you listen to *"I Wanna Come Over,"* when it starts off, there's his snare and what more can I say? He sets it up, its Rock & Roll.

Voted # 1 Studio Drummer by BOTH Modern Drummer Magazine and DRUM! Magazine the same year in 1996, Kenny was dominating multiple media markets including radio in rock, pop and even country, playing on such # 1s as Mary Chapin Carpenter's *"Shut Up and Kiss Me"* and *"Closer to Free,"* the BoDean's Top 20 hit that became the theme for the hit T.V. show *"Party of Five,"* and on the silver screen after movie superstar Tom Hanks hired Kenny to play drums on the theme for *"That Thing You Do,"* laying down the film's signature beat, a gig that came when

I got a call sometime in the mid-1990s from Don Was to come play on another great project he was producing, the soundtrack to a Tom Hanks movie called 'That Thing You Do.' I came up with that signature opening right there on the spot in the studio, and we were instructed during the session to record many different versions of the song because Hanks wanted many different stages of "The Wonders" playing the song throughout the movie: everything from the band learning the song in their garage to the church/makeshift studio where the band recorded the version of the song that wound up on the radio in the movie. It was a unique process, and the first time I'd worked that way, but I understood why they needed to many keeper takes

I remember I must have played that a hundred times with Don in the studio, and it was really cool because I remember I walked into the control room after all these takes, ands Tom Hanks is sitting there and says to me, "That was really great Kenny!" He was looking out at the live room through the glass like a director, or producer sitting at the mixing board, and then he continues, "That was really great job man, I kind of miss the Beret." That's what I was wearing in the video for *"R.O.C.K. in the U.S.A.,"* and I later found out from Don Was that that video had inspired him to sit down and write the script for *'That Thing You Do.'*

Aronoff's reputation for being the go-to gun for hire drew the attention of Alternative Rock Gods the Smashing Pumpkins in 1996 after frontman Billy Corgan had been impressed by Aronoff's reputation as "a true professional. That's why through the years he was one of the highest-paid studio musicians, because if you called Kenny's number, you knew exactly what you were gonna get, and you could literally book it to the minute and that's something that's not always appreciated in the music business, but as you get older and you look at these things maybe from a different perspective, maybe its like a baseball manager who goes "Okay, I know I can slot that guy in at third base every day," because you know what you're gonna get and its beyond solid." Feeling that he "fit right in with the Pumpkins' style of rock too because of my background in Jazz, because their songs were all jams, so I could adapt to all kinds of different things they did on stage during their shows." Touring with the band on a sold-out arena tour around the world, Kenny remembered feeling inspired by Corgan's smart decision to "encourage me to be myself on stage instead of trying to play exactly like Jimmy Chamberlin, which I was totally with because there aren't two Jimmy Chamberlins. Billy had two huge percussion set-ups on either side of me on stage."

That same year, Aronoff got perhaps his career's most fated call, one that would make him the drummer to back Creedence Clearwater Revival's legendary singer/songwriter John Fogerty as he prepared to play his CCR catalog live for the first time in 30 years, declaring once he'd heard Kenny play at his audition that "you're the drummer I've been waiting for all my life!" The 30th and final drummer to audition for Fogerty, Kenny remembered feeling the two were a good match for each other because

> we both are work horses, perfectionists and never completely satisfied. He wanted lots of takes and I always thought I could do it better, (laugh). I really liked working with John and dug the songs I was recording. I really liked and related to his style of writing and how every note I played had to be perfect with regard to my parts, feel, power, and relentless consistency. While we were recording one day, he asked me if I would be into touring with him. I said "Wow, Absolutely!" This was going to be the first time in at least 17 years he would perform the Creedence Clearwater Revival (CCR) songs he had written, arranged, played guitars, sang and produced. I was so excited to be performing those songs live with John. Those songs were a part of my life personally and as a musician. This was the beginning of a relationship making records and touring that has lasted over 20 years and is still going on today.
>
> We are a great combination because we both are always going for it. He calls me his offensive line as in NFL Football. He depends on me to feel every song the way he is feeling it every night and if he wants to play faster

> one night, I play faster. At any given moment in a concert with John, I can get a cue from him to step it up, if that's what he's feeling, and I'm studying this guy every split second I'm on that stage to see where he's at. I keep my eyes on him for the entire show, watching every move he makes, so when he gives me a hand signal or turns around at any point in the show to tell me something, I am there for him. He has a tech that runs notes to my tech at different points in the show, and that's why I have a 16-channel mixer and my tech, Nik (my son), mixes my monitors all night long for me to give me exactly the perfect mix so I can hear John's vocals and guitars. John likes me, no matter where he's at, to "kick his ass," that's his instruction to me every night, that's my job, always. He likes to rock. Nik has to make adjustments on every song, sometimes as many as four or five adjustments throughout one song to make sure I hear what I need to hear.

Entering the Millennium, Kenny remained as relevant as ever courtesy of a personal philosophy he describes as "hard work, driven by passion and education" that allowed him to continue to play with rock legends like The Rolling Stones, Rod Stewart, Brian Williams, and Joe Cocker – but equally as impressive and important – successfully adapt to a new generation of rock and pop that was driven by the hybrid of programmed and live beats played together on hits Aronoff drummed on including Ricky Martin's *"Shake Your Bon Bon,"* Avril Lavine's *"My Happy Ending,"* and Michelle Branch's Top 20 smashes *"Everywhere," "Are You Happy Now?", "Breathe,"* and *"I'm Feeling You."* Taking fans inside his creative mind for an exploration of how he fit his drum hits within that hybrid production model, Kenny first points to the advantage of a norm he's employed throughout his career of writing charts ahead of any gig for the music he'll be performing, explaining that

> the advantage of writing a chart out and being very clear on ideas: it allows me and the producer to be more creative. I'm not slowing him down, I'm moving through ideas, and he's saying, "I like that, I don't like that." I listen, I learn and I lead, but I'm not the boss. The producer is the boss, and you've

> got to keep these talented producers engaged and going, never slowing down the session, and the key to that is: *preparation is everything!*
>
> With Michelle's sound, I was playing around walls of guitars and along with programmed loops, so this was really a new hybrid sound to be part of musically. What was different about recording on these 2 records was my drums were the last instrument on the recording, which was the opposite way I had recorded for years. The pressure was always on the drummer to get a great drum track first and everyone would overdub to the drummers feel and parts. But recording last, this new way, I had to approach everything differently. I had to find the right sounds, right drum parts and the right feel based on what was already recorded. Once I got my drum parts figured out, the most important thing to me was to add my soul, my energy, my vibe to the tracks to make sure the songs didn't feel programmed or stiff. Her songs were definitely pop, but at the same time they still rocked.

Voted # 1 and #2 Studio Drummer by DRUM! Magazine, Modern Drummer Magazine in 2002, and # 1 Studio/Session Drummer by Rhythm Magazines in 2005 and # 4 Country Drummer by Drum! Magazine in 2007 as he continued to put hits up on the Top 20 across multiple charts, including Lee Ann Womack's *"Something Worth Leaving Behind,"* Trick Pony's *"On a Night Like This,"* and Jake Owen's *"Startin' With Me"* and *"Don't Think I Can Love You,"* all Top 10 hits on the Billboard Country Singles Chart, and Puddle of Mudd's *"Famous"* and *"Psycho,"* both # 1 hits on the Modern Rock Singles Chart hits, Aronoff's universal praise was due and his visibility was at an all-time high after multiple appearances throughout the first decade of the Millennium on high-profile television shows including Good Morning America, The Tonight Show, The View, TMZ, Ellen, Saturday Night Live and American Idol, The Voice, CMT Crossroads, Conan O'Brien, Last Call with Carson Daly, MTV, L.A. Ink, Jimmy Kimmel, Regis and Kelly, and his personal favorite, Late Night with David Letterman, where in addition to over 50 artist appearances throughout the years, Kenny was also a regular sub for house band drummer Anton Fig.

> in 2014, after I played on Letterman with John Fogerty where we performed *"Down On the Corner,"* and *"Fortunate Son."* I was on fire when we performed *"Fortunate Son,"* and when John sat down after our performance for an interview with David Letterman, Dave said laughing to John, "John, I don't want to tell you how to do your business, but if you just got yourself a drummer, you got something here (laughs)," to which John jokingly replied, "I'll work on that." I remember sitting off to the side of the stage thinking "Wow, how cool is that? David Letterman acknowledged the drummer."

Arguably for Kenny, one of the decade's biggest spotlight moments came in 2008 when he was asked to be the house drummer for the White House Inaugural Celebration at the Lincoln Memorial for newly-elected President Barack Obama. The kind of elite-level gig the drummer highlights to illustrate just how extreme the pressure is even as he makes it look effortless for the cameras in *below-zero freezing temperatures.* Shivering even today as he reflected back on the first-in-history event, the drummer confirmed that nature was indeed presenting an extra challenge to all of the inherently-normal chaos already a-swirl on stage:

> it was freezing cold, 9 degrees outside! The stage was set up in front of the Lincoln Memorial looking down toward the Washington Monument. In a tent next to the Lincoln Memorial where we rehearsed, I had to wear long underwear and a snow parka and a ski hat with drummers gloves to stay warm. During the actual show, it finally warmed up to 32 degrees (laugh), I wore long underwear and drum gloves and no hat so I would look cool, but multiple layers of cloths. Even the Secret Service Agents were freezing! The joke was, we had heaters the size of my laptop that were basically useless, there was no heat. When I was on stage the day of the show, they had this huge mega-screen facing the stage so that the people talking could read the screen while looking into the cameras and the singers could see their lyrics, and I had the people writing the script put cues on the screen for me so I would know when to count off. "Kenny Aronoff counts off this song."

> That's why gigs like this, are not just about being a great drummer, its about being somebody who understands the entire show, knowing what comes next, knowing when to count off and end songs. I wouldn't be there if the producer and the musical director didn't think they could count on me to do my job and solve problems if they occur. For instance, when the cold weather froze the cables on Stevie Wonder's keyboard and it wouldn't work when he started playing, the house band played the introduction over and over again until he came in. While this was happening, I saw the camera on the big boom come down from the main stage onto me and when I saw that red light come on during that moment, I smiled and looked right into the camera as if I didn't have a care in the world!
>
> When I was playing the Presidential Inaugural Ball, I remember I was in the Green Room before the show, and Tom Hanks walked in, and from across the room, yelled over to me "Kenny! What are you doing here?" Then he says to everybody in the green room – including stars like Jack Black, Samuel L. Jackson, etc – "This show is going to ROCK! We have Kenny Aronoff..." And when we were doing soundcheck, which was on a stage at the Lincoln Memorial looking out over the Washington Monument, Tom was out there listening and actually came over the loudspeakers, and said "Testing, testing, one, two... Kenny Aronoff's in the house everybody!"

After years of wear and tear banging away behind the kit as Rock & Roll's hardest working and hitting drummer for hire, Aronoff at 62 is just as busy behind the kit as ever. Applying a disciplined regimen for staying in world-class shape, he outlines a series of steps consisting of "8 things that make up a healthy life for me: 1. Weight Training, 2. Cario Workouts, 3. Stretching, 4. Diet, 5. Suppliments, 6. Water, 7. Sleep, and 8. Meditation." Necessary to combat the repletion of on-the-job injuries that he's sustained over 35 years behind the kit, Kenny tries these days to play smarter without being any less harder a hitter:

I have to say, I spent a lot of my years crushing my leg when I hit the snare drum because I have this technique where I play super loud, and on one Fogerty tour, I broke 5 die-cast tubes in 30 shows – split them in half! I don't do that anymore, I just won't play that hard, but when the front of the stick would hit the head, the back of the stick or the middle of the stick would hit the rim, but my hand would kind of hit my leg, and it was that ball on the padding of my hand below the thumb would always hit my leg. So because I'd spent years crushing that part of my hand into my leg, which didn't' help the leg either, or the toe because my right foot's fine but my left foot has a little bit of arthritis in just the big toe joint because I don't put my foot down flat on the hi-hat, just my heel and the ball of my foot is on the hi-hat. So when you hit your leg, it sends all that pressure down to that joint, so "Hello, duh, no wonder its sore after 40 years of playing drums.

The expectation of constant and consistent perfection among his peers both in the playing and producing worlds has earned Kenny one of Rock & Roll's most esteemed honors of being house drummer for PBS's Kennedy Center Honors concerts for 7 consecutive years between 2008 and 2014, honoring artists who he also shared the stage with on national television with such Rock & Roll luminaries as Dave Grohl, Chris Cornell, Rob Thomas, Garth Brooks, Steven Tyler, Lady Gaga, Bruno Mars, Brad Paisley, Willie Nelson, Sheryl Crow, Kid Rock, Miranda Lambert, Kris Kristofferson, Norah Jones, James Taylor, Steve Winwood, Tom Morello among others performing for many of his Rock heroes, including The Who, Led Zeppelin, Paul McCartney, and Bruce Springsteen, along with Merle Haggard, Neil Diamond, Billy Joel, Carlos Santana and Sting. Kenny's secret weapon to keeping the dizzying array of artists' drum parts straight was once again his charts, reasoning such organization is required quite simply because

I *CANNOT* fuck up when I perform on live TV shows like the Grammy's or the Kennedy Center Honors. There is no room for one mistake so I prepare and do my homework. You have to be able to read and write music really well because there are changes, adjustments, and re-writes done right up to the last second before the curtain opens with the President, the First Lady, political figures, Hollywood's finest and many of my peers sitting up with the artist being honored that year. I rehearse all the count offs, when to count off, who to count off to, double check my charts, the drum machine tempos, etc and go over all the important transitions over and over again right up to when I walk on stage. Stage managers, producers and engineers love it when they see that I am in the house band or I am performing, because it makes their job easier when I am there and they don't have to worry about me fucking up and if something does go wrong, they know I will make immediate adjustments on the spot and make things right.

My session charts are written out on a piece of paper with a pencil because I'm going to have to make a lot of changes usually, and so I put the first page of the song in my hi-hat side and my head's turned to the left, and the first page is closest to me and the next page is to the left of that. Now, when I do things like the Kennedy Center Honors where I have four pages of music, I take scotched-tape and tape the pages together from the back and while I'm playing, at some point, just reach and physically push each page over on the music stand so it starts hanging over. It hangs over first on the far side and as I get through the pages, I start moving the whole piece, and then it starts hanging over on the right side and I just keep moving it. It's a pain in the butt. I've done some wild stuff where I'm playing with one hand and moving pages around with the other.

Despite all of these trips to the top of the Mountain, Kenny's true personal peak was reached in 2014 when he was drafted to back up his childhood heroes on stage live on national television on CBS's "The Beatles: The Night That Changed America" special. A full-circle moment 50 years to the night he'd first watched the Fab 4 on Ed Sullivan and declared that he wanted to become one of them. That night, he was, and for Aronoff, it remains the crown jewel! I actually got to DRUMS alongside Ringo and share the stage with Sir Paul McCartney, i.e. BOTH surviving Beatles at the same time! It was surreal from front to back, and really was a life-statement for me to have come far enough in my career to be considered worthy of being part of this celebration. One thing I thought Ringo did that was really cool too was initially during soundcheck that day, when he walked in to check out the stage set-up, he objected to the initial way they'd had the band split up into two sections on the far sides of the stage. As soon as he saw that, he stopped the stage crew and said "Wait a minute, I don't want to be that far from the band. I want the band to move in close with me," and man, I was so happy to see Ringo say that. He was all about being in a band.

I got to play *"Yellow Submarine"* and *"A Little Help From My Friends"* with Ringo, and then we all got to jam with him and Paul together on *"Hey Jude"* during the encore, it was amazing. When I performed *"Something"* with Joe Walsh, I played 2 buzz rolls on the rack tom and then the floor tom on beats 3 and 4 in the song the way Ringo had recorded it. When I watch the show on TV later on, the camera showed Ringo looking at me from the audience and he air drummed those rolls as I played them and was smiling at me in acknowledgement. The bottom line is I nailed it and he knew it.

I remember as the show was ending, I walked off stage and right past this roped-off section where Ringo and Paul were sitting with their wives, and Sean Lennon and Yoko Ono, and George Harrison's family, and they were all clapping. As I walked by Ringo, he suddenly grabbed my hand and said "You did an amazing job!" It was and will always rank as one of the greatest nights of my life.

These days, Kenny stays as busy as ever working both with his usual stable of Rock & Roll legends along with playing on a whole new generation of Millennium up and coming artists and bands, courtesy of the savvy decision several years back to open his own drum studio with Uncommon Studios LA, where

Aronoff gives bands looking for his signature sound the same access as any veterans on his discography. Recommending the move as a smart piece of advice for any player who can swing it, the drummer proudly explains that

> as the music budgets have continued to stay small over the past decade, my Uncommon Studios LA has proven itself to be a great and sustainable business model for me as a session drummer as I adapted to the new reality of competing in today's version of the record business. Bringing 35 years of experience and expertise as both a drummer and musician to every record I make, I am constantly trying to improve my sound by listening and learning, using great recording gear and working with great engineers that understand recording acoustic instruments, playing the best beats, grooves, fills, and getting the best sounds for the song I am recording. I have recorded on so many albums and songs in so many different studios across America, playing many, many different styles of music, that my understanding of music and the recording process is vast.
>
> Those assets come in very handy for the large number of independent artists I work with who, in many cases – have grown up in the digital, in-the-box age of bedroom Protools recording – have no idea how to get a live drum sound because they haven't had a chance to even place microphones around a drum kit. Besides playing the drums and understanding the recording process, I have experienced working with many different personalities thrown together in a room. Learning how to get along and be a team player is a huge part of getting hired and making records. I am so fortunate to have worked through the greatest era as a session drummer where w e had huge budgets ad the room therein to experiment with microphones and pre-amps and EQs and effects, plus spend lots of time working on parts and arrangements for songs
>
> I have the "Aronoff drum sound," no matter what I hit or part I play. Every musician has a unique sound and feel when they play. I have a sound that's

unique to me that no one else has, and I have that sound in my head and in my gut. *The Kenny Aronoff sound*, and when I play, I am always trying to get that sound and feel. And if I'm not getting that across through those speakers in a studio when they play it back, then I will always take the time – no matter how big or small the client – to get my sound so when you hear those drums, you know its Kenny Aronoff.

I have also launched my "Evening with Kenny Aronoff" series, which has thankfully been very successful with fans. I'd been working on a one-man show for many years. It came from 35 years of doing drum clinics and writing my autobiography, where I went back and looked at my entire life: every live gig, tour, TV performance and every session I ever did, my personal life, my successes and my challenges and struggles in life. I put together this show to share with people, and talk about what I think helped me become successful: how a kid from a small town of 3,000 people in New England became a successful rock star and is continuing to stay successful. My motto is: I'll never be as great as I wanna be, but I'm willing to spend my life trying to be as great as I can be.

"There is that pyramid of drummers, but there's only one stone on top, and at one time, Buddy Rich was the stone on top, and then at one top Bonham was the stone on top, and I think we all collectively make this pyramid of creative music, and the top stone alternates between different players over the years and makes other musicians grow, and then the pyramid grows higher." – Stephen Perkins

(photo by Gabe L'Heureux)

Chapter 7: Stephen Perkins of Jane's Addiction – Coming Down the Mountain

By all counts, Jane's Addiction was the Led Zeppelin of the Alternative Rock generation. Consider Rolling Stone's endorsement that with the band's "huge, hybridized sound…helped define the soon-to-be-coined alternative (genre)...As much as any band in existence, Jane's Addiction is the true heir to Zeppelin." As dynamically inventive as the boundaries of musical imagination itself, Perkins invented his own style of percussive power that hadn't been heard before or since. Required to compliment the Funk-Rock/Psychedelic/Jazz/World/Heavy Metal hybrid that defined their sound, for Perkins, the fusion of those styles into his playing is a natural extension of his love for

> absorbing everything and then kind of spit it out in own home-grown fashion. I play my beat, but inspired by a mix of my love of Jazz, African, Funk, Motown, and having conversation with people as a musician on my drum set, and knowing when to shut up and just be a pulse, and let them say something. I'm always experimenting with rhythm and hopefully they are catching on, and when an imprint is made on people's brains with rhythm, I love that.

Taking fans back to the early impressions made on his own musical mind as a young child first picking up the sticks, Perkins credits his principle mentor Jim Engle for helping him begin to dissect these outer influences as he absorbed and apply them internally within his own fast-evolving creative cognition as a player. Taking ahold of a talent as unique as Perkins' by the reigns, the drummer recalled that he and his teacher began with the basics:

> My first drum teacher, Jim Engle, who I played with for 6 years between 8 and 14, showed me the traditional grip and showed me how to approach the snare drum in that Military, rudiment sense: "These are the rudiments you use on a snare drum to get your chops together." From there I wondered, "Well, who are the best drummers on the drum kit in the world?", and he said "They're Jazz drummers – Gene Krupa, Buddy Rich, Elvin Jones, Tony Williams – these are the best drummers in the world. They're taking that military approach to the snare drum and using the contraption of a drum set, and if you listen and dissect what they're doing: they are using rudiments – paradiddles and what they're doing with the ride and the snare and the kick drum – and making patterns out of these rudiments.
>
> Then of course, *the feel,* was not just what I thought as a kid was Jazz. No, Jazz was a conversation. Jazz was listening to who is playing what and reacting, and in that sense, you have to swing. You have to leave room for one person to step while you pick your foot up, and then you get to make a step while his foot is up, and you have almost like the Bigfoot walk: you've got

to swing to it. You just can't help it if you're a drummer. I love the linear drumming, but if you talk about Jazz and the way that conversation happens, with the phrasing of a piano and an upright bass and Sax, trumpet, flute, clarinet – especially clarinet. I'm a Jewish boy, and the instrument's sound and feel went right into Benny Goodman, who is a Jewish clarinet player.

The inherent focus of Jazz on improvisation, syncopation, poly-rhythmic elements and swing all appealed to the natural leanings of Perkins' musical imagination and immediate fascination with inspiring a reaction from the listener with what he played behind the kit. Deconstructing this aspect of his attraction to the drums – which has maintained as firm a hold on him as a player to this day as it did when he was a child first learning to play – Stephen begins by explaining that,

to me, if you think about what a drummer can do to a room and to a body and to a hit and to a body's reaction, if you go to Africa or Asia or South America, the rhythm controls the hip movement, and with swing drummers and basically that military rudiment approach. So when I realized that drummers playing in African pop bands that no one in the Western world had ever heard of were making these crazy rhythms, and an East Indian tapas player, listen to those rhythms, and a Latin Tamali player, you realize its not just about Gene Krupa or Bonham because there's so much going on there as far as the fuel of rhythm: what can you fill your tank up with?

So when you dissect that and put it on to a Trap kit, that's the best musical range for playing Jazz, and that's what I got into with Jim Engle. He showed me that Jazz wasn't keeping a pulse, like Motown – which was fantastic – but that Jazz was a conversation, so I thought the drum solo was just tom, snare and floor tom, but its actually Elvin Jones' drum solo was an answer to Coltrane's Sax solo, and the last 48 measures of Sax inspired the next 16 measures of Elvin's solo. He used the phrasing and the melody and the theme and put it into his drumming, and then replicated it with the drums.

As Perkins began translating that conversation outwardly with other local neighborhood musicians, his musical pallet was expanded even more broadly by the natural fact that "as a drummer back in the day, no one was playing trombones or pianos or saxophones in my neighborhood, they were all buying P-basses and Les Pauls, so I was forced to understand the power of AC/DC, Van Halen and Led Zeppelin." Understandably drawn to the drummers, Stephen quickly discovered that beneath the surface, they all were speaking the same basic language within their playing because of the common Jazz roots he had in common with these drum Gods:

> As I looked deeper, Mitch Mitchell and John Bonham and of course Ringo and Charlie Watts, and discovered it was swing. They're influences was Jazz meets Motown. They understood the pulse of Motown and a lot of the early Stones and Beatles shows were based on Motown, they covered a lot of that stuff, so basically they loved the conversation of Jazz as musicians, and you can't help it as a drummer but want to have a conversation with everybody in the room.
>
> Sometimes though in the Rock world, especially as the producers in the late 70s and 80s started to take a little more hold of the sound and the producers guided the band, you heard a lot of the drummers having to back up on the conversation and just play the pulse, and go back to almost a Motown situation where the drums are kind of just not even heard in a way, they're just felt. In Rock & Roll, it was nice when a few bands – including Jane's Addiction – showed up and were able to stir it up a little, and say "You know what, things can be a little more dangerous, in a sense." Just like, of course, if you listen to anything The Who did with Keith Moon, it shows in the recordings that there's a sense of danger because its just dangerous drumming and bass playing, it makes you feel like there's a real sense of freedom and Keith of course swings too, all my favorites: Bill Ward from Black Sabbath, wow, he really swings, all the great young rock guys were

> influenced by great Jazz guys. The soul of my drumming likes in a swing, which is also like the guys I grew up with and the way they played.

Entering his early teens as the 1970s glory era of Hard Rock and Heavy Metal entered its next generation of the Hair Metal-driven 1980s, Perkins would find himself gravitating as a music fan toward the more avant-garde styles of Funk, Punk, Reggae and Goth, a refuge that appealed to Perkins' innately open-minded nature as a player once he started blending them into his pedigree as a player. Soaking up "the impression I got from Allman Brothers and the Dead and other bands that had a great understanding of displacing these rhythms and changing them and working them and people catch on," Perkins began testing these rhythm theories out on the audiences he was playing before in his first High School bands, including Dizaster with future Jane's Addiction bandmate Dave Navarro.

By the time he'd joined up with his like-minded band mates – the master of ceremonies, visionary frontman Perry Farrell and one of Rock's most imaginative bassline composers, Eric Avery – in Jane's Addiction and quickly signed their first record/management deal with XXX. Perkins was relieved to find himself on standing on the right side of the old music industry adage of "surround yourself with good people," because Stephen's tribe were among the brightest in the business at stretching their minds and boundaries in the process around the music the band made together. Creating enough room for the drummer to fully spread his wings and creatively develop into the professional player he became on the band's first album, Stephen recalled of this growth process that

> when me and Dave joined, we were just 18 and still obsessed with basically flash playing, showing off what we could do. And Perry and Eric were into Bauhaus and Joy Division and there was more a subtle approach, so what we brought was this flashy, metallic thing and that was still fresh as a teenager, and what they were bringing was an interesting English songwriting

technique that, as soon we were a band, you can see how of course some of the moments in the studio gave me and Dave a chance to kind of pull out of our inspired metal days – which were fantastic – and kind of take a breath, and Dave Jerden and Ronnie Champagne and everybody was so supportive of what we were after.

They gave us the time, and everybody had great drum ideas, and I was like "Cool, let's try everything, let's try anything that goes." It was a great team of creative people that loved rhythm at heart and I think that shows in the production of the band. We didn't just want to put together a hard-rocking record, we really wanted an experience, and the beauty of the song was so important to Eric and Perry and then of course for me and Dave, the beauty of the player was so important. So that's really what you get is these great players with these great songs. We all had different record collections, we all had different friends, we all dressed differently, and we sounded different, but we all wanted the same thing: really creative, colorful, psychedelic music.

Fans discovered quickly enough they were onto something new to raise Janes' to the top of the L.A. underground club scene overnight, allowing the 18-year-old Perkins to proudly join two bands on stage whom he respected for both their originality and eclecticism musically as much as he did for the equally open-minded audience of listeners they attracted as fans: "At the time in L.A., Fishbone and the Chili Peppers were really the hot bands downtown, because what happened at the strip was GnR and Motley, Poison and Ratt, the Strip ended at Midnight, and we played downtown and our scene started at 1 AM and went all night. Our scene was in a sense, Funk, because Mike Watt was there with there with Firehose, which is quite funky, and then even X was on their 4th or 5th record and was almost finished, but you really just had Fishbone and the Chilis, which is real funky, and so you can hear what was happening in L.A. with *'Idiots Rule,'* and *'Standing in the Shower'* and *'Trip Away,'* we were playing some hard rock funk, and were not afraid of it either."

Reflecting that scene in their sound, Billboard soon reported on the band's word-of-mouth wildfire that "Jane's Addiction became the talk of the Los Angeles underground as their unpredictable and high-energy stage show, gender-bending look, and sonic mix of punk, funk, metal, jazz, and haunting ballads hit a nerve with a diverse rock crowd." Welcoming the world aswirl around him into his muse as a player, Stephen was happy to mirror the tension and nervous energy of his listeners in his playing, reasoning that its always a smart move for a musician to play to as well as for his crowd:

> There's something to be said about pulling from your environment, and making your own style and reflecting what's around you. That's what Jane's did: you can hear Hollywood on the first record, *"Whores," "1%,"* and there it is: you can hear the frustration, "Motherfucker! Give me some more," and when I heard that chorus, I was like "How else can I play the drums to that except shoop bam!" There just was no doubt the drum part was born from those lyrics and that's my style, to listen to the lyrics and react, like John Densmore from The Doors, or Keith Moon from The Who would do that, react.

Hollywood vampires who were rocking the nights at an hour where only the brave enough to walk the cutting edge as music fans dared downtown to catch the band, including future producer Dave Jerden one night, recounting of the Midnight mayhem that "I once saw them play at Scream, at 3 o'clock in the morning, and there were like 3,000 kids waiting in line to get in. We reflected that in their debut album, Nothing's Shocking, the over-all feel of that record to me was that it should reflect the culture- be chaotic, and makes sense at some times, and at others, doesn't make any sense at all. Just constant stimuli coming at you from all different angles, as the culture was doing. And that's what I wanted to capture on the record. They're a band for the future, that's the kind of band they are at heart." Seeking to salute not only his fans in the band's music, but also tribute the bands who'd inspired him before they became his peers on the same music scene, in *"Trip Away,"* one of Perkins' earliest demonstrations of the electrifying energy he was capable of conjuring behind the kit, he proudly shared that

> the beat and the funk were really inspired by what was happening in L.A., and I really think that it honored the Peppers and Fishbone's music and the scene and hanging out with those guys. The Dead were also very important to us, me and Navarro went to alot of Dead shows, and the break-down in the middle of "Trip Away" really felt at home, like it had a Grateful Dead-kind of opening the door to a new kind of atmosphere, and the announcement of Perry before the guitar solo and Perry and Dave singing and playing together. It was really a joyous song, and basically tripping out and getting high and getting out of your skin.
>
> *"Idiots Rule"* was written at the same time as *"Trip Away,"* and you can hear our love for funk and hard funk and Bootsy Collins and James Brown and even Bad Brains, so the guitar riff itself is a fucking funk riff, straight up. And the drums could have been 4 on the floor and a little more simple, but I was in a strange sense inspired by some of 16-note hi-hat work of Stewart Copeland and I don't know if it was New Wave, but there was a lot of 16th note hi-hat going on at the time, and even Larry Mullin Jr. Think about *"No One's Leaving,"* its kind of a U2-inspired drum beat, its a lot more aggressive and recorded a lot differently than anything that would happen there. So there was the Larry Mullens, there was Stewart Copeland, and we were like "Wow, you can play funk that hard? Oh, okay, let's try that!", and for me personally, it was like "Woah, you can do that with a hi-hat?" Really open it up, close it, change it, and really make it part of the song. Or in *"Whores,"* there I've got two hands on the ride, and I'm just thinking on the bongs, how to become more percussive, if I was a Djembe player, and don't think about the drum set, think about the bongo – what would a bongo player be doing? Its how I think with the song.

Rock N' Roll was not a virgin anymore after Jane's Addiction got ahold of her, and as the band began to steal more and more of the market share from the ears of mercurial metal fans looking for something just as hard but a little bit heavier in musical and stylistic substance, Rolling Stone Magazine – who became an instant fan of the band – observed that the were the able to strike the hybrid balance they did because "Jane's Addiction rocked hard (harder than many of their Sunset Strip contemporaries, in fact), but they did so while mixing elements of funk, Goth and world music into the equation, resulting in a deeply personal sound that struck a resounding chord." Offering up *"Mountain Song"* as a demonstration of that harmony screaming in perfect pitch between fan and song, Perkins channeled his inner John Bonham as he came raining down on the toms in the song's opening moments, inspiring one of his Greatest *Air-Drum Hits* in the process:

> I look forward to the moment in *Mountain Song* where we're going back into the verse and I can see everybody's hands go up and do the snare fill, I loved that triplet fill when I was a kid. I thought it was perfectly played and couldn't believe what a hook we have all of a sudden, and it happens every time we return back to the verse with that snare fill. I love to see people do that. I feel not in any way responsible but part of a great moment that makes the show better and makes people join together.
>
> There was a moment when we played U.S.C. in 1986 and a bunch of my highschool buddies had showed up, like "Fuck, you and Navarro in Jane's Addiction, this is insane!" And we were doing *"Mountain Song"* and two of the hard core kids that I thought were hardcore skate punks, I saw them grab each other in like a tango grab and started tangoing together to "Mountain Song," these two punks, right into the pit! It was like "Holy shit, look what we've done to my friends! This is important," because the music electrifies people, and it electrifies us as musicians back and forth. Its not a cliché, there's a real energy exchange and that's what I love about people air-drumming to me. Those moments are just as important as a

> guitar riff or vocal scream and so I really love that moment, and it's a full-circle moment: I thought of it, I wanted it, and the band committed with me and there it is in stone, and people still do it.

As the band headed into the studio and began translating their infectious live energy onto tape, to match their on-stage vibe as authentically as possible in the studio, Perkins confirmed that "the live band in those moments of being spontaneous really were authentic, it was a live situation for us only, and then they'd put the mics on. The first record, XXX, we did live entirely." Maintaining within their musical spirit the constant pulse of a jam band, Jane's players' perfected their parts by constantly testing them out on audiences, maintaining an aggressive gigging schedule where

> we played live all the time – up to 3, 4, 5 times a month – gigs everywhere, 2 or 3 times a week if possible. So our songs, the shape of them, were taking on a reactive kind of sense, where we were reacting off the audience and it changed the songs. There were those moments to change songs, and those songs then went into the studio and they sounded like we were live, because we were. We played those songs live in the studio and then just kind of put salt and pepper on as post-production, so we didn't cut the song separately with everybody listening in the other room while I did my take: we were all there together jamming.
>
> Everything happened in the rehearsal in Perry's garage on Wiltern in Hollywood, everything we worked on, and the beauty of Jane's and those songs and what you're hearing is us listening and hearing Perry tell us a poem or a melody that is phrased in an odd way and what that means to the music, and not to make it feel in an odd time because he said it twice instead of once. You're supporting the line again, there it is, it just happens again, and then of course the guitar solos and the drum fills and me reacting to Perry, that all happened to us on stage and then it became part of the song.

Throughout the band's debut album, *Nothing's Shocking,* Stephen with his drum performances became a painter of musical canvases, and *"Ted, Just Admit It"* may be among his finest masterpieces. From its cascading dances around the toms to a percussive imagination that runs wild about the kit throughout the entire rhythmic vagabondage, the drummer sets a pace where as the tension builds like a woman toward an orgasm, withdraws and then stabs again, drawing the listener into new explosions of musical color that he continued to release throughout the entire work of erotic musical art. A post-punk player as much as he was a punk rocker at heart, Perkins struck a brilliant balance when he sat down behind the kit and set out on his ambitious journey to create the song's theatrical beatscape:

> We wanted to explore dub rhythms, and it was taking what Adrian Sherwood was doing with Reggae and mixing on stage and making records, and Bad Brains had touched on it a little bit. But by adjusting snare effects and using tempos and having fun in the sense of using the drum set and thoughts in the music and then what can you do to make those songs events and then make those events happen by using the sound of the studio equipment? So we listened to a lot of Adrian Sherwood and we said "Let's have an intro for this song," and basically the first two verses, when Perry's telling the story of how now basically nothing's shocking. When I was a kid, they had that one video *"Faces of Death,"* and that was the only way you could see anything filmed with something dying, and now its everywhere, he really hit the nail on the head. But anyway, Adrian Sherwood and the sound of Dub was our inspiration for the beginning of the song, and working with Dave Jerden, who had done *"Remain in Light"* with The Talking Heads and *"My Light in the Bush of Ghosts"* with David Byrne, and a lot of that was happening in what they were doing already. It was more of a more subtle way of doing it on those records, and we were from California and liked to do things in your face, so that's how you get this drum sound and this drum effect – right in

> your face, right to the point where there's no where else to look, and you're in a cave alone with these drums.
>
> That's where we wanted to approach the drum sound, and the whole intro, I worked out a melodic piece with the cowbells and the bongos, and I had these 10 inch concert toms with mics inside of them, and I had 10 and 12 inch cymbalito and metal, chrome Timbali drums with the mics on top, and I had 10, 12, 14, 16 DW toms in front of me, and a Gretch kick drum. I was using a Yamaha all-brass piccolo snare drum, thick cymbals, rock hi-hats and rock crashes, and I had a whole set of actual wood temple blocks, and I have a picture of me at the beginning of *"Ted"* with all that stuff there. Its visual too, I look at it and its like "There it is, there's the sound that you hear," it was really a great chance for me as a young drummer to paint something, and to have that chance.

In creating a movement for the music that felt something akin to being out at sea, throughout the exploratory process of plotting its pace, Perkins remembered he and bassist Eric Avery struggling at first to pinpoint the right pocket to fit into as a rhythm section. In spite of the perfection of the performance that wound up on record, the drummer confesses that because of the song's continually shifting musical tides,

> when we wrote the song, it was a great challenge for me and Eric to find the bass line and the drum part to just fit like that perfectly – it grooved slow, locomotive, it didn't come just like over a jam. We really wanted to work out how it was all going to fit in there, and how are we going to feel like we're on a boat almost and the ground is not secure, because the time signature is in time but its moving and displacing the snare drum and using tom-tom fills, or displacing the toms and using a Timbali triplet into the one. It was just trying some ideas that were inspired by Reggae and Dub drumming, and using that idea out of having this 2-3 minute colorful experience before we pulled it into the song and it became more concrete,

> and as the song grows, I thought, "Let the chaos begin!", but at the same time, I've got to be the guy holding the reigns on those horses. It is like holding reigns: you get to whip them, and they go up and then they whip tight, and they go up and they whip tight. I really try to think visually when I go to the toms and the ride cymbal, its basically if I had both hands on a hi-hat, but I have one hand on a tom and one on a bell.

Following Perry Farrell's story throughout his animated performance, Perkins layered his flashy footwork along with the appropriate percussive punctuations and accents to fully flesh out the musical moods – including all the subtitles and extremes – of the song's personality, beginning by listening for his cues as a player "lyrically, driving next to the lyrics and supporting the lyrics and listening to Perry's pulse rhythm and the way he punches is almost a percussion player with his words. So I can play off him as a percussionist in a way, and as the song gets heavier and goes into the 'Sex is violent' tribal drum part. What you got there is a lot of single-headed tom toms and a musical drum experience while Perry's chanting 'Sex is Violent, ' then its got my timpani roll, and the whole time during that tom part, I'm actually rolling on a timpani with a nice, fat mallet, so that's what you're hearing. Then, the second half of that tune was cut separately where I just put up like a 4-piece." As much a storyteller with his drumset as Perry Farrell was with the song's lyrics, the drummer reveals that

> *"Ted"* to me has this elastic feeling, based upon the telling of the story and the lyrics support the parts, and that's why the parts change all over the place, because of the lyrics telling the story. Same with *"Three Days"* and *"Then She Did."* Lyrically, that's what happens, and that's why the songs go places. Maybe *"Mountain Song"* doesn't because lyrically, Perry's chanting the same lyrics over and over, so that's how *"Mountain"* became a repetitive song, because the lyrics are repetitive. And if the lyrics don't repeat, as a poem, and things don't happen ever again in the poem, then the music should follow that. That's important I think as far as a story, Bob Dylan's got 13 verses on one song, so how do you get through that? You have a great band!

Perkins' tour de force behind the drums would later be hailed by Spin Magazine as the album's "most booming moment," from "its dubby intro to its hard-swung, slow-motion funk groove to its convulsive breakdown." By the time Perkins had reached this peak in his performance and was preparing to propel into one of the most hypnotically dazzling thunder of toms ever to storm down on Rock & Roll since John Bonham's Led Zeppelin heyday, he reveals that vs. sitting behind the starting gates with both feat at the ready behind two double bass drum beaters, in reality, his lightning-fast syncopation came courtesy of

> a single bass drum actually! Dave Jerden was so excited about the challenge of making every note come out clear, I think we had 24-inch bass drum and he took the front head off, and stuffed it with blankets, black-dot head, wooden beater, and the big tunnel of microphones.
>
> My favorite part of the song is the drum break between the verses when I go crash, tom, crash, tom, snare, and there's that moment where it was like mechanical, it was linear, and it was still emotional. There was still emotion in it even though there's like a liner, mechanical approach to that moment, because a lot of my drumming on that song is so boomy and then all of a sudden, it gets straight. On stage, we have a great time, because the intro we can stretch it (or not), and then at the end where Perry's singing "Violent," he likes to take that to a new level and I start doing different tom work.
>
> It could be mostly floor toms and kick drum on the end of the song, but to me, playing it live is recognizing that swing and not playing it too fast, and recognizing the peaks and valleys of the heavy verses, and there's a ride in L.A. at Magic Mountain where this pirate ship goes up one direction and then goes up the other direction, and if you sit in the back, you feel like you're losing your stomach like 20 times a minute. That's my approach, because if I can be an egg rolling down the hill, not a ball, and it doesn't always happen, but that's my goal. It doesn't mean I have to make it so extreme, but there has to be that feel, and then the bass player goes "Holy smoke, that's

what you're doing? Okay," and then Dave Navarro goes "Okay, cool, now my solo can be more elastic."

Perkins' power would be on equal display throughout "Nothing's Shocking" as "Jane's Addiction gave Los Angeles punk the majesty of arena rock," SPIN Magazine would later declare, correctly crediting Perkins as "their steady engine." A Ferrari that roared onto the open highway in *"Ocean Size"* – another of the album's master works – with such horsepower that the drummer remembered the band required a literal roadmap of sorts to chart the full immensity of the song's musical adventure:

> *"Ocean Size"* was a really great memory of working as a band. We actually put up a chalk board because there were so many parts, and wrote down every part and then we started subtracting how many times each part happened or adding or selecting moments that were important or events, and then taking those events away if there were too many, and so we knew the power and the tempo, and the riff was the power. But then there was gonna be the acoustic and the surprises, the quiet to the hard punches, just like a big ocean wave crashing on you. These moments are unpredictable in a way, and that's how the song was kind of written with this "I want to be on an ocean," kind of a boat feeling, and letting the floor kind of move around in a way.
>
> Jane's Addiction I think always had a lot of power, but it wasn't "Go home and write something," it was more like "Go home and make love with your girl really hard," so the music had this punch but it wasn't negative, it was a positive punch, "3, 4 BAM!", so when the band's at its best, and we can support when Perry says, "3,4" all our problems goes away, that's how it feels. We save *"Ocean"* usually for the last song of the whole set, because we feel it just like you do. That's the moment where everything breaks, the levy broke. The songwriting and arrangement – which I loved and I think is lost today – we really worked on it, like *"Standing in the Shower Thinking,"*

> we spent weeks on that. *"Ocean Size,"* we spent a long time on that, and it's a 3 minute tune but there's all these parts that happen and we had to work on it. I respect bands that still have that energy to put the time in, because these songs take time, ours took time, and the feel of them comes from a great band that wants to jam together.

While he displayed the muscular side of his playing on the latter hits, Stephen revealed a softer side on beloved ballads like *"Summertime Rolls"* and the band's anthem, *"Jane Says,"* a still-timeless touchstone of alternative rock that first introduced Jane's Addiction to the radio waves, and highlighted the personalities Perkins' paints within his performances, perhaps most poignantly on the stripped-down instrumental backdrop where Rolling Stone in their 4-star review later chronicled the song's evolution as "a holdover from the rawer and more abrasive independent album that the band released last year; from the strummed acoustic guitar that carries it along to the song's acid-etched portrait of an addict, the song is a worthy Left Coast successor to *"Walk on the Wild Side."* Showcasing his eclectic sensibilities as a composer with the selection of Steel drums that actually sang along as a harmony to Perry Farrell's lead vocal, the drummer shares of how his own part found its voice within the song's broader musical conversation that

> we already had a version of it on XXX where I just played Bongos, and we did it almost every night at every show, and basically I just played bongos and sat there with the fellas. But when we did it in the studio, Warners wanted *"Pigs in Zen"* and *"Jane Says"* off the first record, so we re-did *"Pigs"* and tried to do a weird version compared to the rest of the record. We recorded it differently, and placed it at the end of the record and it wasn't on the CD, it was only on the vinyl, so we tried to make *"Pigs"* special from the XXX version. There was just something different about it, and then we started working on *"Jane Says,"* and realized how beautiful the song was coming together lyrically, and I broke down that kick-snare part and abandoned the bongo, and started bringing the song to life.

> Once the kick and snare was in place and then electric bass, there started to become this other melody and I think we tried guitar parts and maybe even tried some vocal parts, and we all just thought to fill the void in the song with something haunting and melodic, and so I went to Guitar Center and bought a steel drum – which I still have – and we picked out the notes that worked, and I came up with a melodic piece that included maybe 3 solos, but really a piece that would change off the first half of the verse, the verse itself and then there was the chorus. And when we heard it back, we really felt like it add this haunting part to the melody that then became joyful, because there is a joy to the song, but there's also sadness: "I'm gonna kick tomorrow…" So the notes that we picked out really supported the lyric.

With *Nothing's Shocking,* the band would gift fans with the first of what the BBC later concluded were "the most intense, mind-expanding albums ever heard," the second of which was a bookend that would be studied for generations to come. With *Ritual De Lo Habitual,* Stephen's hometown paper, The LA Times, declared that "Perkins may be the most powerful, rhythmically inventive drummer in rock 'n' roll," a dynamism on full fiery display on the record's opening burst of brilliance, *"Stop!"* Leading with a piece of advice he offers to any drummer aspiring to meet Stephen's speed on the kit, the beatmaster recommends following the feel he took,

> especially for a fast song, where the number one thing to do is to make it feel still sexy, still behind the beat, but charging. There's a magical, mystical moment where you're gonna be charging and its still behind the beat, but "What the fuck is going on right now?" Like *"Ace of Spades,"* dude's behind the beat but he's fucking charging! So for me, the trick is for fast music is to sing the bass line, sing the guitar riff, that's what I'm playing to and that's what I'm singing in my head with the guys. Its like 1,2,3,4/1,2,3,4/1,2,3,4, and I can't think numbers, I can't think "How fast is the tempo?" I'm thinking "What should the song feel like to the kid in the audience? Why does it feel good?" That's what I got to say to myself, and then the kick

> drum pattern comes in: kick-snare, kick-snare, kick-kick, kick-kick-snare, kick-kick-snare, kick-snare, kick-snare, kick-snare... It comes easy because I'm singing it, and I am listening to the bass line and the guitar riff and I'm trying to drive them a little faster but still somehow be behind the beat to it feels sexy and its not easy to get behind the beat on a fast tune.
>
> So its really about singing the bass line and the guitar riff and the vocal part, singing it, while you play, and play to the song with that bass drum. Don't even think about what your foot's gotta do, don't even think about the double-stroke of the snare, its not even part of it anymore. You have to sing their song, so it was easy, I just played to the song and the bass drum starts to dance, I've got my heel up. I'm the kind of bass drum player where I wear my spring really loose, and bring my pedal up a little higher – that comes out of the box and I bring it up – and I cock the beater back a little, but my spring is really loose and it's the combination of interplay between the kick/snare/hat and I guess in a way its got a second-line New Orleans type of thing going on. If you just had that on snare and just kick drum, and just did that for a couple minutes, it would feel like you're walking down a New Orleans alley.

Driving a Mack Truck from behind the drum set as he triumphantly pounded his way through the freedom-themed anthems like *"No One's Leaving"* and *"Ain't No Right,"* where Entertainment Weekly was so blown away they described the impact "as if careening speed metal had mated with rhapsodic mysticism," Perkins' officiated a marriage of controlled explosions of chaos over top of solid rhythm foundations designed to support the glory of his band mates' soaring performances:

> Again, it really is about singing a song. If you listen to the bridge on "No One's Leaving" and the second part of the verses, I'm singing along with that bass line in my head, and there goes my kick drum and snare drum.

> How does a band that does *"Ain't No Right"* do *"Of Course"* and still get away with it, and not fake it, because we were generally into the Grateful Dead and the Allman Brothers just as much as we were into Zeppelin and Sabbath, it was all important.

Perkins singled out *"Obvious"* as an exception to the album's trend of more plotted songwriting exercises that grew organically into "the most unusual Jane's track because that was the one that was a jam-oriented song," Perkins reveals, adding that the direction for the song during its writing fit its title because "that song is one of the most jammed-out songs in our whole catalog, and you can really hear it in the playing, and its loose and responsive – its call and respond – it's a conversation between the guys, and I love the modern drum part and the way the modern sounds of the guitar, it sounds I guess unearthy in a way, in the atmosphere, away from earth. *"No One's Leaving,"* no way, that's not a jam-song at all, *"Then She Did…",* not even a chance of jamming on that. Even *"Ain't No Right"* wasn't a jam song because of the two parts. But *"Obvious"* was a full jam of us." Written against the classic Rock & Roll backdrop of the open road on their first national tour leaving Los Angeles, the drummer fondly recounted his memory of

> writing that one when we were on tour opening up for Love & Rockets in 1987, and writing every day during sound checks, grooving on that, and then Perry singing, and then the drum fill comes in, and that signifies the next part. If you think about the rhythm part, the snare march that is pre-bridge in a way because it only happens for 4 measures, that was very Love & Rockets and Bauhaus-inspired in a way, the way I approach it. Kevin Haskins, Love & Rockets/Bauhaus is one of the great drummers, I got married in his house and he's a part of my family, and I love the guy, and a lot of my drumming – when I think about Joy Division, Bauhaus, Suzie – these really great choices and really unique moments and then stick to them. So I thought of Kevin during that snare roll.

> So that song came out of a jam and a lot of conducting from Perry's vocal cues, or drum fills. It's a repetitive tune, and there's 4 or 5 parts that are in a way all replicating the other part, just played a little differently. So there is that playful jam that you hear to that song. That's kind of why we don't do it that often on stage, its not one that we've really ever rehearsed or put together, because its such a jam tune, its kind of unusual to play onstage because its a lot of uncertainty, "How long does this part go?"

Arriving at the moment on the album that would take Jane's Addiction mainstream, the instantly-infectious *"Been Caught Stealing"* gave rock radio programmers the excuse they'd been waiting for to throw the band into heavy rotation, resulting in run of 4 weeks at # 1 on the Billboard Modern Rock Tracks chart, and a huge hit MTV music video. Praised by Rolling Stone Magazine as "a real jewel" for being a "shuffling, upbeat bouncer," Perkins' hip hop rock festival of fun between the kick, hi-hat and snare would drive the song's fuzz bass hook and Dave Navarro's funk rhythm while Perry's celebration of thievery made the song catchy enough to make anyone think stealing was cool for 3 and a half minutes, a tribute he recalled, to

> this huge influence on me from this band called Trouble Funk, which was a Washington D.C. Go-Go music band. So if you listen to what they're doing and then listen to *"Stealing,"* or *"Pets"* from Porno for Pyros, there's a lot of that Go-Go beat, which is no hat, kick/snare/roto-tom or kick/snare/bongo the whole time. Then there's a guy on keyboards, and another guy with a mic going "Come on, put your hands in the air!" It was like 1981 Washington D.C. late-night funk music, so that was a influence on the drumming. So I was just 17, 18, thinking "Man, it would be great to write a song without a hi-hat!" Then you take the aggression of Eric and Dave and they're not playing what funk dudes play so it changes my pattern.

Kicking open the door for their fanbase to flood Alternative Rock into the mainstream, *Ritual De Lo Habitual* took Jane's Addiction's Led Zeppelin allegory to mythical proportions, in the process making *"Three Days"* the *"Stairway to Heaven"* of its generation. Once again seeking to channel his inner-Bonzo into the ground-breaking beatwork he would hammer out on the kit, Perkins proudly pointed out that while

> I can never play like Bonham but I love his approach and I love his beats and I love his ideas, and Tommy Lee – one of my favorites – does it the same way. For instance, "Home Sweet Home" is a ballad but he's fucking playing it hard as possible and it works, so what I did for "Three Days" is I kind of wanted to have this power beat through the verses, and then as the first chorus hits, off to the ride and basically supporting Perry.
>
> My approach in the drum part was to grow from a seed into a small plant in to a strong tree and then into an old Redwood (laughs) basically, and so you start with the hi-hat and the kick drum, and then in a triplet and then the kick-snare-hat Bonham-style "Physical Graffiti"-type drumming where its like powerful.

A musical orgy where each player instrumentally seduced the listener in deeper by the listen, Stephen remembered the important role crowd reaction played in developing the song's expansive musical landscape into full bloom by the time it was laid down on tape. Born out of one of the band's transcendent writing sessions where moments of truly original inspiration like *"Three Days"* landed in their laps, Perkins detailed an organic evolutionary process that followed where

> the band wrote most of our songs in a short period of time, and as the songs were played over and over on stage in different situations, like 3 in the morning in downtown L.A. of 4 in the afternoon in Las Vegas in the sun opening up for Love and Rockets or closing for Iggy Pop, whatever happened, the songs started to become something different, and *"Three Days"* was a wonderful experience to write. We had this club in L.A. called "Scream" and "Scream" happened on Friday or Saturday nights and moved to different clubs throughout L.A., and you couldn't find them unless you

> knew. But they had this one spot downtown for a week or two and they'd let us rehearse there all week and the show was on Friday night, so our rehearsals were from about 11 PM to 5 AM for a whole week and that's where we wrote *"Three Days,"* on the night shift.

Majesty swept throughout the musical landscape of *"Three Days,"* each player a warrior roaming the outer realms of his ability looking for new territory to conquer, and in Perkins' corner of the instrumental kingdom, as he served the storyline Perry Farrell was weaving throughout, the drummer felt his most important priority was to let the lyric guide his rhythmic reactions:

> So it was about the poem, and Perry sang, *"True hunting's over,"* I heard that and went straight to Africa, and I said "Goodbye cymbals, goodbye snare drum," and I just worked the toms 14, 16, and that was my goal for the next 2 ½ minutes, reacting to Perry, "All of us with wings," tom fill, and back off, and orchestrate with Perry. What's he singing about? "Okay, pull back, he's not talking about it yet... Oh shit, he's here, he's talking about it, let's get excited: floor toms, no volume..." Because I was trying to support Perry while of course listening to Dave and Eric, but my guide was Perry, and I wanted to ebb and flow with him.

Beyond Bonham, Perkins' pallet of available derivatives to pull from had by then become a second-to-none collection among his peers, rich with eclectic choices that were an extension of his own growth as a player with a boundless curiosity to discover, absorb and incorporate new styles of music into that repertoire. A challenge because he had to balance his anchor as a Rock & Roll drummer with the wind at his back as he sailed into more experimental territory in the now-legendary drum charge that led and dominated the second half of the song:

> The hard part was, by this time, I was past rock music. I was listening to Sabu Guide and Babatunde Olatunji, African drummers, and taking these African beats – *"Ain't No Right," "Mountain Song"* – beats that don't belong in a rock tune, they belong on a djembe, and making those into rock tunes.

That's kind of where the tribal drumming of *"Three Days"* fits into that category, where I think it not only supports the poem where he's talking about something that is, to me, can conjure up tom work. Then *"All of us with wings,"* I started to feel like it was starting to get time to get to the meat and back to the beat, and then of course, we knew after the long poem was Dave's guitar solo and then as me and Eric found our part and what we were going to do to support Dave, Dave – like Perry earlier – was my guide, and if Dave solos more on the higher notes, I work over to the ride and start going crash heavy. Then I might go to the hi-hat or bring down the volume, and then half-way through the solo, bringing it back down to the toms and letting Dave have a little story where Dave's reflecting musically on Perry's poem on the downpart of the solo, then the solo comes back up.

That's the excitement of it live too is it changes nightly, and he changes, and I change and back and forth, and on stage, there was always a drum solo with a Trap kit. But in the studio, we were having a fantastic night recording, and during that part I thought of gun shots and anvils and metal and linear, less swinging, straight playing, a lot of me banging on the one and really making it straight-ahead because we knew what was next and what was gonna be pounding on your chest before Perry's announcement. And then when Perry announces, *"Erotic Jesus,"* bam, that means the fucking gates broke, and okay man, and the drums there to me are almost in a way independent of the music.

I'm supporting Perry and the guitar part, but after that, I really feel like rocks are coming down the hill, and you're in a car looking up, going "We're about to get knocked down here!" That's my feeling, the rocks are falling, and there's a peaceful moment before the next announcement, which is to reflect on what has just happened and it really is about Perry's experience in bed with these two girls, etc. So you know how that is, you take a break and its back into it, and as the song gets more courage by the lyrics, the playing is more frenetic in a way and aggressive and emotionally charged, and then

> the final, beautiful guitar solo with the floor tom. To me, like I say, I like to use that word announcement or event, because the song is a story, but how do you put your foot down and say "Now, listen to this!" in the middle of the song. It Zeppelin can do it… (laughs) Then after the final guitar solo, you blow the kiss goodbye, the very final, gentle lay off.

As the song faded off into the same dreamy climax listeners had shared, they drifted off into the gentle and inviting opening chords of *"Then She Did."* A representation of Perkins favorite kind of creative moment to experience with his band mates where, vs. the understandable tinkering with genius they'd invested in the writing of songs like *"Ocean Size"* or *"Three Days,"* the band became a vessel for a song that he remembered arriving fully formed:

> *"Then She Did"* is one of the highlights for the whole band because of lyric and music joining as one, and it really feels like the song was never thought of, it was just born, it was there. Like we didn't really work on it, it just happened, and we really did work hard on that, but it sounds so beautiful, and playing that is so emotional that we really don't play it often.

"Of Course" hung in the most abstract wing of the album's gallery of artwork, with a bumping waltz beat coming courtesy of Perkins' tapping into his own authentic ethnic background to channel what in the studio became "a great experience exploring that Jewish melody in the intro – me and Perry are both Jewish – and having that violin solo go throughout it. With the waltz and the lyric, it seemed to really fit hand in hand and really make sense. Percussion and drum wise, it was one of the highlights of my life at the time, making that, in the studio for a few nights and listening back and of course, having the great band that is Jane's Addiction to be part of it. It wasn't just a drum piece, it was a great song with some really interesting drum parts." Aware of just how spellbinding a mood hung over the song throughout its inspired writing and recording, Perkins proudly agrees today looking back that

> that was just an incredible situation, because the song itself was written on a camper on the Love & Rockets tour, and all I had were brushes and a pillow, so I did started playing that pattern, and Perry wrote this great lyric and poem about his brother. So when we got to the studio, it seemed real simple and kind of boring – in a way – just as we had it. So I spent the next 2 or 3 days with Ronnie Champagne, the engineer, and our producer Dave Jerden, with all sorts of different talking drums, tympanis, chimes, bells, I think I had some marching cymbal, gongs, and finger bells and ice bells, and I wrote this beautiful drum piece, especially the intro, where I had a lot of room to say something.
>
> Then as the parts changed, bring those soft drums back in and big drum fills and I had single-headed 12, 14, 16, 18 rack toms right in front of me, and it was also using a Swish Knocker with like 15 rivets and putting that through a sound machine, that's my cymbal, and I just had a great time and have done it ever since then. I'm inspired by that, and on Jane's records and even solo records, doing drum pieces that are layered drum stories, because of what took place on "Of Course." We did it live a bunch on that tour.

Cover songs are always a tricky proposition of a band of Jane's Addiction's clairvoyant talent at interpreting existing styles through their own unique filter and coming out with something entirely original, so expectations were high among fans of what the band's re-invention of the Grateful Dead classic *"Ripple"* would sound like as the final track on the star-studded *"Dedicated: A Tribute to the Grateful Dead,"* which featured a superstar collection of musical salutes from Elvis Costello, the Indigo Girls, Suzanne Vega, Dr. John, Midnight Oil, Lyle Lovett, Warren Zevon, Dwight Yokam, Bruce Hornsby and Los Lobos before closing with Jane's.

Ironically, the track would serve as one the band's last time making music together in the studio for almost 10 years – or ever again with bassist Eric Avery – and a fitting farewell as they were able to put aside personal differences and unite around the mutual love flowing throughout the band for The Dead: "Me and Navarro and Perry and Eric were all very deep serious Dead Heads, we loved the Dead, we loved the music, we loved the vibe, we did shows with Bill Graham, he helped us promote Lollapalooza's first year in San Francisco and Sacramento, and the song itself is such a beautiful, sad tune." Serving not just as an acknowledgement to The Dead, for Perkins personally, the song served as his chance to pay homage to the spirit of his brother, also a longtime fan of Jerry and Co. who Stephen actually credits for helping the band begin shaping what became their eventual rendition of the classic:

> My brother passed away right after the first Porno record. He sang on *"Pets"* and a few other tunes, but my brother made me and Perry and the other fellas a tape because he was the biggest Dead head of all of us, and it was of 40 different *"Ripple"* live, studio, demo, fast, slow, acoustic, electric. Then at the end of the tour in England, we ended up going to the Kinks' studio in London and there we were surrounded by the vibe of the Kinks, and it was our last session with Eric. He never recorded with Jane's Addiction again after that, and we were inspired to do a mash-up so to speak, like the Dead would do on stage where they're playing one tune and then a melody of another would fly in, and that tune would show up and then later that night, the other tune would show back up, and they would book-end it over the weekend. It would start Friday night with a tune and end it Sunday night with the last verse, I'm not kidding, the Dead were like "If you're here for all weekend, we just book-ended two songs. We never finished the first song from Friday, but we're going to finish it right here." They were book-ending songs between 4 day shows, so we tried to do that kind of experience and drop ideas and songs and rhythms from other songs throughout, and a lot of the Deadheads really dug that and it didn't get in the way of the song.
>
> It was just weird, cosmic musical exploration if you're on board, and the Dead were doing that and we were simply very aware of that, and my brother was too. So we took 3 or 4 Dead tunes and Perry took almost like an Elvis

Presley approach, a 50s angle to the vocal, it really kind of brought back the Memphis sense of humor in a way, the shuffle to the lyrics to kind of loosen it up. I brought the drums, which were inspired by another tune we broke into at the very end, *"The Other One,"* and then the guitar player starts doing *"Bird Song"* in it with a little guitar riff, so we got really a mash-up of the original arrangement and melody, Perry bringing this Memphis shuffle to the vocal part, the tom-tom rhythmic drum part inspired by what the Dead always did, which was second-line Memphis/New Orleans-inspired feel. Its like an African/Creole vibe that was happening in New Orleans, and you really hear that New Orleans sound creep into a lot of the Dead rhythm, so I kind of regurgitated that whole New Orleans-tom tribal thing, and so the imprint of all the Dead moments that we loved. To recreate that swing which they already had in the guitar part was really what I wanted to do in the tom fills, and the whole time I recorded, I was thinking "Mickey and Billy, they're gonna hear this... Be direct, be interesting, make your choices and then play it," that's the way I thought of that.

Its really a sparse performance if you think about it: it's a drum part and some guitar lines, it wasn't overdone in any sense, but it was played well with a lot of feel and we all were in this magical place, even though the band wasn't in such a great place. Me and Perry were already talking about Porno, and I think Dave and Eric might have been talking about Deconstruction even and what they were going to do next. So there was a sense of a broken band in a recording studio where it didn't affect the sound because we were so feeling responsible to do a great job because there was no doubt in our minds the Grateful Dead were going to hear this. So about 6 months later, before my brother passed away, Jerry Garcia did an interview with Rolling Stone, and they asked him what he thought about "Dedicated," and he said the highlight for sure was Jane's Addiction, and my brother flew over the fucking rainbow. Then later in the end, they said "What about the music of the 90s, like Living Colour?" and he said "I'm not sure about Living Colour,

> but I really like Jane's Addiction," so Jerry mentioned us twice! My brother passed away not long after that interview came out. Then since then, I've played with Bobby Weir, hung out with Billy and Mickey, played with them, Bob Wasserman, I played his wedding with Bob Weir in the band, this whole Grateful Dead thing has really been taken into my life, and its just magical and I wish my brother was here to experience it with me. So "Ripple" was really a salute to the greatest experimental band I think of all time.

Using his drum set as a springboard to jump right into making some Infectious Grooves following Jane's Addiction's split in 1991, the jamboree Stephen joined was a sound new for its time, a cutting edge he was an expert at riding within the wave Jane's had been the past few years, and with how sick he got behind the kit on *The Plague That Makes Your Booty Move,* the results made an addict out of mainstream critics like MTV, who noted that the chemistry between bassist Robert Trujillo, "Mike Muir of Suicidal Tendencies and ex-Jane's Addiction drummer Stephen Perkins) is a provocative synthesis of funk and metal." A musical relationship that began as an extension of his personal ones he developed with the members of Suicidal Tendencies

> opening for Jane's in 1990, they did about 10 shows with us, and so I started becoming friends with Robert Trujillo and Mike Muir and the rest of the guys, and Robert and Mike said to me, "Look, we're making this hard, funk record," and said "Yeah sure, for one thing, I'll play percussion no problem because you've got a drummer, so I don't want to show up and start playing drums," so I started recording with the Infectious guys and did percussion on the whole record. Then they had maybe 2 or 3 tracks that needed drums so I did the title track and *"Pump It Up"* and *"Bring it Back to the People"* on a trap kit, those 3. So that record was done in like 2 weeks of just hanging out with the guys, and musically I really loved it and the combination I thought was really ahead of the game there of putting that hard rock metal guitar tone next to a funk guitar player, and then taking that West Coast funk bass playing and putting that into it. We took a lot of time to craft

those tunes so people were surprised when they listened, but it wasn't like "Why did they do that there?" No, it made sense.

So I was really into it, I loved the record, I loved the attitude and thought Robert was just a tremendous bass player, and when Jane's did our last show in Hawaii, Robert and Mike flew out to the show and I was backstage, and they were like "Fuck, you broke up, I can't believe it! By the way, we're going on tour with Ozzy opening for a month, wanna come?" And I was like "I'm in man!", so 10 minutes after Jane's broke up I was in Infectious Grooves, and the next week we were practicing and getting ready for the *"No More Tears"* tour with Ozzy. It was just the greatest tour. I was torn up about Jane's, but I was back on tour with Infectious and having a great time, so it was a great way to heal. It really did heal me from the Jane's experience.

People were more about the whole experience of Infectious Grooves, that was really cool to me, and it is surprising to see where its at today that we can go out and play gigs if we want because people have wanted to hear it and see it. I think when something is just ahead of the game – like Jane's or Infectious was – bands that hear something that not everybody else is hearing yet, years later, its like "Wow, listening back, that shit was amazing!"

Me and Perry already knew we were going to do Porno, but he wanted to finish *"Gift"* with Casey, and wanted to take a year off, and so the timing was perfect for me to do Infectious Grooves, which took me to another level as a power drummer and as a guy that was able to – in a way – take my rock roots and bring those more to the surface. Because the record was only 40 minutes but we played for an hour and 20, so we started doing covers, like "Immigrant Song" and had a good time with that, and it just became a great physical experience. Mentally, I loved being out of the Jane's pain, and it was great to make friends with Robert, who I'm still close to, and Infectious played with Metallica and the Chili Peppers about 8 months ago

> in Detroit and did a show in L.A. in 2014. We've actually been doing them lately with Jim Martin from Faith No More on guitar.

Coming off the carnival of fun he'd had out on the road with Infectious Grooves, Perkins was one of the most in-demand free agent drummers in Rock, with Modern Drummer painting of this high profile in the early 1990s that at "just 25, Stephen Perkins already has his own sound. His snare carries a signature crack. He's pure bombast at one turn, passive the next, but always in touch with the emotional side of music." Deciding to return to the mothership creatively that he and Perry had been piloting together for much of the past decade, this time they combined their cosmic energy to set Porno for Pyros alight.

With Porno for Pyros, Stephen's drumming would take even more of a center stage role in supporting and elevating the power of Perry Farrell's lyrical landscapes, acting as "the anchor of the band," Variety would observe, "laying down a continuous barrage of African-inspired beats and rhythms that propelled many of the tunes." In pointing to what derivative influences he was drawing from in basing his rhythmic sensibilities around the latter direction, Perkins' points to gems from the band's self-titled debut like

> *"Pets," "Blood Rag," "Orgasm,"* there's a lot of that good old funky tribal drumming, but based upon Trouble Funk, just great funky, weird percussive music. I think they had kick and snare and hat, a guy on bongos, a guy on roto-toms, a guy on djembe, cowbell, a guy on bass and a guy on keyboards – that was the whole band, and it was just so percussive.

Going platinum on the strength of the continued Perkins-Farrell team, the success of Porno for Pyros confirmed the drummer had a loyal fanbase of his own, one who was now beginning to follow him in and out of his associations with Jane's Addiction with the same hunger to hear what new direction his playing would guide them in. On the band's follow-up album, *Good God's Urge,* that tour took Perkins and his bands on an organic tour around the world where he let his natural exotic backdrops influence his rhythmic choices and beatscapes throughout the album. Writing the album with geographical muse in mind, Stephen points to the record's lead single, *"Tahitian Moon"* as one such example of art imitating life where

> while the first Porno record was written in Los Angeles, but the second Porno record was written around the world: we went to Tahiti, we went to Bali, we went to Mexico, we went to Figi, we went to Hawaii, spent some time renting a house in Malibu, and all those experiences went into the songs. That's the real gem of the second Porno record is real life experiences that you wouldn't think would happen period: like Perry getting lost at sea at Sunset on a surf board, and we couldn't find him! And when he washed up, he had sea urchins all over his feet and legs, he was a wreck, and we wrote the song that night.
>
> Those stories became lyrics and poems which became campfire songs on those trips, with a bongo and a little hay shaker and Pete Destefano with his acoustic guitar and me and Perry. So *"Bali Eyes"* and *"100 Ways,"* a lot of the tunes on that record, started out around a camp fire type of atmosphere, literally away from our instruments – so to speak – and then we brought it back to the studio and kind of figured out what would work best for each tune. That was opposite of the Janes' records and the first Porno record, which was a live band on stage rehearsal back and forth and then going into the studio to play. This was a more creative way of looking at writing music and producing it, and it turned into a really great vacation. I wouldn't recommend it for a hard-working band that doesn't have the time to do that, but the songs are really post cards from those days. So *"Bali Eyes"* was written in Bali and *"Tahitian Moon"* in Tahiti and *"Dogs Rule the Night"* in Mexico and on and on, and each trip gave birth to a song, and an experience that went right into a lyric, and that led the way for the second record.

As an artist, Stephen's pallet by that point had begun fusing existing rhythmic styles in such original ways that they produced new musical colors entirely, adding new mixtures of natural percussive playing and splashes of electronic overdubbing to "confidently blend weird improvisation with gorgeous melody, giving the album both depth and beauty," Mojo would later applaud. Reflective of a period Perkins had entered as a player where he was drawn to the possibilities of innovation such creative combinations invited:

> I had started by then to get into hybrid drumming, which was half electric/half acoustic, and I had electric pedals doing kicks and snares and possibly shakers with my left or right foot on a backwards D.W. pedal – one of those upside-down ones – and then I also started wearing pads on the kit. So the drums had started becoming a little hybrid for some of the tunes, *"Thick of It All," "Wishing Well,"* and on stage, it was mostly kick and snare and cymbals and then hitting pads. I went full-force when I joined Tommy Lee's band Methods of Mayhem, full-force hybrid, but this was the beginning of that, and it changed my approach to drum sets.
>
> The title track, *"Good God's Urge,"* I actually played on the kitchen table with my hand and an egg shaker! That's how we recorded that song, just because it was born that way and every time we tried to do it electric, it seemed like we were trying to hard, and didn't catch the real spirit we had at the campfire, so to speak. So we went back to that, set up at the kitchen table at the house in Malibu where we lived for about a year, and this was an amazing house. The Band had Scorsese in that house with them when they filmed *"The Last Waltz"* and a lot of the footage of them playing Billiards and pool in there house and then Clapton did a record there, and The Who, Elvis, so we stayed there to record the record.

Finding a chemistry with bassist Mike Watt that he hadn't had since Eric Avery left the pocket, the drummer was so excited by the eclectic groove the pair kept together that he rode it out of the success of Porno for Pyros' second album and straight into a spin-off side project, Banyan. With their debut album, the duo brought an improvisational sensibility and stylistic focus on Jazz and Funk to the forefront where instruments like Trumpet, Clarinet, and Saxophone were as much the star as guitars, and the core of the musical melting pot was held down by Perkins and Watt:

> Mike Watt – who was such a great fit – joined forces with us and that's when we started Banyan because the drumming of Porno and new songwriting technique was keeping me away from the drum set. Not that I was bummed out in any way, because it was a new experience and a new way to write music with a bongo and shaker and go back and explore the drum kit to relive the song. So I started Banyan with Watts so we could really play without a singer, and didn't have to worry about stepping on a song, or ruining the seam or subject matter by overplaying or underplaying, there really are no rules when there's no singer. I really love the fact that I've got a poet in the band, and Perry's fucking amazing, so I want to support those poems, and I couldn't find somebody to write something as beautiful as him so why even try. And so Banyan was this musical exploration so we could overplay, underplay, left and right, because we're not really supporting a poem. So in a way, the change of Porno forced me into more of an instrumental exploration as a drummer, and I really appreciated with where I started to go by dipping into Bill Buford and even early Genesis. Anywhere that I could find the drum kind of in your face in the mix, not really considering pocket at all times and more of the lead instrument as a guitar player or maybe a piano player, and for that reason, Porno was a wonderful machine of songs, but they were becoming more produced and less played.

Pushing Perkins's as a player into open territory no doubt being traveled for the first time within the expansions that was their circle was exploring, guided Billboard would later highlight by "an anything-goes aesthetic that touches on elements of jazz, funk, rock, world music, and even hip-hop, the second album from this Stephen Perkins side project somehow flows even more cohesively than its impressive debut…(showing) its diversity without sacrificing cohesion…A multifaceted album that isn't afraid to take chances." Precisely what was driving Perkins' as a drummer by that point based on the new frontier where the music the band made together had shown him he could travel:

> Everything I did in playing with Mike Watts and Nels Cline and Money Mark over and over changed my playing. Playing with Rob Trujillo and the guys in Infectious before the Porno records changed my playing from Jane's, and here was a great moment for me to have a transition for me without even being in my own garage and working on stuff. I was out on tour with Infectious and had to become this new player that was almost more aggressive and more percussive. I heard that music going in that direction, and that's what I wanted to do for that music: its hard, its interesting, its scattered, its unpredictable, and what Infectious Grooves did for me and to me and with me is what I brought into Porno, and then of course, everything Banyan was going through – all those shows with 2 sets, 3 hours a night – I played so many shows with no singer, and I was setting up the drums in the front, and set up all four of us in a row. So I became more of a story teller, because I had to find a story in my 8-minute jams onstage, because I didn't want to be a jam band, I wanted to be a band that made music with a lot of playing going on with a lot of personality. My favorite players are personality players, and its not the guys with the chops, it's the guys that leave an imprint and you can hear a lifestyle. I love drumming to stick out, not as anything to step on a tune, but to increase the value of a song with a great moment of drumming, or whatever instrument it might be.

Taking his newly discovered love of hybrid playing into a new sound entirely when Perkins joined up with the brilliant Frankenstein that was Tommy Lee's *Methods of Mayhem*, where Industrial, Hip Hop and Metal all teamed up in the same hybrid to create a sound that kept Perkins on his toes at all times. Putting his coordination as a drummer to the maximum test, Variety in their review of the band's live debut show would spotlight the drummer as "a mesmerizing presence behind his big kit," a compliment he is not shy about admitting he earned the hard way: "It was me and him, and he wanted to reproduce the sound of his record onstage so I had 5 or 6 electric bass drum pedals in front of me, and then 5 or 6 packs of cymbals up high, and then real cymbals and a real snare that had a trigger on it. So basically I had a click in my ear and I would use the first kick to the far right for the verses, and then move to the second kick closer to me for the choruses, and then for the third pedal for a different bass drum sound. He wanted all different bass drum sounds, and then I'd be moving my left hand from the real snare to a pad above me that's the other snare, and then I had to move my right hand to the floor tom which was another electric pad, and it was fucking crazy like that for every song." Teaming two equally-revered and respected Titans of Thunder behind the kit not for a drum-off but a drum along that had heads banging hypnotically all over the summer shed circuit in 2000, Perkins picks this out as a personal highlight from him as a fan of Lee's, a drummer who once again challenged Stephen to play at a peak only reserved for the elite:

> We worked out three songs where he got on his kit and his kit was somewhat like mine, a little more acoustic, but he still had electric sounds, and we played to a click at high tempo and had 3 drum solos together. It was high energy techno rock drumming, and a lot of the songs were backbeat heavy but with electric overdubs, so I had to recreate a 24-inch crash ride where I would just ride that and try to be Tommy Lee, and meanwhile, with my left hand, I'm trying to hit all these digital-sounding ones. I just loved it, and the rehearsals were epic because it was me and Tommy from like noon to two, and then the band would show up at 5 or 6 and then me and Mixmaster Mike and Tommy would keep going with them to midnight. So touring with Tommy was just an epic experience, forget it, playing those songs nightly, the focus and the fucking party, its all there!
>
> As soon as we started talking about getting back together as Jane's, of course, everything you do goes into the experience of what you're going to do next, and playing with Tommy changed by drumming because he's meat-and-potatoes and I'm more of a pitter-patter kind of effect. He didn't

> want any kind of playful ghost note with the kick or snare, and so I had to and to and loved to and was honored to try and do it and nail it.

That return to the mothership in 2002 to record to team back up with Perry Farrell, Dave Navarro and new bassist Chris Chaney would introduce Jane's Addiction to a new generation of fans, and re-establish the relevance of their brand of 3-D psychedelic funk metal courtesy in part of the futuristic edge Perkins brought to his beatscapes for the band's 2003 reunion album, *Strays*, where every member of the band was in outer space anyway to be working with Pink Floyd producer Bob Ezrin. The perfect co-captain to take the band exploring out into their next musical frontier, Ezrin was an sonic architect at some of Rock & Roll's bravest, boldest and successful missions in such expeditions.

From *"The Wall"* to what critics would eventually hail within the hypersonic sound he made via his collaboration with Jane's as one that "offers compact, arena-ready songs that are simultaneously nimble and sturdy, with madcap displays of metallic crunch, funk-pop, industrial sizzle and spacey atmospherics," as USA Today would later note, with Rolling Stone adding that throughout, "Stephen Perkins' drums…(are) constantly demanding more." Bringing the best out the band musically as he always had, the drummer remembered synching up with Ezrin right away when the band had first worked with him when

> Bob did one Porno for Pyros song before the Jane's record for a movie called "Dark Blue," and we had a great time, and rented an old Ludwig and wrote a cool beat together and did percussion together, and so I just loved him. So when we did the Jane's record, I brought in like 5 drum sets and timpani, and he was like "What are you doing?!!", and I was like "Hey, you want a 26 inch bass drum, and I've got an 18 inch too, and I figured let's bring it all down and use it!"
>
> I was excited, and he's a responsible producer - and you've heard great stories of Bob and what he's done for bands like Pink Floyd and Alice Cooper – and

> what he did for us was understand how to work with everybody. So he's like, "Okay, Perkins likes to show up at 2 in the afternoon, and Perry likes to show up after dark, and Navarro likes his Chicken and Broccoli at 4…" Then musically, he sparked ideas for us and affected change in our playing.

Perkins' beat bounced all over the walls of guitars throughout the band's Grammy-nominated single *"Just Because"* with the kind of dazzling drum play throughout the kit that reminded fans why his unique blend of power, technique and imaginative parts was still as electric a part of the Jane's Addiction experience as ever. Catchy from the opening riff and drum build up that felt like riding the opening incline of a roller coaster before diving into the rush of Rock of the hardest sort that the drummer revealed was

> the very last track, it was the end of the year, and we didn't have it. We had stuff that didn't make it to the record, and didn't yet have that one that felt like us onstage, and Bob had said "Why don't we do one that sounds like you guys are on stage while you're playing!" So we started doing gigs, we opened up for the Chili Peppers in Korea and Japan, and then did Fugi Fest, and played a couple of the new ones, and then got home and Bob's like "Now go to a rehearsal place and start writing."
>
> So we moved into Clown Studios in Santa Monica and this was the first time in the whole time of Strays where we were actually in a rehearsal place writing, not in a studio with headphones and glass. Now, we're playing like a band, and we wrote *"Just Because,"* and it felt like a band again – we played and toured – and brought that element to it and that's how the song was born, and it became the first single.

It really is, in a sense, very orchestrated, but dangerous-sounding, and the riff on the bass was impossible to play, and the guitar riff and the intro was to me like an announcement, and the drums are locomotive and rolling, and there's the beautiful, big single-headed toms – I had 13, 14, 16, 18 – single-headed, I took the bottom heads off.

Stephen's gift as a speed demon racing away behind the kit at the kind of lightning-fast speeds that broke sound barriers was alive and well on another of the climax of *"Hypersonic,"* an explosive performance that Entertainment Weekly would single out as a "dizzyingly tight piece of metalcraft," and one that the drummer confessed was so challenging is

> almost impossible to play live if I think about it, but if I just fucking sing the song, I start playing without even realizing it. But if I do try hear the beat, it might not sound like it should. I'm the kind of guy to whom its important to make your personal best every day, but also not to live in judgment. You're a body, you're not a machine or a tool, you're a person, so I've come to realize that when I don't hit the way I should or the way I wanted to, even though you might not know – no one else might know – it doesn't mean it's a failure, it's a chance to get better, and go "Okay, that's something I need to work on." I'm not afraid to buy into that work, and that's also part of me: it doesn't just all come natural and I can't just sing any tempo. I work at it, but I find the best way to make it feel good is to sing it and play with the song, and try to work the tempo into that song. And as I get older and better, I realize "Wow, that was really hard 10 years ago to come up with this, or hear that and replicate it." So I don't hold myself in judgment, its just my body, and its something I've recognized.

Boasting bionic performances throughout the space rock masterpiece, longtime fans were over the moon alongside Millennial teenagers who were flipping out over the super-hip *"Superhero."* Another smash from the record that gave Jane's 8 seasons of raised profile among that generation as they grew up through High School and College loyally watching HBO's monster hit *"Entourage,"* it was a phenomenon the drummer remembered the band was grateful to become a defining part of the soundtrack for:

> With *"Superhero,"* we wrote the song in the studio with Bob and never once do you think a song will go somewhere, except that you want to make a

> great song and make it sound weird and modern, and approach it and hit it, and as far as the parts, they were played funky and they're kind of straight forward, and the mix is really elastic and very colorful. The color and shininess of the show and the sound of that song, it just went hand in hand. Its strange today in the business that you don't get a song on the radio, but then again, it can be played 5000 times in a month because its on a TV show. So we really did enjoy the casual moment of turning on the T.V. and hearing our song, which nailed it and just happened to fit. We thought it was a really fun show and cool and it really did work visually, and playing it live is surprising because a lot of people know that fucking song, and you forget how T.V. really can just reach in to so many households and have a bunch of different people listening to your song all at the same time. How often does that happen?

Still pushing the acoustics of aging and modern arenas to their electric limits after touring throughout much of the past 15 years, Jane's Addiction's sound remains as vibrant and timeless as ever. Showing as much grey as died green hair throughout audiences that now transcend generations as teenagers to fans who look as old as the vintage concert T-shirts they proudly wear as badges of loyalty to a band they've been an extended members of for the better part of 30 years. Attacking the drums with energy equal to his 18-year old beginnings as the band – and Rock & Roll's – most groundbreaking and sound-shaping beatkeepers, Perkins' practices a ritual of readying himself for battle behind the kit by maintaining a Zen headspace when he walks onstage facing thousands of screaming fans each night:

> To me, on stage, you have to be relaxed when the song starts, laid back, don't even project the next 8, 10 minutes of what's gonna be, because you're not the tree yet, you're still the seed. You have to grow every time, and just because I let subtly grow into a tree on a recording, I don't have the patience to do that every time I'm on stage. So I have to really relax at the beginning, laid back Bonham, glorious chorus, now the tribal poem and tell the

poem with Perry every time, so its emotionally exhausting if you want to do it right. Not physically, but emotionally, because *"Ain't No Right"* is like 4 minutes of charging and that's not exhausting if I'm connected with the music. If I'm not connected, its just physically laborious and then it is tiring, whereas, if you're connected with the lyrics, you have this special type of drain on you that's emotional, and then with *"Then She Did"* and *"Ted"* and even *"Summertime,"* its my job to emotionally support it and be the pillow for Perry until he needs me to be the gun.

It takes a lot of work to get it right, and that's what I love about Jane's Addiction, is we don't do that many shows, and it comes out pure when we do because we can support those lyrics and those journeys, because it's a real journey from here to there. And if we really are connected, its emotionally charged, and I think that's what you hear as far as the patterns and my influence from African to Bonham, its all there, but it's the emotional connection is what makes it so exciting. We've been doing *"Nothing's Shocking"* complete, sooner or later, its time to do *"Ritual"* complete. Still, I don't want to be known as 1991 and *Ritual*, I don't want to be holding onto that, I want to be holding onto what I can do tonight on the drum set. As a painter, you wouldn't want to look at your paintings from 1986 and then 2016 and see the same strokes and colors, you want to get better and change.

Prescribing the same ambition for any young drummer looking to get in the game based on a desire to follow in the Olympian-like footsteps of one of Rock & Roll's great live entertainers behind the kit, where Perkins has always mirrored the excitement of his studio performances and then some, a thrilling skill that the Hollywood Reporter recently took note of during "Stephen Perkins' mighty drum solo" at a recent sold-out concert. These days, Stephen's favorite fan to entertain is his own 6-year old son, who he often uses as a barometer for whether he's keeping his energy at the same peak level he's always set the bar at:

> I have a 6 year old so I can't tour as much, and how many more summers does Jane's Addiction get as a band? So we should be out every summer, and my son has seen me play many times with Jane's and different shows, and he shakes his head and moves his arms like a fucking octopus! And I'm like, "Yeah, absolutely right! That's the way daddy plays," I don't play like other people: I go nuts and I try to somehow in all that chaos focus on kind of a repetitive melody drum part, and so my impression on him was this octopus thing. That makes me want to play better, to know he just saw that and that's what he thinks of me.

Dressed up at this point in his 30 year career with all the appropriately due accolades and honors Rock & Roll has to offer, from a Star on the Hollywood Walk of Fame to Variety's acknowledgement that his beats have made such a permanently indelible impact that, through present day, Perkins' band's "reputation as godparents of the alternative nation has remained rock solid… Its biggest hits, like *'Been Caught Stealing,' 'Jane Says'* and *'Stop!'* still receive regular play on modern rock radio alongside rockers who were toddlers during the band's heyday." Billboard in their own recognition of the drummer's Bonham-esque relevance to Jane's continued glory has asserted that "Stephen Perkins' tribal and powerful drumming style served as a main ingredient for the wide-ranging sound of alt-rock greats Jane's Addiction," while even media as mainstream as the Wall Street Journal in modern times has celebrated Perkins' longevity as he continually "proves to be one of rock's great drummers!"

While he welcomes the acknowledgements of all he's accomplished up to this point, he's a bigger fan of those who point to the fact – as the LA Weekly recently did in their assessment of the 20 Greatest Drummers of All Time that Perkins' # 5 ranking was due because he's "not only held down this signature sound for the L.A. band's two-decade-plus career, he's elevated it and evolved with it." Closing with a projection rather than reflection about where he'd like to see himself in continue to head as a beam of inspiration and influence shaping drummers for all the right reasons:

I'll be 49 in two months, and I still care, I really care, about my reputation as a drummer. Its not an ego, I just want to be part of the world that makes an impression on people where they air-drum and need and love that moment. I love to be part of that. If you can make an impression like that, and the drums are that powerful that you can conjure up some great, magical, positive feelings. That's what keeps me going too, that I have a little bit of control to make things better in some way.

For me – and some drummers don't look for this – but for me, it's the chase of that personal style. I want to be Stewart Copeland, I want to be Keith Moon, I want to be a style drummer, and that's my quest. So I love that I can find my inner sound and let it out and I have somewhere to do it, so my advice is follow that inner voyage you have, and it is hard to be different. Its scary and people don't appreciate different all the time, but when we play a song or jam or write a song, hopefully you get better every day and learn what not to do and what not to repeat and what works best. They just come out of me, and its amazing, like "Wow," and if it happened to me, it can happen to them.

I like to be in the moment and I think if you're a great musician or artist, you can live in the moment, you want to be connected. So that's my advice: stay connected and follow your heart, because the business is ever-changing. I want to reflect my mirror as a drummer, look what happened to me today, last year, good, bad or ugly, and put that into the performance and the moment and that's what keeps me happy and hungry. Its not the payday or the competition, it's the inspiration.

"I like to see myself as a drummer who can play anything and everything." – Steve Smith, 2015

(photo by Andrew Lepley)

Chapter 8: Steve Smith of Journey – Vital Information

Often a band's namesake is a metaphor for their music, and Journey is no exception. One simply has to turn on *"Don't Stop Believin'"* to hear each instrument with its own voice telling its own story. Listening to the drums sing within the song's percussion is a feat that belongs to Steve Smith, one of Rock & Roll's great kings of swing. A true Jazzman at heart, Smith traces his roots back to the same source that inspired so many of finest Rock drummers of the past half-century:

> My interest in drumming started before I actually picked up the sticks for the first time, and I think it came from my mother, who had some Gene Krupa recordings in our home, and my folks had seen Gene live and I remember them talking about that, and when I would go to the 4th of July parades in the little town of Whitman, Massachusetts where I grew up – which is about 25 miles South of Boston – when the marching bands would go by, I remember that had a very big impact on me. Especially the sound of the

> bass drums and the snare drums just really spoke to me, and I was probably 5 years old when I first felt that kind of excitement with the marching bands.
>
> Then when I got to the 4th grade, I was 9 years old, and there was an assembly at my school where somebody was demonstrating instruments, and each one of us could choose an instrument if we wanted to. That's the point where I chose the drums and knew I wanted to learn how to start learning how to play the drums. My first teacher was the 4th Grade music director, but my parents and I – and I think especially my parents – knew that he wasn't a great drum instructor because he wasn't really a drummer. So my parents were smart enough to get my a private instructor, and as luck would have it, I wound up studying under a guy Billy Flanagan in 1963. He was already in his 60s by then, and so his heyday would have been the 30s and the 40s during the Big Band era, and that's the style that he taught – it was what I would call a very traditional U.S. style of drumming instruction. So for the first two years that I played, I only played on the practice pad, not a drum set, and I learned how to read music and I learned good hand technique, and really just how to play from a technical point of view – with all the rudiments and sight reading, etc.

Earning his way to a full kit through old fashioned dedication and hours of practice, Steve remembered an incremental process whereby "after two years, he told my parents that I had earned the right to have a snare drum (laughs), so then I got a snare drum and basically played that only for one year, and then eventually in the 6th grade, I finally got my first full drum set for Christmas!" Growing up a self-described "Big Band freak," as Smith progressed in his studies throughout high school under Flanagan's direction, he immersed himself deeper and deeper into the genre's stylistic fundamentals at a prodigious level:

> I got into Jazz time playing and syncopation, and I learned how to play the ride cymbal, so my studies really – in a way – prepared me to be a Big Band drummer, which was great training. Being a Big Band drummer, you can

> really play anything after that, so I'm grateful for the fact that I had such a good instructor in those years – Billy he had that much to offer as a teacher. When I was playing through my High School years, I was playing in concert band, playing in the marching band, and played in a local college Big Band and then was playing with some garage bands too, but nothing on a very pro level. I did join the musician's union pretty early on and was able to do Professional gigs – I worked for the circus band and a concert band that would play in the Gazebos in the parks around the area.
>
> So I got professional experience early on and the beauty of having a good education and being able to read music was at 16, 17, I could play with musicians of all ages and that really sped up my development because they could give me valid feedback of what I was doing right or wrong in my playing. Especially in those years, that was not uncommon to grow up with that experience, but when time went on, it became more and more unusual to find a good local teacher because that generation of drum instructors that I studied with started to die out and they were replaced by young people that hadn't had that kind of rigorous training and were just teaching people to play beats, and that isn't going to really help you become a great musician.

While learning the live side of is trade, Smith studied by watching live drummers, making the regional rounds "during those formative years, where I would go to see Buddy Rich when I could, and even in those early years before I had my driver's license, my parents would take me to see Buddy and Elvin Jones and the Stan Kenton Big Band and Woody Herman Big Band, and Count Basie's band with Sonny Payne. So I was fortunate that I got to see all of those groups, and then of course, being a teenager in 1967 when Jimi Hendrix came out with Mitch Mitchell on the drums, that's when I could start to hear Rock & Roll music. I really couldn't relate to it before that because in those years, I couldn't relate to Ringo and Charlie Watts and the Dave Clark 5, because the drumming just seemed so simple. Of course now, I love that music, but with Mitch Mitchell and then Ginger Baker, I could relate to Rock drumming and

Rock music finally." That connection would prove crucial in his future fusion role as Journey's drummer, and as he began discovering the genre as a player, Steve absorbed a whole new generation of influences:

> Once I started listening to Rock, my influences in those years – along with Jimi's drummers – were John Bonham and Carl Palmer and Ian Pace from Deep Purple, and then from the U.S. side, it would have been Dino Danelli, Carmine Appice, Don Brewer from Grand Funk Railroad, and Michael Shrieve from Santana, I loved Santana.

By the time he enrolled at Berkeley School of Music in Boston, the renaissance of the early 70s Jazz influence – ranging from veteran legends like Miles Davis and John Coltrane to the modern pioneer players of the day like Weather Report and Chic Korea – loomed large over the musical and social culture of the student body. Shaking up Smith's sensibilities and style as a player as well as that of his drum set, he remembered that

> when I started Berkeley in 1972, my drum set up was a clone set-up of Buddy Rich's kit, but when I got to college, that style of playing wasn't really en vogue. So I went through a pretty substantial conceptual shift going to Berkeley. What was hip in those years was the way Tony Williams was playing with Miles Davis and the way Elvin Jones was playing with John Coltrane and the Weather Report. So I really radically changed my drum set and went in the direction of getting an 18-inch bass drum and put my cymbals up pretty high with a severe angle on the cymbal stand, and that shift in direction came in some teachers in some ways but mainly from the student body, my peers. That's the kind of music we were trying to learn how to play was not even big band, but small group Jazz from the 60s, and if you look at the timeline, it was pretty relevant because Miles Davis with Tony Williams was only a few years before I went to college, so that influence was still very strong.

At Berkeley, I had some amazingly great instructors: I studied with a teacher named Gary Chaffee that was into expanding our rhythmic pallets by learning how to play with odd groupings and in odd time signatures, and he had a big influence on me and my peers at the time. I studied with him over a period of two years, and studied with Allan Dawson, who was a great, great Jazz drummer who helped me learn how to play song form and develop more coordination and better hand techniques – he was a fantastic influence as well. But at the same time that we were studying and developing this Jazz concept from the 60s, there was a profound influence of what was going on in Jazz fusion of the early 70s, because in a way, I really became quite out of touch with what was going on in the Rock world during those years. My focus was on the Jazz of that time, which we now call fusion, but the Jazz of that time started to become very influential to me and the student body. So between 1972 and 1976, if you know the history, throughout that time, from 1971 to 1973 are the years of the Mahavishnu Orchestra with Billy Cobham – who was rated as like the premier drummer of the world during those years. Then from 1973 is when Chick Korea did "Return to Forever" with Lenny White, who became a big influence of mine, and Tony Williams had developed various incarnations of the Tony Williams Lifetime and I finally got to see him with The New Tony Williams' Lifetime with Allan Bosworth on guitar, and Tony had developed a radically new way of playing the drums that was profoundly different the he'd played with Miles Davis in the 60s, and that became a huge influence.

Then the rise of Steve Gadd as a studio musician and his recordings with the various Chick Corea albums he did became influential, as well as Harvey Mason, the West Coast kingpin of the studio scene. His recordings with George Benson and the Breka Brothers and Brothers Johnson, and Herbie Hancock's "Chameleon" album, and then there was also a European influence from Manfred Eicher's label, that had Jack Bassinette playing on some great records and a drummer from Norway named Yan Christensen. The

> influence was very big at the Berkeley College of Music back in those years because Gary Burston was one of the main teachers, and he was recording for ECM and Pat Metheney was his guitarist. Then Pat made a great record with Jaco Pastorious and drummer Bob Moses – who was kind of a local legend in Boston – that became Pat's debut album, "Bright Size Life." So all of that became profoundly influential, and slowly the fusion concept seeped into my playing and I'd say the rest of the student body.

Steve's first "big break" as a professional player would come four years later in 1976 when he landed a gig keeping the beat for jazz violinist Jean-Luc Ponty, a now-iconic virtuoso who throughout his career has played with everyone from Frank Zappa to Elton John on the rock side to jazz-rock fusion giants the Mahavishnu Orchestra. Popular enough as a player to sign a solo record deal in 1975 with Atlantic Records, as Ponty went about assembling an A-list band to back him up, he took a chance on a 23-yeare-old unknown drummer, reflecting Smith's already-accelerating maturity as a player, a once-in-a-lifetime opportunity he jumped at when

> In 1976, I had the opportunity to audition for Jean-Luc, who had just left the Mahavishnu Orchestra, and I was able to get that gig and that's when I left Berkeley to start touring and recording with him. Previous to that, I'd toured a lot around the East Coast and Midwest with some Big Bands who were made mainly Buddy Rich and Maynard Ferguson alumni, and we toured everywhere so I had a lot of touring experience by the time I started playing with Jean-Luc. I was 22, but I had played quite a few gigs before that, but never internationally, that's what changed with him.
>
> When I started playing with Jean-Luc, I still had a relatively-small drum set, and played fusion but with a smaller, jazz-type kit, and after the first tour – which was 2 months long, October into November and December – of 1976, he asked me if I'd get what in his words was "a Billy Cobham drum set," and of course, what he meant by that was a big, double-bass drum set

that would have a certain look and a certain sound on the stage. So in January, 1977, I bought a set that had two 24 x 14 inch bass drums, 10-12 and 13-inch rack big-rack toms, and 16x16x18-inch floor toms, so big drums. I had never played double-bass drum before and had never played big drums before, but to have a big drum set like that fit the music of Jean-Luc Ponty perfectly. So that was a big change, and I went from playing mainly clubs and small concert halls to playing theatres – our first tour had been a club tour but than after that, he quickly moved up to playing approximately 1000-2500 seat theatres and he was selling out and very popular in those years.

So I liked playing drums with that kind of energy and volume, and I was playing much louder than I'd ever played before to keep up with him and the volume of that group, and Daryl Stuermer – who went on to be Phil Collins' and Genesis's guitar player – and Allan Holdsworth played with us for a little while, and the second guitarist was Jamie Grazer, and Alan Zabad on keyboards, and we started with Tom Connolly on bass, and then Ralph Armstrong from the Mahavishnu Orchestra. So all of 1977, I toured with Jean-Luc, and the fact that we had a big stage and then a light show and a big P.A., that did influence me quite a bit and I loved playing drums like that with the powerhouse approach and the big sound, and we got to tour all over Europe and the world.

The equivalent of getting a Master's Degree as he learned the ropes of recording and touring at the level that Ponty operated at, one whose requirements of Smith as a player demanded a practice regimen in between gigs to keep his chops at their constant and consistent best. Detailing the discipline he developed as he racked up invaluable studio recording experience on *Enigmatic Ocean,* which Billboard later hailed as "one of Jean-Luc Ponty's finest accomplishments," adding that "quite impressive is the insightful and passionate drumming of Steve Smith." Giving Steve his first number one as a recording artist when the album went to the top of Billboard Jazz Albums Chart, his credibility was growing among peers, a pressure that the drummer managed by way of good, old-fashioned habit I cultivated of practicing every day, even from a very early age, 9 and 10 old, and I practiced every day because I enjoyed practicing, and still do – I practice every day. Really the best way to get results is to practice every day, that's in fact even more important I believe than how many hours you put in, because even if you do 1 or 2 hours, the fact that you're doing it every day means you're constantly developing, whereas if you take a bunch of days off, and then you put in 4 hours, you're not going to get the same kind of results. So I just continued with that approach of practicing a little bit every day, and on the road that was difficult and it took me a while to figure out how to practice on the road. I finally eventually figured out how to practice with no drum set, basically just a practice pad but still playing as if there was a drum set in the room, and playing my feet on the floor and developing a technique that didn't even require a pedal, for instance. So I can play the rhythms and play what I want to play pretty much without the drum set because I am the instrument anyway, the drums' are just the loud speaker that's going to amplify what it is that I'm thinking and hearing and feeling.

So touring on the road really helped me develop that concept, because I could practice in my hotel rooms and without a kit, and my focus of what I practiced also I think really helped my development, because I would – and still do – practice the music I was playing. So it was not just an esoteric kind of technical practice, it has to do very specifically with Jean-Luc, I worked on his music and always would be developing parts of a particular tune I might be having trouble with, or how to transition from this part of a tune to the other. So my practice was well focused and I figured that out very early on, to practice that way, so that way while on the gig I can sound a little bit better at what I'm doing every night.

By 1978, Smith's run with Jean-Luc Ponty came to a close after "basically, I got fired from that band along with Jamie Grazer and Daryl Shermer, and it was a good lesson because the 3 of us had become very close friends and we were feeling like we weren't getting treated well in that situation, and so I think there was we were complaining a lot about the situation, and Jean-Luc didn't want or need to deal with that, so he fired the three of us. Now, as a band leader today, I totally relate to him and he was completely right and we were all wrong because we were just young kids and had a great gig and were getting paid pretty well at the time – I think we were up to $400 a week, which was the going rate. I think we were pretty out of line, but we were so young and we didn't realize that, so I learned a good lesson: that that has no place on the gig. If you accept the gig, just enjoy the music and play and if you're unhappy with the situation, leave." Though he'd learned that lesson the hard way, the opportunity freed Smith up to make a fresh start in Los Angeles, and with his next gig, establish the credibility on the Rock & Roll side of the aisle as a player that would eventually qualify him for consideration to replace Aynsley Dunbar in Journey. Leading up to that shot at the brass ring, Steve found his foot in the door when he hooked up with Ronnie Montrose, a result of the networking skill Smith recommends all aspiring drummers develop as an essential tool for navigating the record industry as a journeyman player first making your bones:

> After we got fired and then I was back in Boston just trying to figure out what to do with myself, and I had a good buddy – David Locheski, who was a sax player, and we had been playing together in the Boston area since High School – and we were in College Big Band together, and he said "Hey Steve, why don't we move to L.A. and get in the music business." I had met quite a few people from L.A. since Jean-Luc's business was based in L.A., and I tracked down his road manager – who I'd become friends with – and the apartment he was renting had an empty room and I asked if we David and I could live in that room, and then there were two other people in the other two bedrooms – it was a 3-bedroom apartment. So that's what got me to California, and the rent was like $90 a month back then (laughs), and we went out then look for auditions, that was really the next step, and one of those was the Ronnie Montrose solo band.

> My room mate, Jean-Luc's road manager, was also working for Freddy Hubbard, who was one of the great Jazz trumpet players ever, and I auditioned for him within a week of arriving in L.A., in January of 1978, and I got the gig, and that gig was still with the 16-inch bass drum, and exactly everything that I was playing when I was back at Berkeley School of Music: the small jazz group with the acoustic bass and acoustic piano, and I could do that, but also, I had heard about this Ronnie Montrose audition up in San Francisco, and somehow I got myself an audition, and got that gig too. That was a real crossroads, trying to decide: "Do I go back to playing the acoustic Jazz or do I keep going with this more fusion rock direction?"

An important cross-roads for Smith that would ultimately set him directionally on path to his signature jazz-rock fusion style, Steve decided to head in the new direction of Rock & Roll, a fateful decision that helped the drummer develop and sharpen his rock sensibilities "because Ronnie Montrose's album, *Open Fire,* was what I would call Rock Fusion, especially the way he wanted to play the music live, which was much more aggressive and he told me he wanted me to do what Simon Phillips was doing with Jeff Beck and to really express myself and it was really exciting for me and I wound up taking the Ronnie gig. Here I am, this 23 year old kid, to be playing with this rock guitarist who had great time and great tone, so the groove always felt real good playing with Ronnie."

In what would prove to be an ironic twist of fate, Steve would come face to face with his future bandmates "on Journey's very first headlining tour!! We went on the road with Ronnie Montrose as the second headliner, and Van Halen as the opening act. We were playing the same venues I'd played with Jean-Luc that everyone does on their first headliner, like 2500-seaters, and I watched Van Halen every night, and that would be my warm-up. Because I'd get my practice pad out, sit on the side of the stage, and jam along with Van Halen and get my hands in shape, and would be playing my feet on the floor getting warmed up, and sometimes Journey's original drummer Ansley Dunbar and I would do that together and would get ready to hit the stage. Then I'd go out and play with Ronnie Montrose, then after that, I'd sit back and watch Journey play." An eye and ear-opening experience in every way, beginning with the band's brilliant blend of Jazz fusion with a brand of Progressive Rock & Roll their very own that dazzled Smith from first listen:

> Journey was a revelation to me, because I'd never heard of them but of course I knew of Greg Schon and Gregg Rolie from Santana and Ansley Dunbar from Frank Zappa, and on that tour, they were playing the music from the *Infinity* album, which had just come out, and it was Steve Perry's first tour as their new lead singer, and he was amazing. The music that filled out the show was from their first few albums, Look Into the Future and Next, and it was all this great progressive, fusion rock music, so I was pretty blown away by them and very impressed by the musicianship and the writing. It was a fun tour with all 3 bands together, and me and the guys from Journey all became pretty good buddies hanging out and having a good time. I got to be pretty good friends with the Van Halen brothers Alex and Eddie, and Michael Anthony – we all seemed to hang out quite a bit.
>
> I really enjoyed watching Journey's show every night and I would stick around and watch the entire set because it was always exciting and entertaining to me, and I loved Aynsley's drumming. Again it goes back to the Mitch Mitchell thing, he really played from that same concept and was like a Jazz-Rock type of drummer, and in fact, Aynsley had even tried out for Jimi's band, and so I really enjoyed listening to him and the whole group.

Taking an important detour following the conclusion of the tour with Journey and Van Halen, Steve once again decided to start a new chapter in his playing profile, taking a momentary break from Rock & Roll to head back home to his first love of Jazz drumming. Returning to his native Boston to reunite with some friends he'd grown up learning to play with to form the roots of what would later become one of the most celebrated Jazz Fusion groups of the 1980s, Vital Information, Smith felt the move was the right one because

> once the Ronnie Montrose tour was over, all options were open and I was open for anything. I wasn't thinking, "I wanna just go in the rock direction," and in fact, I was still playing a lot of Jazz all throughout that time, and came back to Boston once a year with my roommate Dave Wocheski, who was playing with Freddy Hubbard. I had a third character in this trio named Tim Landers, who was a bass player and he and I really grew up playing together, I'd also met him in the College Orchestra program at our high school. He lived in Boston, and we played together a lot and that was one of the reasons I developed good time, because I had a bass player partner to work out with. Tim had moved to New York and was playing with Billy Cobham and Al Di Meola. We would all meet up once a year in Boston and play gigs under the band name "Not Bad for White Boys," (laughs). We would always bring in great guests too, so I had Dean Brown, Daryl Stuermer and Barry Finnerty, Mike Stern – all friends of ours from Berkeley or that we'd met touring. So that continued through the Montrose and Journey years until 1983 when I was able to get a record deal with Columbia Records and that group became Vital Information.

Steve would return to the Rock & Roll ring in answer to a call he'd received in the late summer of 1978 that he accepted to join Journey, staying loyal to a trend followed of taking the kind of smart career directions that later inspired Drum Magazine to conclude that "the choices Smith has made in his career beginning with his fateful break as the drummer for everyone's favorite '80s rock powerhouse, have been, for drummers off all stripes and styles, a professional model worthy of serious consideration." Vs. any sort of pressured audition process given the band was already familiar with his playing from the previous tour bill they'd shared with Ronnie Montrose and Van Halen, Smith recalled an easy-going invitation extended courtesy as well of the fact that

> we'd all got along personally on that tour, so I think the guys in Journey knew personality-wise things would work out, and it wasn't until August of 1978 that I got a call from Herbie Herbert asking me if I'd be interested

in joining the band. I was still playing some gigs with Ronnie but that was winding down, and my birthday's in August, so I remember I was actually home visiting my folks when I got the call. I was just about to turn 24 when I got that call from Herbie, and I was very excited about that because I thought musically the band was great, and so I told him right away I was very interested in doing it, and he told me to keep it quiet and that he'd get back to me and eventually did make me the offer, "We want you to come out to San Francisco and join the band."

There was no audition or anything, it was just "Come out and start rehearsing," so I did. I ended up going back to L.A. right away, packing everything up, leaving that apartment and moving into Neil Schon's house at first until I got my own apartment in Mill Valley, just outside the Bay Area and started rehearsing with the group. It all happened fast and was very exciting, and it wasn't financially-motivated on my part, it was musical, because I went from $400 a week with Ronnie Montrose to $350 a week with Journey and a million-dollar debt to Columbia Records for their 5 years of unrecouped albums and tour support. So before anyone made any money in that group, I became a band member and signed on to pay back that million-dollar debt, and being young and naïve, I didn't even think about it.

With this next evolution in his playing would come an elevation as well courtesy of the innovations joining Journey would bring to Steve's approach to drumming, drawing from both his Jazz and Rock tool kits as he slid into the saddle world-class drummer Aynsley Dunbar had just vacated. Filling those shoes proved a natural fit for Smith based on both his own Jazz background as well as in part on the beat blueprints Dunbar had left him to follow in his earliest days learning the band's back catalog and how the drums conversed individually with each player instrumentally:

For the tunes from *Infinity* and those early years I was playing with the Journey, we were still playing the instrumentals and earlier fusion-based

> material from the first 3 albums, I played essentially exactly what Aynsley Dunbar had played. Those drum parts were perfect for the music, and the difference really was the groove, and I think the fact that I'm a U.S. drummer in general, I had this kind of rock/R&Bish type of feel to my playing, simply from growing up in the U.S. and having Jazz not only be my basic influence, but the R&B music and groove rock music. And that's what the guys in the group heard in my playing, that it had a particular kind of groove to it that was a free and funky kind of rock groove that has more of a deep pocket to it, and that fit Steve Perry's voice and his time feel.
>
> So our time feels really connected, because Steve Perry, coming from Gospel – which is his main influence and very obvious a thing to most people – Steve's probably 90% Sam Cooke and 10% Jackie Wilson. So he was not a rock singer as much as he was a Gospel and R&B singer, and I mean in the same way Sam Cooke started out a Gospel singer and then became an R&B singer, just like Ray Charles started like that as well. So Steve's got a groove that is amazing, and he needed a drummer that could match that groove, and that he could connect with rhythmically, and I could do that. Neal Schon still wanted a drummer who could stretch out and play Jazz rock with, like Aynsley could do, and I could do that because I had the Jazz and Jazz fusion background, so I understand why they asked me to be in the band.

Teaming up with super-producer of the day Roy Thomas Baker to shape what would fortunately for both Steve and the band be their commercial break-out album, the three-million-selling Evolution, which broke the Billboard Top 20 for the first time on the Album Charts, the drummer recalled an air of excitement as he uprooted from L.A., moving to Journey's home base in the Bay Area in September, 1978:

> My first rehearsals were simply to learn the back catalog that they already had, and we played a few gigs, then went into the studio, and if you've never

> heard this recording I suggest you check it out, because we did a King Biscuit Flower Hour which you can find on Joel Selvin's website. So you can hear me playing some of the early *Infinity* material and there's guests too, so Tommy Johnston is on it, the Tower of Power horns, and its like a Bay Area jam session. That was my first time in the studio with the band, in November, 1978, and then we started writing material for *Evolution.*

Detailing the stylistic adaptations he made within his playing approach upon joining the group, Smith in deconstructing this transformation, began by conforming that "when I first started playing with the group, I had to make a major shift in my drumming concept, because I had played mainly Jazz and Jazz fusion, and even when I was with Ronnie Montrose, I was playing in a fusion style. What that means is that I wasn't playing drum parts exactly, I was playing time feels, meaning that the drumming parts were more or less improvised from night to night, and there'd be a lot of variation to the beat and not a steady, repetitive drum part. That's what I was used to doing, but when I started playing with Journey, I realized that didn't work for that group and that I needed to play compositional drum parts, and I think during this first couple of months, that's what I figured out how to do. So again, it was a big shift in concept, like "The verse has this particular groove and pattern, and there's a fill that goes with the chorus that adds another pattern," and I really honed in on that." Along with learning to think like a story-teller within the parts he picked to accompany the rest of the band's songwriting, Smith loosened up a bit as well within his feel as a player, explaining that this adjustment was necessary because

> the other thing was the time feel of the group was very open and relaxed, especially in those early years, and Ross Vallory had a lot to do with that. The bass players they'd been playing with had this sort of Jazz fusion edge, where they were up on the front of the beat, really pushing the beat, and one of the keys I think to the big, open Journey sound is that Ross plays the bass in a way that is very open and in the middle of the beat, even toward

> the back of the beat. So I had to adjust my time-scale so it was very open, middle of the beat with not a lot of forward motion that I was used to using, and just sit on the tempo and allow the notes to have their full value. That was a concept that Steve Perry talked about, "Allow the note to ring," so if it was a half-note for example, "Allow that note to ring the full two beats before the next note comes in, and just allow things to sit comfortably." So that took some conceptual and technical adjustments.

With the group "now committed to completing their transformation from jazz fusion/prog rock mavens into arena rock superstars with their fifth album," Billboard felt the group was aided in this transition because "thankfully, former Ronnie Montrose skin-beater Steve Smith soon brought his college-trained jazz fusion background to the table." A group effort from front to back, Steve remembered the band's writing process as an open sharing of ideas where

> when we wrote, we wrote as a group, so there were no demos. Nobody brought in a song that was finished, so all the songs started as some kind of a groove or guitar riff or bass line or melody or chord progression, and then we went from there. The publishing split really reflected the fact that we were all working together to write the music, and some people were able to get copyrights for the actual songwriting credit because the songwriting laws said you could copyright melodies and lyrics but not drum parts and chord progressions, so most of the time, I didn't get songwriting credit, but the publishing made up for that because we were all throwing the ideas around.
>
> So for the most part, Journey songs came out of jamming and working on riffs and chord progressions, and usually, the last thing that would happen would be the lyrics, but during the group jam/writing sessions, Steve would be there singing melodies and (phonetics), and sometimes he would pick up a bass and play a bass line or sometimes he would even sit down behind the drums and play a particular groove. So he had a lot of ideas and was proficient enough at drums and bass to get his ideas across, but Neal Schon

> came up with the majority of the riffs that we used, and Craig Rollie had a lot of ideas with keyboard lines as well.

Producing in the process what iTunes would later hail as an "incredibly articulated" collection of songs that launched their tradition of rock power ballads, an arena where the band would rule rock radio throughout the early 1980s, kicking of with their first Billboard Hot Singles Chart Top 20 hit, *"Lovin', Touchin', Squeezin',"* Steve remembered that serenading leading singer Steve Perry's soaring vocal performance was another adjustment for Smith given that the simplicity within

> playing very slow ballads, I wasn't used to that either. I was used to a lot of mid-tempo and up-tempo tunes, and we played a lot of ballads, so I had to work on getting my body clock to comfortably slow down and play those ballads, and in those years, we never used a click track for anything. That wasn't unusual, I don't think any bands did back then – it just wasn't part of the concept to use a click, so we developed what I called "a good band time and groove," and that was an interesting transition for me. My approach was try and keep the feel open and relaxed, and then just find the parts that made the music work.

Each new Journey record was cleverly framed by a thematic title symbolic of what new revelations the group would decode within their next studio odyssey, and with 1980's *Departure*, the arrival of a new era of mainstream rock domination would begin. This movement would become courtesy in part because of the successful transition the group had made within its rhythm section, Rolling Stone Magazine noted, to "Steve Smith's steady…drumming," arguing that his style of playing "has proved to be an addition by subtraction: goodbye to Aynsley Dunbar's virtuoso technique. In the past, the group's good moments came when Neal Schon and Dunbar took off on extended jams, but now Journey works best as a band. And they've never rocked harder."

Proud of the fact the group had gelled to firmly into a musical unit as songwriters and performers in such a short time, the results included the band's next Top 40 hit and still one of the most rotated songs on Classic Rock radio today, *"Any Way You Want It,"* a song Smith remembered standing out during its recording because " its got in a way some weird little accents, and I picked up on all these off beat accents. I was just playing what felt right." By 1981, the band was on the edge of a new frontier of popularity, and would effectively re-imagine Rock radio in their image with Escape, the 12-million-seller that marked the band's first # 1 album on the Billboard Hot 200 Album Chart and blasted the band off into another galaxy orbiting atop the charts as Rock & Roll's biggest overnight stars with their first generation of mega-hits: the always-iconic *"Don't Stop Believin',"* *"Whose Crying Now,"* and *"Open Arms,"* which ascended to # 9, # 4 and # 2 respectively on the Billboard Hot 100 Singles Chart.

Beginning with arguably the most celebrated anthem, *"Don't Stop Believin',"* a pop culture touchstone whose musical spirit is as driven by its passionate drum marathon pumping toward victory as it is by Steve Perry's soaring vocal or Jonathan Cain's glorious lead piano chord progression, the song has kept a crowd cheering their favorite sports teams on through a thousand late innings, third periods and fourth quarters, and proved the perfect soundtrack to Tony Soprano's send-off on the final scene of the last episode of The Sopranos, as well as being the closing number to the wildly successful *"Rock of Ages"* Broadway Show in recent years, and moving a million ringtones with the Millennium generation of newest Journey fans, the drummer revealed of its creation that

> that drum beat presented me with a particular challenge because I couldn't play the melodies that I was hearing while playing the drum set right handed. So on that particular song, I wanted to keep the hi-hat going through all the drum melodies, so I had to learn how to play it open-handed – like Billy Cobb. So while my right hand is playing all the cymbals and the toms, my left hand just keeps steady time on the hi-hat.

> That beat was inspired by more by Terry Bozzio, and of course I had my own ideas, but Terry was in a band at the time called Group 87, and he was playing what he was calling "industrial beats." It would be a little bit of new wavish/punkish groove but he'd have all these moving melodic parts in the drums, and so I had been experimenting with that idea inspired by him. And then out of that, when we were developing *"Don't Stop Believing,"* I started trying some of those ideas as a counter-point to what was going on melodically and rhythmically with the chords and guitar riffs, and basically I went home after some of our rehearsals, and worked out all of those parts at home. Then I brought them back the next day and played them for the band at rehearsal, and generally, that was my process: I worked out most of my more complex drum parts at home, because in the rehearsal studio we were writing and there wasn't a lot of time to work out specific drum parts.
>
> So whenever I'd come in the next day and play it, I'd either get no reaction – which is fine – or I'd get a smile, which was fine, or if the reaction was "What the hell are you doing?", then I knew the part didn't work so I'd scrap it. But as long as there was no reaction or the smile of like "Yeah, that's cool," then I would keep it. With *"Don't Stop Believing,"* I don't think anyone really noticed what I was doing until we got to the studio and then Kevil Elson – and Mike Stone – they really featured that drum beat in the mix, and I think it because a pretty big signature part of the song.

Steve would show off his rock chops on a song so popular it might as well have been a hit single even though the band never officially released it as one, especially given how much Classic Rock radio and live demand the song receives among Journey fans from every generation, with *"Stone in Love,"* where the drummer detailed playing off Neal Schon's instantly-infectious guitar lead: "I think I was responding to the guitar riff more than the vocal on that one, and in fact, most of the drum groove is a response to the riff. So I was thinking more of orchestrating what Neal was playing." The cinematic dimensions of another of the album's smash singles, *"Whose Crying Now"* were fleshed out rhythmically, Smith recalled, in "a basic kind of Mick Fleetwood type of beat, but maybe with a little syncopation in there to go with the bass parts, but some of the accents didn't follow to the downbeat."

"Open Arms" is precisely how FM Radio received what has since become the most-played rock ballad of all time across all radio formats, a dreamy love song that closed a million Prom dances and inspired the band's hometown paper, The San Francisco Chronicle, to vote the song "first ballot inductee into the Make-Out Music Hall of Fame." Expressed perfectly in every one of its musical performances, including an ambient drum sound where Steve debuted a new approach he was bringing for the first time to rock balladry based on when the drummer explained was

> the approach that I took in the studio, which was what I would call a stripped-down type of approach, where I would leave a lot of space between the notes in order to allow the reverb to ring out on the toms. And it was a concept that I was developing while in that situation, it was specifically tailored for the music of Journey, and inspired by the music and by what seemed to be the best type of playing approach for the music.

Designing his in-studio drumming deliberately for arenas to ensure that fans got in the band's live performances precisely the same sonic feeling they did within the album recordings of their songs, the drummer remembered that in the course of creating space within the song's astral musical galaxy,

> there was a pretty organic learning curve that I went through myself, and then was encouraged by members of the band and by our producer Kevin Elson to play like that, and in fact, as we went from theatres to small indoor arenas and outdoor ampetheatres, it made more and more sense to play like that because then there was a clarity to the playing that would translate to 20,000 or 50,000 or 90,000 people. So I think it was a combination of the studio and what worked live that I developed that concept of leaving a lot of space, and conceptually, drummers that influenced me in that way were

> Nigel Olsson, for instance, who played with Elton John, or the drummer who played *"Little Help From My Friends"* with Joe Cocker at Woodstock, Bruce Rowland, on something like *"Open Arms,"* which has that same kind of feel if you think about it.

Voted by Kerrang!'s readers as the "Greatest AOR Album of All Time," Journey were the uncontested kings of Album-Oriented Rock radio by 1982, with radio in effect orienting itself to their albums by the near-constant rotation of a growing Greatest Hits collection that with the arrival of Frontiers in 1983 would add to that domination with a new wave of hit singles that featured such fan favorites as the Top 10 hit *"Separate Ways (Worlds Apart),"* another of the band's instantly-timeless ballads *"Faithfully," "Send Her My Love"* and the 1985 Top 10 hit *"Only the Young,"* the latter of which Smith banged out on a monster-sized kit he designed to withstand the power he brought to bear in hammering out hit after hit in the studio, and on stage night after night on tour after sold-out arena tour during the late 1970s and early 1980s:

> I used the same drum set for *Captured, Escape* and *Frontiers*, and it was a Sonar drum kit with two 24x14-inch bass drums, 10, 12 and 13-inch rack toms and a 16-and-18-inch floor toms with all Remo clear Ambassador heads on the toms. I liked the open sound, they had a very big, very open resonant sound. The kit had an Oak finish, and I used couple different snare drums, including a Sonar snare drum and a Slingerland snare drum and this wooden Radio King snare drum, and I used all white Ambassador heads on the snare drum, probably with some tape on the head because we had the snare pretty in tune, and I didn't play ring shots, I just played in the middle of the drum and there was a little bit of tape on the head. My ride cymbal was a 24-inch Zildjian and then I had 18, 19-inch crashes, all A 24-inch Zildjians. It wasn't until 83 that I started using K Zildjians live.

Turning specifically to highlight performances from an album where Rolling Stone Magazine noted in their review at the time that the band "takes care to maintain an equally-high level of musicianship" as previous outings, Smith begins with the charging tom-tom progression he galloped out of the gate with on the album's keyboard riff-driven opener, *"Separate Ways (Worlds Apart)"* as an example of that musicianship in practice literally as the band wrote it during a soundcheck on the road. A product of a routine from which many of the band's biggest hits had been produced out of the band's reactions to one another's ideas during jam sessions on tour,

> I remember we came up with most of that song at Soundcheck the Saratoga Performing Arts Center, which they call SPAC, its in New York. The orchestration of it is something that developed over time, but it started with a bass drum and then toms, and then goes into the beat and all of the various elements of the song, we spent time in rehearsals on all of those details and to develop the arrangement. Then of course, my drum fills were trial and error until I came up with some that really felt compositional and like they really worked for that tune.

Setting the pace with his opening rim count off for another of the band's most prized hits among fans from the album, *"Send Her My Love,"* Steve's delicate playing throughout his performance around the kit was stylistically an approach he remembered drawing on his Jazz roots to help create, proudly confirming that "that was inspired by Tony Williams playing on a Miles Davis album called *In a Silent Way,* and that's one of the first times that you'll hear that beat where the cross-stick is playing all 4 beats in the measure, is on that album. And I'd played that beat lots of times in different Jazz gigs, because it's a very popular Jazz-fusion groove, and so it fit quite literally to the tune."

Rated # 1 All-Around Drummer for 5 consecutive years in a row by Modern Drummer Magazine during this era, Steve made another monumental career decision in 1985 to depart Journey and focus full-time on his solo Jazz fusion band, *Vital Information.* Signing a solo deal in 1984 with Columbia Records, the band began a prolific run of releases for a band that the Jazz Times in recent years concluded "has for decades been an enjoyably high-octane amalgam of fusion jazz laced with funk-rock grooves." As the band's creative director, Smith has thrived on fulfilling a goal he first set for himself back at the end of his 80s Journey tenure:

> I like to see myself as a drummer who can play anything and everything, from Ray Price to Zucchero to Bryan Adams and Mariah Carey and then back to the Indian music I'm playing now, but to be taken seriously by the Jazz clubs and Jazz promoters that do the Jazz Festivals, it took a while to make that transition. But that was my intention after I left Journey, to really develop that side of my playing as an artist, and I really haven't looked back since then. The term I came up with for myself is I'm a U.S. Ethnic Drummer who can play any style of music.
>
> It made sense to form the group because I still wanted to play Jazz, everything has always been an option for me, any kind of music, and I still make Vital Information records 33 years later. I enjoyed playing the music of Journey and playing with the guys in the band, but ultimately its not as satisfying as when I'm playing with Jazz musicians and musicians I can relate to as Jazz musicians. There's just, let's say, a camradarie and a brotherhood that happens, and I relate to that better, so the band for me would be a reality check. To be in the rock world of playing and living in the Journey bubble, in a way, that was my experience of being in the group. It was a bit like being in a bubble because you were surrounded by the hysteria of that popularity when we'd go on tour, and in some ways, it was very isolating to be in a group like that, and its hard to have normal relationships. People that want to talk to you in a day-to-day way that is not highly influenced by the fact that I'm a member of this band that was very popular at the moment, so there was a certain touching down to reality that happened when I got back together with my old friends playing music that we found exciting and challenging and interesting. So being able to be together again felt comfortable and

grounding to me, and so the music was a big part of it, but I'd also say that grounding was another element to it.

I never wanted to lose my Jazz drum chops, and its easy to lose them when you don't exercise them. I actually know a number of players who have, and it will catch up to you if you don't exercise those chops – you start to think slower and you start to play slower. You have to think real fast when you play Jazz, that's a big part of it: you have to be in the moment and have to be able to respond instantly, and if you don't, you'll lose that improvisational ability. I do think Jazz is one of the most challenging kinds of music to play. I'm now involved with playing with Indian musicians, and I think it's a similar – if not even more demanding – concept of playing, and I like that. I like engaging my mind and thinking about what it is that I'm playing and responding to what other guys are playing, and you have to be able to think fast and have the chops to be able to respond to what's going on around you. And when you play parts over and over again, that can deaden your mental capacity after a while.

There's something else that happens, is that you become very precise and you want to play the parts better and better every day – that's the challenge – but in Jazz, that would actually be anti-Jazz, because you *don't* want to play the same parts every night. You want to play it differently, you want to be creative and push yourself and re-imagine the music from night to night, and dig into a wellspring of creativity. So that's what drove me to play with those guys, and over the years, I've heard from a number of musicians that they didn't listen to Jazz until I put out the Vital Information Records, so that's interesting.

On the other hand, when I did try to leave Journey and then go have my career go in the direction of the Jazz world, it took me many years to convince people I wasn't succinctly a rock drummer. It was a very difficult transition, and at this point, people know me more as a Jazz drummer than

> a rock drummer, and in fact, Charlie Watts came to see me play a couple years ago, and he knew me as a Jazz drummer. So one night I was talking to him back stage, and told him that Journey had opened for the Rolling Stones for 3 shows – including one at RFK Stadium and got booed off stage by the Stones fans. I remember he was so shocked, "You're the drummer for Journey? I had no idea!" I took it that was a successful transition that people now know me more as a Jazz drummer than a rock drummer.

In 1996, Smith treated fans to a reunion of the band's classic line-up when he rejoined his Journey bandmates in the studio to record *Trial By Fire,* which produced the comeback Top 20 hit *"When You Love a Woman."* The kind of ballad that reminded fans the group hadn't lost its musical mojo, it was a discovery that the drummer remembered the band made for themselves "right before we did that album, we got together and played one day just to see what it would be like, and there just that instant chemistry happened again. There really is something to be said for a band's chemistry, because you can replace guys with better players, but its not going to sound the same. It was very natural in itself and was really an interesting situation, because we all just got back together and it fell together and sounded like Journey instantly. So it was great, it was really fun. It was a really healing process to go through that, and musically, it was pretty satisfying."

Treating a new generation of Journey fans to the same thrill in 2015 when Blabbermouth announced that the band was "welcoming virtuoso drummer Steve Smith back into Journey, marking the first time he will perform with the band since 1998. Schon and Smith have always remained close friends and musical collaborators. Smith has lent his incredible talent to several of Schon's solo albums, including critically acclaimed *'The Calling,'* and, most recently, *'Vortex.'* Schon was thrilled when Smith accepted his invitation to rejoin Journey." Citing his relationship with Schon as a one of the primary reasons he made the decision, Smith added that he took a full-circle view of sorts of the opportunity after patient lobbying by his former bandmate:

The motivating factor behind my decision to tour with Journey for a 2-year cycle, really it goes back to the relationship I have with Neal Schon. We've stayed together over the years and done a lot of work together on his solo albums, and that's always been a fun and very creative process. During those times where we've been in the studio and working together, he's always asked me if I'd ever felt like coming out and touring with the group, which for many years I had no interest in doing at all because I was so busy developing my career as a bandleader and as a sideman playing with a lot of really great musicians. So I was not interested in going on tour with Journey, its just something that wasn't on my radar even.

Then I was invited to be a groomsman at Neal's wedding, and I hadn't really spent any time with Neal, John and Rodge together for quite a few years, so I didn't really know what it would feel like to interact and be together, but when we did, we had a really great time and it was fun and relaxed and I could see we'd all moved into different places in our lives and I knew I could feel comfortable working with them again. So that was a step towards this decision to tour with them.

Then, because of the recent changes, that changed the situation because before, when Neal would ask if I would come on tour with the band, it also meant I would be as a full-time member, and that doesn't appeal to me at all because I very much like being an independent artist and bandleader. So they said "How about a two-year cycle?", because that's how the band usually tours, one year of heavy touring and one year of light touring, that's their system, and I said "Okay, as long as there's no issue with me also doing my other projects."

That included one where I was on a recent cover of Drum Head Magazine with Zakaria Hussain – the preeminent tama player in the world, an amazing virtuoso. He's 63 years old now, a little bit older than me, and he's so popular, we just did a 4-week tour, and I was the first non-Indian to ever tour with the band. We played Madison Square Garden, Boston Symphony Hall, Chicago Symphony Hall, and sold out, so that's unprecedented, and it was mainly drumming, all drumming.

But I'm very proud of the Journey catalog and the music we created, and I feel like it holds up over time, and still sounds relevant, and with that shared history, I also thought "Well, its an opportune time to do it, plus I'm 61 years old now and not getting any younger," because just physically, the demands of playing that music seem like something I can handle right now, but in a couple years, I don't know if I could handle it. Then, because we have a lot of fans from a number of different generations, that started to play into my decision too.

So I'm looking forward to fans that we played for in the 80s coming to hear the group, and of course, experiencing what its like with the new generation of fans, because that's a phenomena that's happening with Journey that's really exciting. Then, for me, that my kids have never seen me play with the group, that's kind of a payoff too, because they've grown up knowing about my history with Journey and in a lot of ways, having the benefits of the lifestyle that that helped me have as a musician, so they've grown up with that in their lives but yet have never seen me do it. In fact, they've all gone to Journey concerts and seen the band without me! (laughs) So it will be fun for them to come to a Journey concert and see me playing those hits.

Staying as busy as ever between his various musical projects, Steve took time out to put his experience and knowledge of rhythm history into an educational forum with the release of "a DVD I've got out called ***Drum Set Technique: History of the U.S. Beat***, that also traces the history of drumming from the early years of Ragtime and Marching Bands through the Jazz era to the present, and that kind of insight is always valuable for drummer to know so they can make good choices and be well informed." Closing in that spirit by sharing some of the gems of wisdom he's picked up throughout his amazing playing career with the new generation of drummers, Smith begins with the basic bedrock importance of bedside manner as a player:

> Be easy to get along with. A lot of the drummers I know are the easiest to get along with people, and are sometimes even the diplomats in the band that try to help the different band members work out their differences. As a drummer in the group, we really control so much of the music: we control the overall dynamics, the tempo, the groove, and its an important job, and if you have your skills together, there is work for good drummers. And by having those skills together to me means being able to read music, being able to play with great time (with or without a click track), and then being creative and being able to come up with good parts.
>
> All of that comes with study, practice, and playing experience, so as much as I recommend studying and practicing, of course, playing music is really where the rubber meets the road and where your experience comes from. So I see it all as a cycle, I study, I practice and I play, and during playing, some things work and some things don't, and if something's not working, it gives me something to practice and a reason to study, and I try to find the right balance between studying, practice and playing where I continue to have forward motion. All of that helps me improve as a musician and develop better and better technique, and the main reason for developing great technique is to be able to get a beautiful sound out of your instrument, and for you to not hurt yourself, and not have injuries.
>
> Finally, I see a lot of young students when I do drum camps, the majority of them hit the snare drum far too loud, and because they put a pillow and a hole in the bass drum, they don't get a good bass drum tone, and so the bass drum a lot of times is not feeling like the foundation of the kit. Then they play the cymbals much too loud, because one of the keys to the success of the drummers from the 50s and the 60s – like Earl Palmer and Hal Blaine and DJ Fontana – they could do a lot of things that's becoming a

lost art. # 1, they played the drum set with a beautiful, internal balance. So that way, if there's literally only one mic on the drum set, they have a perfect balance between the bass drum, the snare drum and the hi-hat, or the snare drum-bass-drum-cymbal, and the tom fills. So they really knew how to mix themselves, just by their internal balance, and that's something that lot of people do not think about today. So that internal balance and learning how to play a bass drum without a pillow in it – just two heads with a nice, beautiful tone – is becoming a lost art.

"It's the same thing that drove me when I was 13, and it's the same buzz that you get when its really happening, whether its studio or live, it's the same exact feeling." – Taylor Hawkins, 2017

Chapter 9: Taylor Hawkins of The Foo Fighters – Times Like These

Imagine being a drummer who steps into a band where the lead singer/guitarist simultaneously happens to be regarded as one of the greatest drummers of his generation and you'd be sitting where Taylor Hawkins was behind the kit when he joined up with former Nirvana drummer Dave Grohl three years into his one-man-band The Foo Fighters in 1997 after Grohl had played drums himself on the band's self-titled debut and follow-up, *The Colour and the Shape.* Though Hawkins joined the band in time to play on the band's entire road show and a few tracks off *There Is Nothing Left To Lose*, by tours' end after playing Grohl's drum parts night after night, as the group attempted to record head into the studio to record their fourth studio album, Hawkins revealed that

> we were really having a hard time figuring out how to be the Foo Fighters. It was 2002, and we had tried to make this album *One by One* and were having a hard time making it, it just wasn't working, and Dave took off to go do Queens of the Stone Age, and at that point, you know, he never said it, but I think the future of the band was definitely in jeopardy. I don't think anybody knew if we were ever going to make another record.

A pivotal point for the band that hinged on how one crucial last recording session would go for the troubled album, as Taylor took charge of finding his own voice as a drummer within the band on his first outing recording original music with them, the answer to whether the Foo Fighters would forge ahead came in the form of *"Times Like These,"* a victorious anthem that turned out to be as ethereal in its creation as it was inspiring in each of the band members' performances. A chance to break free of the doubts he'd been privately having about the band's future, Taylor poured everything he was feeling into a performance whose urgency, energy and sheer excitement reflected a sense that everything was riding on the line:

> In being reflective at one point or another, Dave wrote that song about "We gotta stay together and we've got to be a band," and it had something to do with a new start for his life, he'd just met his wife. So it kind of had that feeling and meaning behind it, and that record was the album's final recording. Me and Dave went back to Virginia with the intention of just recording two songs. We were going to record *"Times Like These"* and re-record a couple songs and attach it to the album that we had been trying to make, and just kind of hodge-podge together an okay record. So when we got to Virginia to literally cut two tracks, we got there at 6 o'clock at night, and our producer Nick Rasculenez had gotten to the studio a little bit earlier, and we just put up a drum set and kind of got a drum sound right then, and Dave said "Fuck it, let's go for a take on something!", and that was the first song for the final session that I recorded.

I literally did it in 2 or 3 takes, and I think there was a certain excitement of just going "Here's what I am as a drummer, this is what I sound like. I'm not going to sound like Dave, I'm not going to sound like anybody. If I try, I fail," and I didn't think about it, I just went and played how I play: which is on top and driving and its slightly out of control the whole time, and that's me and the way I play drums, and I think in a way, that was the first time where Dave just kind of said "Fuck it, that's the way this band will feel," and went for it. So that song was a new beginning for the Foo Fighters, and really a new approach in a way, where we said "We are who we are, and let's catch that. Let's not try and be anything but us," and at that session, I think there was a lot of excitement and nervousness and I was kind of kind of going through what turned out to be the beginning of a good time in my life: I met my wife, and was feeling good about life again, and there's that excitement on that track.

The funny thing is I didn't even know how the chorus went, because Dave does this thing where he writes choruses sometimes in bars of 3, and I didn't really understand that, so if you listen, I'm doing a snare fill in the middle of the choruses, and that's just because I didn't know. Had I known how the vocals went, I wouldn't have done that, and it turned into a hook, in a way, out of ignorance of how the song goes, and there's a beauty in that: grabbing stuff on the fly and having it be there. Every note doesn't need to be planned out.

Not an exception to the rule, but in fact the norm of how the Foo Fighters have come up with many of their most inspired musical parts over the past 15 years, Taylor confirms that "a lot of them actually happen that way, because we don't really know what's going on half the time. We play music, and Dave'll kind of hummed melodies, and sometimes you don't know." An approach that requires one of Rock's most exciting drummers to stay standing literally on his toes at the ready when the band's writing as they record – an approach reserved for only the most gifted of bands vs. the normal process of writing ahead of entering the studio – Hawkins admits that this process of spontaneous inspiration is a mixed bag:

> Its exciting sometimes and its frustrating sometimes, because there's times where Dave's trying to explain something to you, and he knows how it should be, but its not all right there in front of you. I think some of the results can be mixed sometimes, but you do get really exciting results – as we did with *"Times Like These."*

The foundation of their now-intuitive bond as bandmates was first laid during the recording of Hawkins' first album with the band, and first time in fact in the studio period, a learning curve where the drummer readily credits Grohl with "kind of holding my hand through that." An anxiety that every musician no doubt feels their first go-round in the recording environment – which any will concede is a far different experience from playing live – Taylor remembered feeling inspired by the encouragement he received from his bandmate after Hawkins admitted feeling initially defeated by the experience:

> That was my first time in the studio, so I was just generally fucking scared, and really wasn't pulling it off to begin with. That was me settling in and learning how to record in the studio, because you first get there, and you're whole life's kind of leading to a moment, and sometimes your life leads to a moment and you're just not ready yet, and I just really wasn't ready. So with the first record I played drums on, *Nothing Left to Lose*, I only played on half of that record.
>
> So I'm the one who said to Dave, "Dave, I'm not ready for this, you play drums, I'll watch you," and just watched Dave a lot and learned a lot from watching Dave. I learn a lot from Dave all the time, but Dave didn't want me to not be on the record, he just couldn't deal with that: he wanted me in the band and didn't want it to turn into a situation like the old drummer, and I think he was also battling "Can I let someone else play drums on my record? Maybe I just can't, maybe that's the problem with these drummers,

> that I just can't give it up," but I feel like he made a conscious attempt to say, "No, fuck that," and then said "You're not going to give up, I'm going to help you get through it."
>
> So he kind of gave me the space to grow, and I love that whole record, even the tracks I didn't play drums on. There's "Next Year," which was beautiful, and I didn't play drums on that one. So I think mostly the better drum parts on the record are Dave's drum tracks, so I only played songs on half that record, but the songs I did play on – out of all of them – there's a couple of things I'm really proud of. One standout for me, and its actually my favorite Foo Fighters song of all time, and will always be, and that's "Aurora." The drum performance I'm very proud of. I hear things I would do different now, but I also hear things I can't do, it was just such a moment. I love that dearly, and I think *"Generator"* is crazy, a little bit out of control but definitely there's a good energy to it. "Breakout" is me playing drums, and once again, is a little bit out of control.

Though he may have need a confidence booster in the studio drummer headspace, Hawkins had already been sitting behind the drums since he first discovered his musical talent as a 10-year-old kid, a true surprise given his recollection that "there were no musicians as it were though, nobody else played instruments - we had a piano but nobody played it." Reflective of his unique talent behind the kit, Taylor remembered his journey to that instrument beginning when

> my neighbor Ken Kunio had a drum set and guitar and I was always messing with his guitar, and getting really into music at the time. After a couple months of messing around with his guitars, he said "You should try the drums," and at first I said, "I don't care about the drums, I don't want to play the drums," and he persisted, "You should check it out" and sat me down on the kit. So I sat down, picked up a pair of sticks, and he showed me the one, simple Rock & Roll beat that is at the root of every Rock & Roll beat: "Boom, bap, boom boom bap," and I could just play it. I wasn't

> a prodigy by any way, shape or form, and today, I see 10 year old kids on the internet doing shit I could never do, I wasn't like Tony Royster Jr. or anything (laughs), but pretty quickly, I could play the simple 4 on 4 Rock & Roll grooves that are basically the basis of every Rock & Roll song.

Accelerating quickly as he discovered the ability to mimic what he heard on the radio on the drum set, Taylor was reared as a player by teachers he identifies as "the main three to begin with were Roger Taylor because I loved Queen, Stewart Copeland because he was such a badass, and my brother was a huge, huge, huge Police fan, and then Neil Peart because he did long drum solos and had the most drums, and he was great of course. Those were my first three drummers that I "studied" and a lot of what I do on the drums probably in some way, shape or form comes from one of those 3 guys." Bitten by the bug to become one of them, a wide-eyed Taylor knew before he was even a teenager that

> I wanted to play in a band by the first day that I sat behind the kit, I wanted to be in a band. I wanted to be Roger Taylor or Stewart Copeland or Neil Peart or Phil Collins or Larry Mullen Jr or Kenny Aronoff. I wanted that, I wanted to be in a Rock & Roll band. I wanted to play in a band, and the first thing in my mind was "Wow, how cool would it be just to have a band?"
>
> So that as my first thing, was just trying to form bands, and the first guy who I really started getting into music with was this guy named Sean Davidson, who now is the front man for YES, how funny is that? We started together, and both wanted to be in bands at the time, and decided to be in one together.

Already at the performance level of convincingly covering Alex Van Halen's drum parts in 9th grade at a Battle of the Bands talent show at Laguna Beach High School in the later 80s, Taylor would discover his knack for generating hurricane-force winds behind the kit, as his hands and feet kicked out beats with a speed that turned even his own head looking back on it now: "I don't know if I need to get any faster, I don't think I could. I don't ever think I'm going to be as fast as I was when I was 19, 20 years old. My hands were so fucking fast, faster than they are now, and that's just from being fucking spaz!" Pouring that passion into developing his skill as a performing drummer, Hawkins points to the timeless garage band as the ideal launching pad for any aspiring drummer to really begin getting their chops together:

> As far as learning to be a drummer on stage, I would say if you're in High School and you get a band together, learn a zillion covers, learn arrangements, learn how other people play songs, learn feel, learn dynamics, and learn a lot of people's drum parts because that's how you get good at being in a band is playing in a band. And the only way people are going to really want to hear you when you're a kid is playing covers. If you can play the hits of the day man, you can get a band together and do dances and all sorts of stuff like that, because Van Halen for instance, that were a cover band, The Beatles, were a cover band.
>
> I think about when I was in High School, I have this cover band Chevy Metal, and we go out and play and have fun and entertain people and even make a little money when we want to, and if I would have had that model when I was 12 or 13, 14, I could have been driving a killer used Mercedes and living in Highland Park when I was 16. (laughs) If I would have had 3 or 4 guys that were good musicians, and said "Okay, we're learning 300 of these covers, and we'll write songs and get our band together, and every once in a while, throw in one of our own songs. But we've got to learn how to play, we've got to learn how to entertain and learn how to put on a show." Learning is so important, and just sitting in your garage practicing for that one gig a year, I don't know...

Linking up around this same age with what would become his mainstay High-school band Sylvia, the drummer self-effacingly describing his group as "a Jane's Addiction rip-off sort of band, not very good, and we were kids." After gigging around Southern California locally for a few years, Taylor's first "Pro" gig as a drummer would arrive when he'd just reached legal drinking age after Hawkins landed an audition for Canadian pop star Sass Jordan:

> The Sass Jordan gig happened after I was working at this music store, and I was buddies with this guy who was friends with the owner, and he referred me to Steve Salas, and they said they were going to Europe to open up for Aerosmith, and Steve was a real hard ass, and I was brand-spanking new, I really was, I didn't know shit from shinola, I had no idea what I was doing. So he was just tough, very hard on me, but I needed it really and the Sass Jordan gig was definitely a eye-opening experience.
>
> I went from being in my own bubble thinking I was the greatest drummer in the world to like realizing I had no idea what I was doing at well, at the tender age of 20 or 21, and I had my ass handed to me, but again, I needed it. I needed to find out that I was not the greatest drummer in the world and that was definitely eye-opening.

A little less green and ready for a new scene after coming off the road with Sass in 1994, Taylor's training camp would come in handy when he wound up saddled to a shooting star after he landed an audition for a spot in fast-rising Alt-pop darling Alanis Morrisette's world Arena tour just as her *Jagged Little Pill* album was beginning to take over the mid-1990s. A wonderful exposure platform for any drummer to be sitting upon, Taylor was asked to play a central role in helping to cast the band, a responsibility he excitedly embraced after

> I got the Alanis gig and I got asked to put that band together in a way. I auditioned, and me and the guitar player Jesse Tobias got the gig, and then Chris Chaney the bass player came a little after that, and then I brought in this other guy Nick Lashley from Sass Jordan. She basically said "Okay, you're the band, I'm going to go out and do a promo tour, just get the band together." So me and the guys just sat in a room and took her songs and sort of turned them into live performances, and I don't know if you ever

> saw that band live or footage of us, but it doesn't sound anything like the fucking record!
>
> Her manager was smart though, and had said to me, "Taylor, make it a Rock & Roll band," because she'd made this record that was really cool and unique for its time, but for her to come off like a real deal Rock & Roller, she couldn't have this sort of playing the tracks Janet Jackson kind of band behind her, because it would have been very contrived. But we were this scrappy little band trying to sound like The Who and Jane's Addiction and the Chili Peppers and Led Zeppelin and Pink Floyd, so we took her record and made it for a band like that. Then she came back after being gone for 3 weeks or a month, picked up the microphone, and we jammed the whole fucking set without saying a word, and she killed it! She killed it man, she was a real singer, and she could really be in a band, and that was like a little band it really was. We had a blast.

Boarding the bus for what was to be his next big Rock & Roll adventure, as Hawkins' view behind the kit was transitioned overnight from smaller venues like clubs and theatres to sold-out Arenas, the band brought Morrisette's songs to life in a visceral way for fans. Capturing a look at this time in Hawkin's journeyman years as a drummer cutting his teeth on the road, Rolling Stone Magazine noted in a cover story from the audience in 1995 performing "with confidence, Morissette leads her crack four-piece backing band – none of whom played on *Jagged Little Pill* – through looser, more explosive versions of the album's material. Her young band comes from journeymen backgrounds: Guitarist Jesse Tobias, a former member of Mother Tongue, was very briefly a Red Hot Chili Pepper before being replaced by Dave Navarro; guitarist Nick Lashley and drummer Taylor Hawkins played together in Sass Jordan's backing band. Then there's bassist Chris Chaney, whose prior gigs include time with '80s soft-pop star Christopher Cross. In a 65-minute set, Morissette and the band play everything on the album." Shaking his head still seeing stars as he looks back years later on it all, Taylor admits it was

> a pretty amazing time, to see that sort of ascension that quickly, it really was, and the best part for me was I was kind of on the outside looking in a little bit. We were in the band, but we're not really "the band" so we weren't sitting there arguing about set lists and so it was fun to be part of it, but at the same time, being relegated to a certain position at the end of the day was a great way to see something like that happen without actually having to actually take the responsibility of it. I didn't have to take any responsibility for it, but could still be part of it, just sort of on the fringes, and that was great.

Drawing rave live reviews throughout his performances around the world with Morisette, the buzz soon enough reached the ear of Nirvana drummer and newly-minted Foo Fighters lead singer/guitarist/songwriter Dave Grohl, who was facing a similar dilemma as Morisette had of needing a band to bring to life a record he'd recorded almost entirely by himself back in his Virginia basement studio. Stepping into the shoes of a drummer whose shadow already loomed large over Grunge, Taylor was unintimidated and ready to take the next step up in his rise toward stardom as a drummer in his own right:

> I went right from that to the Foo Fighters, who was already a pretty successful fucking unit when I got there. They weren't where we are now, and we hit the road hard, and it took us 2 or 3 records to get to where we could play arenas and stadiums. When I first got in the band, it wasn't like that. It was band and crew all on one bus, and we were kids still in our early-to-mid 20s, but we were working, and it was fun, we had a really good time.

One of the true elite masters of speed syncopation playing in Rock & Roll since he sat down behind the kit in the Foos, on his first full studio outing with the band, Taylor had this talent on display throughout hits like *"All My Life,"* the lead single from *One By One* LP, that remains a fan favorite to this day and one of the drummer's as well:

> I like *"All My Life,"* it sounds crazy and out of control, that it doesn't sound perfect and that I'm spazzing and it sounds aggressive. That's one of those

> that people just go fucking crazy when they hear that snare crack at the top, that still gets the blood pumped.

Even though it would go on to win the Grammy Award for Best Hard Rock Album, Hawkins doesn't hold the album up quite as high among his favorites from the band's catalog, blaming his dissatisfaction not on his playing but rather on the sonic disappointment that *One by One* is not our best-sounding record, and its not our smoothest performances ever, it was cut in like a week and a half, rushing, so Dave could run off and do the Queens of the Stone Age tour, and that recording in general just sounds like a band fighting for its life. I think that's great, and think it's a real picture of something going on during that time."

Recording the album's debut single, *"All My Life,"* would prove the start of a performing-under-pressure trend of Grohl and Hawkins pulling out what would turn out to be lead hit singles at the last minute, with Taylor confirming that " *'All My Life'* was written on the fly. Me and Dave were at his house in the middle of the Nothing Left to Lose tour to do some demos, and he had that one, it had a different intro but we mapped the song out. And that intro came from Dave just riffing away, and that's one thing Dave really knows, he really knows when we've got something." The dynamic duo would pull off another 4th Quarter miracle on their next studio album, *Echos, Silence, Patience and Grace* when Hawkins revealed " *'The Pretender'* was a last minute addition to that album, which was really kind of difficult to make." Elaborating on what made the recording environment challenging coming off the heels of the *One By One* sessions:

> *On Echos, Silence, Patience, and Grace* LP, some of the arrangements on that album were expansive, where they were done on Protools, and the guy who was producing it, Gil Norton, was really into making everything perfect. I didn't tend to like the feel of that record, because we would sit around and there's songs that didn't make that record just because we didn't by the time of working on the kick drum pattern, after so long, Dave and I were

> both just like "Fuck this song," and we killed it. We actually killed a couple songs on that record, and Gil Norton went away on vacation for five days at the end of making that record, and Dave was like "I've got this song," and it was one where we'd kind of jammed on that intro, the Beatle-y kind of intro thing, and then we fucked around with that a little bit, and then Dave literally sat there on the guitar and played me the whole song.
>
> Then he told me, "Everybody's coming in tomorrow, me, you, and Nate, and we're just going to do a live demo of it, and we literally went in and did a live demo of it and then Gil came back, and went in there right away and tried to start fucking changing everything. And Dave was like "Nope, nope, sorry, we're doing it like this and we're doing it in one day, we recorded it," and that's what we handed into the label, and what became the single.

Heading in the opposite direction sonically on 2014's Sonic Highways, *Wasting Light,* the Foo Fighters went back to Dave Grohl's roots working with producer Butch Vig in favor of a far more organic analog sensibility of off-the floor approach to making the album where Rolling Stone Magazine would observe of the back-to-basics recording that it produced "eleven tracks of fuzz-box brawn, mosh-pit-hurrah choruses and iron-horse momentum, *Wasting Light* is the best Foos album since the first two, Grohl's all-solo 1995 debut." Hawkins would earn some of that spotlight where the momentum was concerned given Taylor was behind the drum performances this time around that would win praise as well from his own corner of the musical universe, where Modern Drummer complimented the way in which "Hawkins attacks the kit with speed and power, but also with grace and textural nuance" while "*Wasting Light*...blasts a return to the past...taking shape in an all-analog process that required Hawkins to perform nearly perfect drum tracks live to tape." A spontaneity he welcomed following his less-than-satisfying experience working on the band's previous album, Taylor confirmed that

> after working with Gil Norton on the record before, Butch Vig definitely brought a calmness to the process, and was like "Yeah, you know, if Dave

> wants something one way, sure," and he's not going to argue with Dave about a song, he's just not. Other people would, but with Butch, he wants you to do less, so if you're going to really get something extra in there, it better be fucking good or interesting, because he want it if its something that's been done a million times.
>
> The cool thing about Butch and the cool thing about Dave is they're drummers, so constantly, you know when you do something that impresses them, they'll go "Oh wow, that was cool." Because he's a drummer, if I do something kind of fancy Dave's never heard me do before, he'll let me know pretty quick, like "Woah, that was cool, that was weird, I've never heard anybody do that before!" So I'm always kind of looking to do that to Dave, and its kind of similar with Butch.

Earning 5 Grammy Award nominations including Album of the Year, the band would win four, including Best Hard Rock Album, Best Hard Rock/Metal Performance for *"White Limo"* and Best Rock Performance and Best Rock Song for *"Walk,"* while *"These Days"* – which would peak at # 2 on the Billboard US Alternative Songs and Hot Rock Songs Chart was an example – as Modern Drummer would highlight – of the unique trust that ties the two drummers together as the core creative pocket of The Foo Fighters, noting that "Hawkins plays burly rhythms in step with Grohl's guitar…Some listeners may not be able to tell the difference between Grohl's elephantine pummel and Hawkins' lithely propulsive groove and speed-demon fills, but much of the Foos' magic lies in the duo's twin yet separate identities. Best friends enamored of each other's skills, Grohl and Hawkins lay the foundation for every Foo Fighters song." Putting *"These Days"* through those very paces, Hawkins remembers recognizing the song as something special from first listen:

> We'd been doing demos and Dave came in and said "I've got this thing," and he played the whole song for us on acoustic guitar, and we went in the studio, said "Okay," made sure everybody knew the arrangement and did

> a take of it. This was just the demo, but it *pretty* much is exactly like the album version, we just played it once. The song just spoke for itself, and there's not a lot to it, it's a very simple song, sort of like Dave's sort of Tom Petty/Americana rock side.
>
> There's this guy named Gersch who takes care of our drums situation, and he has a bunch of old Gretches, almost 95%, 60s and 70s Gretches, like this one fat kit is 24 inch bass drum, and then there's 15, 16 and 18 floor toms and there's the 22, and the 10, and 12, and even the quicker version. So kind of depending on the song, if we were doing *"Matter of Time"* or something kind of fast, we had this set called The Little Race Car Kit.

In recognition of how far the band's wave of popularity had rolled across the Atlantic by the time Taylor was celebrating his 10 year anniversary with the band, when word reached back stateside that the Foo Fighters had sold out London's famed Wembley Stadium in 2008. A primetime event that, in addition to the back-to-back nights of 165,000 screaming fans in attendance in the crowd being broadcast live via Satellite across the United Kingdom, and later in the U.S. on Pay-Per-View the show went off so spectacularly, standing in the wings waiting to walk into the controlled pandemonium of the crowd, Hawkins confessed that

> I was scared shitless, I'm scared shitless every time man. That gig there was scary, because when you walk onto that stage and all those people are there and something about the way that place is is like an optical illusion! There's literally thousands of people at all times surrounding you, and its strange man, it's a strange trip. Its one thing when you're playing a Festival, because we've played to 100,000 people at a Festival forever, but when you're there and it's a Foo Fighters show, there's something about that place, and you just kinda gotta go for it and stick together.
>
> Its hard not to let your adrenaline and all that other stuff kind of get ahold of you, and you generally don't play quite as well when you're too excited.

> There's a fine line between having a lot of energy and being too excited. I just stay physically in shape to do those Foo Fighter gigs!

By the second decade of the Millennium, the Foo Fighters were one of the biggest classic or modern rock bands in the world, with over 10 million records sold and a multi-generational fanbase that kept the band in relevant, regular rotation on both Classic and Modern Rock Radio around the U.S. Seeking to take the capital they'd built up on the road around the country to both celebrate and explore their collective roots as a band, the band embarked on *Sonic Highways* in pursuit of an ambitious concept reflective of both their intuitive chemistry as a band of musicians and songwriters where – on the spot in each of the cities the band stopped to record in – they would write, work up and record a different song for the album. On top of that pressure, all the impromptu performances were being recorded as keeper takes for the album, and their tracking was being filmed for an HBO series documenting the behind-the-scenes creation of the album.

Kicking off the album's release with a week-long residency on Late Night with David Letterman, the kind of booking reserved only for Rock royalty, where Entertainment Weekly praised a highlight moment where Grohl and Taylor shared drumming duties and "he and Hawkins dominate the song," while the drummer is credited for helping keep the concept moving musically – especially throughout the filming of the series – where the Hollywood Reporter's reviewer made clear the climax of the episodes came when the band culminated their musical exploration of any given city in song, noting that "even for those who will have enjoyed the history and stories from the rest of the hour, there's a sense of relief when Hawkins counts down the beat and the guitars fire up." Throughout smash singles like *"Something for Nothing"* and *"Congregation,"* both of which reached # 1 on the Billboard Mainstream Rock Chart and the U.K. Rock Charts, Taylor felt a refreshing air of creative freedom that remained a wind at the band's back throughout recording:

> This record has that sort of ideal of the arrangements are going to be expanding and kind of going in a longer direction, which kind of goes with the H.B.O. show and the vibe of the whole concept. So I just feel like these songs are definitely our most sort of expansive, they're long, a lot of longer songs, but a couple of them we didn't use a click track, and just kind of went for something more feel-oriented, and there's a couple songs that are very worked out."

Having become "quite possibly today's most vital living, breathing rock & roll band," in the esteemed opinion of Rolling Stone Magazine, the band brought that kind of life to their takes by carrying forward the old-school record-making aesthetic they had pushed with Butch Vig. Entering into an era of freedom within their production process where Taylor revealed an overriding theme where "on *Sonic Highways*, we did it without click tracks or anything like that, and just went for it. I think we're more and more the band getting away from 'What's perfect?', and the more fucked up the better sometimes, you know? So Dave says that to Butch a lot: 'Its just not fucked-up sounding enough,' and I've gotten so into that aesthetic that like, that Birds of Satan record, we made that in a week. All those drum tracks are one or two takes, we didn't even think about it, no click tracks, no nothing. With the Foo Fighters, I think we went for perfection to a certain degree for so long that we're starting to kind of care more about feel, vs. perfection. It's a funny thing, because for me, that's growth as a musician." As he continues to mature as a player along with the band through each new studio adventure, Hawkins speaks with the veteran perspective of many of his own personal heroes when reflecting on the process:

> When I was a kid, I would see in Rolling Stone Magazine that "Charlie Watts gets best drummer of the year," and I would say "What are they talking about? What about Neil Peart?" But now, the older I get, the more I try to understand and am starting to understand why Charlie Watts was so brilliant: and that was because of his feel. He just makes something that feels great and feels like Rock & Roll.

> Once again, we're recording mainly on tape, and we're not utilizing editing the way people are able to nowadays, which is perfecting what's imperfect, and we're keeping all the imperfections, the feel, and the driving snare hits, etc. So looking at the last record, were a lot of the songs were sort of tight, all 3 ½ minute songs, this is kind of the opposite, but done with the same sort of natural feel.

"Congregation" showcased a glorious example of the by-now signature charging guitar-drum introductory burst of energy that Taylor credited as a team effort between he and Grohl where both drummers throw their best beat ideas back and forth in a largely intuitive process where " when it comes to the Foo Fighters, me and Dave definitely work on that together. It changes every time, and I'm sure every band leader has an idea of what he wants his drummer to do, but Dave can actually sit down and show me – and quite well, which he really doesn't do that much."

Keeping the beat to a massive tour in 2015 and 2016 to celebrate the music they'd made with fans worldwide, the New York Times noted of the band's two drummers' twin engines of energy that, in a healthy competition on stage, "Taylor Hawkins…(is) the band's only member whose stage energy even begins to approach Mr. Grohl's." In 2017, the Foo Fighters would return to the studio and the road with the same sense of inspired purpose with their latest studio album, Concrete and Gold, with Taylor dazzling a whole new generation of fans behind the beat. Spilling his secret for summoning the same physical exertion he did on stage in his mid-20s now that he's entered his mid-40s, Hawkins relies on a combination of experience, exercise, and natural excitement for playing to pull it off night after night for months on end:

> I think I have a somewhat better sense with each year that goes by of being a band drummer, and that comes just from playing with your band. But you have to be playing all the time. I don't really practice much, I've got to be honest, and I used to hear buddy Rich say when they'd ask him how

he warmed up before a show, "I keep my hands out of my pockets." So I think practice is good for sure if it makes you comfortable. I hate to say this, but I like to play and practice and everything, but I think getting better is getting a better perspective on how to play with other musicians. So a band practicing together all the time, yeah, I get that.

A lot of that stuff we play is pretty fucking technically challenging, where I'm singing a lot of the time and playing drums, so that's really like learning muscle memory. And muscle memory is important to be the best you can be as a band. When I get up on stage, even though I know *"All My Life"* just as good as my memory responds, but your body kind of forgets it a little bit, so you're just kind of like running around to each drum trying to make it like on time, because your mind knows that your muscle memory is kind of out of practice.

If you want to continue to play aggressive Rock & Roll capably as a drummer with a certain amount of energy, you have to stay in shape, and that's practicing and exercising but its also taking care of yourself. I look back at what my lifestyle was when I was in my 20s and I can't believe what a total fucking shit I was, first of all, but second of all, if I ate like ate and party like I partied and smoke like I smoked, and lived like I lived back then, I couldn't do this job now, I just couldn't. That's why a lot of guys burn out. You have to be done doing hard drugs and hard drinking by at least 40, it doesn't make you feel very well after that if you're not taking care of yourself.

When he's not on the road with the Foo Fighters, the multi-talented Hawkins stays busy with two other bands, The Birds of Satan and Taylor Hawkins and the Coattail Riders, pulling double duties in both projects as drummer and lead singer. Freeing Taylor up to pursue a path that Billboard correctly argued has packed the inherent potential to be a slippery one in the past for other signature members of mainstream bands where "of course, side projects are notorious for being fun for the musicians and not for the listeners," before concluding that, thanks to his considerable talent for keeping things fresh, "this album doesn't fall into that trap." Happy to have the outlet to stretch his wings as a singer and songwriter, the drummer takes great comfort in the fact that

> to be honest, its such a less pressured situation, it doesn't matter, so I can go as bananas as I want, but at the same time, I still want it to be a good song. So I think my approach is roughly the same, although I'm wearing a different hat and kind of have a clearer picture of what I want the drums to be like, than I would when I play in the Foo Fighters because there's just a little bit of guessing, and then flat out asking and then "Wondering if I'm doing this good right now and are you happy?" Because sometimes you think you're not making the boss happy, if you know what I'm saying...

In giving fans some tips on how to just that no matter where they are in their career as a professional drummer, Taylor begins with practical basics like "learning to play to a click track, that's a good thing, you've got to know how to do that. Because if you're going to try and get work, as a studio musician, you better sound real natural and real comfortable with a click track, first and foremost, because unfortunately that's pretty much the way people make music. And it doesn't matter if they're going to tour the shit out of you anyways, you still better sound good before they start touring you. The other thing is enjoy music for music, because I'll tell you, if you want it to be a career, you can work as hard as you want forever, and if you're trying to be a Rock Star, that might not necessarily happen. That's just the way life is, so enjoy music for music's sake most importantly, and enjoy doing it for yourself."

Ranked on Rolling Stone Magazine's 100 Greatest Drummers and no doubt high on the lists of favorite drummers among a whole new generation of aspiring beat makers just now starting to learn the instrument by teaching themselves how to play along with Taylor's records as he himself did at that age, in digging back through his catalog, the drummer proudly points to "certain things that I'm definitely proud of – I think there's one or two things from most records. I like *'Aurora'* a lot, I like *'All My Life'* and *'Times Like These'* a lot. I like the first thing we did on the Birds of Sage record, and there's a song we recorded in Austin on Sonic Highways that I'm really proud of. There's also a couple songs I wrote with the Coat Tail Riders, including one called *'Get Up I Wanna Get Down.'*" Looking toward the future, whether its with the Foo Fighters or his own side projects, Taylor remains driven by the same pure rush Rock & Roll has always given him as a drummer:

> It's the same thing that drove me when I was 13, and it's the same buzz that you get when its really happening, whether its studio or live, it's the same exact feeling. Just because there's a bigger paycheck or people perceive you as being super-human rock star guy, that bullshit doesn't mean anything. The money's good because now I don't have to have a real job, so the idea of getting up and going to the studio and searching for that same high, trying to get that perfect buzz, its something you're always kind of searching for, exactly the same as when you were a kid. So I get to do that for a living, and I'm so fucking blessed! Nobody deserves what I get, that's for sure, I get more than I deserve, but I guess my point with that is I realize how grateful I should be and how lucky I am that I get to play drums for a living.

"We all met in the 8th grade in Junior Highschool. We were learning to play our instruments and learning to be a band at the same time, so there's your unique sound...We were all students of early American Rock & Roll, and we pretty much stayed there." – Doug 'Cosmo' Clifford

(photo by Grady Clifford)

Chapter 10: Doug 'Cosmo' Clifford of CCR – Creedence Clearwater Revisited

If you dig deep enough into the subterranean stratum of any American rock band's roots, you'll find a little Creedence Clearwater Revival woven into the musical make-up of their D.N.A., at least any rock band that made their mark in the past 50 years. Consider the Rock & Roll Hall of Fame's note that "the term 'roots rock' had not yet been invented when Creedence came along, but in a real way they defined it, drawing inspiration from the likes of Little Richard, Hank Williams, Elvis Presley, Chuck Berry and the artisans of soul at Motown and Stax. In so doing, Creedence Clearwater Revival became the standard bearers and foremost celebrants of homegrown American music."

For Doug 'Cosmo' Clifford, who at 69 is still touring the world treating generations of CCR fans to the band's greatest hits playing next to his best friend from Junior High and co-founder Stu Cook, Cosmo still shakes his head at what a long, strange, magical journey his life behind the drum set has been, one where he modestly quips "I just consider myself very lucky, quite frankly, in the company of the drummers in this book, I don't know what I'm doing here (laughs)…" Getting the greatest kick out of seeing the Millennial generation in the crowd singing along to his band's songs, discovering CCR on their iPods and Smartphones the way he had Little Richard 50 years earlier on 45s and the radio, the legendary drummer confirms that

> those are the things that mean the most to me. Its hard to explain, and the older I get, the more I appreciate being able to play at the level we're playing at. We have more young people in our audiences now than older fans, shall we say, and Creedence Clearwater Revisited plays 20-some odd songs that are all hits we think is a pretty-good line up, and its great still being there on stage with the fans just right in front of you, where you hear and feel that energy. The bottom line is bringing the fans to shows so they can hear what you're doing and see what you're doing and get the whole perspective of what it is that we do as a band.

Meeting original bandmate John Fogerty in the same Junior High class some 50+ years earlier, Doug confessed that even though he didn't yet have a proper drum set, hearing the future CCR frontman's raw musical talent at play that day, he knew there was something cosmic at work. Drawing the drummer toward fate was what he remembered as a flawless performance of

> Fats Domino being played on the Steinway in the school's music room one day when I was walking down the hall of my junior high. I still wasn't a proper drummer yet, but I was a very outgoing guy in school, a bit of a class clown in a lot of ways, I could make the kids laugh, while John Fogerty was on the other hand the complete opposite: an introverted, skinny kid

> with no self-confidence. So I remember stopping in the door way and see John now is playing some Little Richard stuff – note for note – with all the little embellishments, and I remember I was really enjoying it. So he finally stopped for a second and I walked in and said "That's Fats Domino and that's Little Richard, note for note," and he said "Yeah," and so the very next thing I said to him was: "You wanna start a band?"
>
> So the next thing John asked me what instrument I played, and I said "I play the drums..." Well, I didn't play drums! I wanted to, and I was working my way to that end, so then he says, "Well, actually, I play guitar. I'm looking for a piano player," and I said "I know the guy! His name is Stu Cook, he's my best friend, he plays Classical piano and he hates it, but he'd love to be in the band. His dad's a rich lawyer, and he has an enormous room in his house with a piano, we can practice there." Well, a couple things here: I didn't ask Stu if he wanted to be in the band, first, and second, I certainly didn't ask his parents if we could practice on their beautiful piano, but I guess I had it all figured out. So with that hurdle out of the way, I asked Stewart if he wanted to do it, and he said "Yeah, he'd love to," so we became an instrumental 3-piece trio with piano, guitar and drums.

Clifford, prior to that fateful encounter for all 3 musicians, described his first drum set as "a pencil eraser bouncing off my books and my little brass lamp, didn't have a drum set, just that old bass drum." With the radio and vinyl records as his first teachers, a young Doug proved resourceful in assembling his first kit, one he fashioned from the classic duplicity millions of teenagers pulled off when listening to Top 40 while they were doing homework, arguably concentrated a little more on the former than latter. With Clifford even going so far as to turn his bedroom desk, school books and pencil into a make-shift kit so he could play along to whatever song that came on, recalling that

> my first drum set coming around this time where the drum sticks that I put in my hands were pencils, and I would set my books up on my desk in

my room, and back in the late 50s, they had these metal lamps made out of wrought-iron that were very sheik, if you will, and this was a brass lamp with a flex-neck. In other words, you could bend it and it would stay in that position, so I used that as a cymbal, and would watch the drummers on TV and occasionally see somebody live, not that often, but then I would be doing my homework, and one of my favorite songs would come on the radio, and I'd turn it up just a little bit and try to listen to what the drummers were doing, then play it on my desk-top drum set. So I basically taught myself to play by listening to Top 40 radio, Country, and R&B radio, and these were the real thing: real R&B, not soul and cool Jazz or any of that. This was Howlin' Wolf and Jimmy Reed and Lightnin' Hopkins, this was the real, basic blues music. The same with the country stations: these were all the great country acts, the roots in other words, but I spent most of my time listening to Top 40 because they were playing a lot of Rock & Roll. But Top 40 radio also incorporated a lot, because Percy Faith would come on with his Orchestra, songs like "The Flying Nun," Ray Stevens and his comedic run-down, it was a real mixed-bag, it was really very, very broad.

See, nowadays, each station is specific to a certain genre, and there are so many things to choose from, but growing up in the era of radio I did, there were like 3 things: Classical, if you so desired, which was on the FM side of the coin, or Top 40 and Country. The thing that was cool about the Top 40 part of it was all the songs that were being played were hits: they went from 1 to 40 and back again. Then they would play new songs that hadn't made the charts yet, so most of the things that you're hearing are a formula if you will: first of all, that you better be musical if you're going to spend the time or effort to put in a note, you better be in the right spot and it better work with both the vocal and/or the movement of the song, where its going – say from A to B. Those aren't choruses, but 1, 2, or 3 positions, because as the song moves, you put a break in there, some of that stuff Little Richard's band used to do. They would jump times, especially when a solo would come, you're going along and then he would scream and the band would all jump up together, and then when they'd come back to another verse, they'd slide back together. It was a really interesting thing, and these were seasoned cats, these were guys from New Orleans, who'd been around the Jazz scene and were pioneers now in this new medium of rock & roll, so they really knew what they were doing.

Going back even further, as a young kid, I remember I had just this fascination with Rock & Roll Music. This was 1953, and I was 9 years old, and rock was just starting to emerge. There was a TV show, it might have been American Bandstand, where kids would dance, and the first time I heard it, I was hooked at least as a fan of the music. I had my little work chart, at the end of the week, where I got an allowance based on how much I had done, and all of a sudden, I ended up filling the ledger because I really had something I wanted to spend money on, and that was buying records. In those days, they were 78 RPMs, pretty fosselistic really, but I was just fascinated by it. The first record I ever bought was by Etta James, so this is at the very beginning, coming over from the Jazz side and Big Band side into this new, kind of dangerous medium, Rock & Roll. My dad hated it, I remember I could never play it when he was around, and my mom had been a singer briefly on the radio in her teen years in Oakland, so she'd had a taste of it, and then gotten married. This was way, way back before I had an instrument, back when I just had a love for music.

The second record I bought was "Bo Diddily" by Bo Diddily, and that's where I think my indoctrination for drums really started, with that great rhythm that opens the song, that hypnotic thing, and I loved it! I'd play it over and over again, and play parts of it, where I got pretty good at dropping the needle down on sections without it skipping. Soon after that, we moved up to the Bay Area in 1958, and I had more than the 2 records I'd mentioned by this point: I had *"Rock Around the Clock"* by Bill Haley and some other classics, and even though I'd packed that box very gently, I'm

> sure my Dad slipped the mover an extra buck and said "Drop this box as many times as you can before put it on the truck." I remember when we got to the new house, anxiously grabbing the box, and hearing this rattling sound and thought "Oh boy, that can't be good," and when I opened it up, the records were all smashed to hell. So I had to kind of start over, and as things emerged and the technology changed, the 45 was created and also the long-playing on 33 and a 3rd album.

Learning by feel, something he brought so masterfully to his playing throughout the CCR catalog, a young Cosmo remembered channeling his inner Gene Krupa – arguably one of the most influential drummers of all time – as he listened, mimicking what he heard on the radio and record, teaching himself by "trying to imitate a sound/feel, because I'm a feel guy, and whatever it is, I guess it's a gift, but I am a feel guy and I can take a song and make it feel the way I think its supposed to, and even back then, that's what I would aspire to do. I had all these references of different songs and styles of songs and the way they were played, and I would just use that as sort of my library, and then try to imitate whatever I could. A lot of the stuff was very technical – especially a lot of the footwork with the New Orleans guys – so I would maybe take some out, but would still find the key beats, and came at that cross-cut feeling, or swing. I can play a Texas swing with the best of them, and I was able to use that little trick, but not too much with the Creedence stuff, that's for sure." Vs. Jazz, Clifford gravitated more toward the sorts of rhythm and blues that would come in time to help define Creedence's groove:

> For me, as a kid, I liked the R&B stuff better because I liked the grooves and what the drum did, and how it made me feel, and I still get that feeling when I play. Its an amazing thing, because when it hits you, it hits you! Then I would just sort of tap around on my desk, and if my mom would come in or certainly if my dad came in, I would either be screwed or have time to make a quick move on the dial and turn the radio off. I already had a pencil in my hand (laughs). But that was sort of the process of it, and

then a neighbor gave me a marching bass drum, and I knew that it looked a lot bigger than a lot of the kick drums I'd seen on T.V., but the big band drummers were using huge, huge bass drums.

Then, what turned me on to being a drummer, which came with just the snap of a finger, is one night when I watched a special on Gene Krupa – and I remember he was playing out in the middle of a big Baseball field, and had his kit set-up – and they never showed the band but they were playing off screen. And Gene came out in this white sport coat and calypso tie, and his black, greasy hair – which reminded me a lot of Elvis – and I just went "God, this guy is like a movie star." Then, once he started playing, he was not just sitting down and playing drums, but also walking and rhythmically playing around the kit, including cymbal stands and things like that. It was just so beautiful, and it wasn't a lot of really fast rolls, it was rhythmical, Bo Diddily's type of thing where he really found the rhythm within the tempo. Then of course when the band when into the chorus, he sat down and banged away and then got back up, and I was GONE! That was it, and I started saving my money for drums now, and got some additional jobs and sources of income to be able to keep buying records as well, but I had found my calling, and I was 13…

By the time brother Tom Fogerty had joined John, Stu and Doug in the band, they had already logged enough time practicing together as a 3-piece to have given Cosmo an accelerated education behind the kit, reasoning that the absence of a vocalist in the band's first incarnation "was, for me, a real help in getting my musicality together, because we were missing a lead singer – which is a critical role- so I'd come up with fills that felt good in certain spots where there might be a vocal, or something to take it up a little bit and add something to it, but without coming in doing really flashy roles, etc. I did things that actually rhythmically moved the song, and that's what I tried in Creedence. I took it a step further in, say for example, '*Who Stopped the Rain,*' where I have a lot of fills in there, and its not so much a rhythmical thing as it is a back and forth between the vocal this drum part that I came up with. John didn't like it and I had to fight for it, because otherwise, it sounds just like another protest song, and I wanted to embellish the song in places where he wasn't singing."

As the band spent their early 20s in the late 60s toiling up and down the West Coast playing dives as The Golliwogs and then CCR, the muse for many of what would become their most popular hits took shape. With hundreds of shows under their belts perfecting arrangements and other features of what would truly make the covers Creedence recorded – including Screamin' Jay Hawkins's *"I Put a Spell on You"* and Marvin Gaye's *"I Heard It Through the Grapevine"* – feel like their own, Clifford proudly points to the band's hit-making rendition of *"Susie Q"* as

> a real classic example of what I brought to the table was our first hit, *"Susie Q,"* which is of course not an original song, but we were playing that at the clubs. Before we made it we were starving, doing 5 sets a night, 6 nights a week for not very much money, so when you play that much music in a night, in a week, in the same place, you have to stretch out the material where you can. So the original *"Susie Q,"* by Dale Hawkins, is a rock-a-billy song with the drummer playing 8th notes on the hi-hat, so what I did was changed up the beat and made it quarter-notes, which freed up a huge amount of space and opened the song up completely. Then the accents in-between which would have been on the 8th notes on the cymbal I played on the bass drum instead so it sounds like a train, and I play that throughout the whole song. *"Grapevine"* has become a favorite in more recent years too, because I do a drum solo on that one. I never did before, but the last couple years I've been doing it and having fun with it, so that's at the top of the list.

"Lodi" would prove a prominent example of art imitating life as Clifford remembers it as one of the band's many wild days on the rock & roll frontiers as an unknown band, recalled in classic lines like "If I ever had a dollar for every

song I sung, every time I had to play while people sat there drunk." Shaking his head as he remembered being there in real time, the drummer confirms that

> it was one specific gig that that song was referencing. We did all those gigs you play at the dives, and places where you had to watch your back, things like that. But the one you're talking about, what happened was: we went into this bar, and there were about 8 big dudes in there, all farmhands, and they didn't like us, we were city boys and they kept telling us to turn down and we wouldn't turn down. You could just feel them staring at you, and I don't think there was a woman in the place that I can remember, just these guys with chips on their shoulders. So we finished the night, did four sets, went up to get paid, and they said "We're not paying you." And we said, "What do you mean you're not paying us, we played for four hours," and they said "You were too loud."
>
> Then they said, "You boys better leave NOW!" So all of a sudden, the bell goes off, and Stu had just bought a beautiful new Bassman amp, and Tom Fogerty had a station wagon that was our vehicle to hall our shit around in, and so we realized that as fast as we moved, its not gonna be fast enough. They'd give us an ass whipping that would be not so pretty, because these guys were all big and they out-number us 2 to 1, and don't like us. So we sped out of there, because we thought they might follow us down the road and run us off the road and kill us or something! So that was the inspiration for that song, it was a real eye opener, and a beautiful song came out of it. Its one of my favorite songs because of the swing, that was definitely a swing song.

Highlighting one of CCR's most celebrated and enduring radio hits, *"Down on the Corner"*– driven by Cosmo's signature cowbell beat– as another song that owed its inspiration to the band's real life adventures on the road finding their way to stardom in the later 1960s. Ironically a song that he and his bandmates were initially resistant to over stylistic objections, the drummer overcame his doubts about the song's place in the CCR catalog by applying the kind of creativity that Billboard argued made he and bassist Stu Cook "as good a rhythm section as any American white rock & roll band of the '60s ever had, on songs where the beat, not to mention the textures of the bass and the drums, counted for a lot." Taking fans back to the night he left practice with a determination to come up with a beat that would make the song work, Clifford began by

> it was probably one of the more unique songs that we did. People loved it, and it was the story of us basically, we were the four kids on the corner. Before the cowbell part was added, in the beginning, we said "This isn't a rock & roll song," because it was like a calypso song, and I didn't want to sound like Percy Faith. Calypso was kind of big for a while in Top 40, and I didn't want to go there, I wanted to still be recognized as a Rock & Roll band. So we sort of complained about it, "Why are we doing this?", and the parts weren't working. So what I would do a lot, is take a little Sony Mono Cassette Recorder to work, put it on the floor in a place where it picked up the drums, guitar, and everything, and it was actually a pretty decent little note taker. It had a limiter in it that almost gave it a cool sound.
>
> So I would take it home, and make footnotes and say things about it: "Well, I want to work on this, I want to work in this section, blah blah," and I didn't have much of anything going for *"Down on the Corner,"* and what I was sort of told to play just didn't feel right for me. So I took it home, and worked with it, and came out with the way it came out with that cowbell at the beginning. I changed it up a little bit over the years. I play a little bit more of an accent now live with Revisited, and it works real well. We sort of way-slowed it down, which I don't necessarily agree with, so Stu and I go back and forth sometimes and I'll give something here, and him there, so it all balances out. So now I kind of like it a little bit better.

Consistently and correctly credited as one of the bands who defined the soundtrack to the Vietnam War – reflected not only in the subject matter of touchstone anti-war movement anthems like *"Fortunate Son"* – as well as the haunting *"Run Through the Jungle"* and other Creedence classics that have been used as part of the backdrop of countless movies depicting the late 60s counterculture and life on the ground of the Viet Nam, with prominent examples including The Big Chill and Forrest Gump. Rolling Stone Magazine raved that the anti-war anthem *Fortunate Son* "rages against class-based draft inequality with rare, beat-driven fury: Even Dylan couldn't pen a protest song that makes you wanna dance." Taking up the topic in general to explore his role in keeping the beat to many of the greatest hits of the anti-war movement, Cosmo proudly paged back to the moment the band knew they had hit the nail on the head with a song very much designed to

> get to the pro-war generation, that was our target audience. We already had the other ones, but we were able to get to a mass audience with that one. You have a very, very, very small group of people who are already there, they were the lunatic fringe, but we got to the masses and there was an important message. We lived through the Viet Nam era and understood and knew what it was about.
>
> To give you another little insight into it, revealed, it's the same foot pattern as *"Proud Mary!"* *"Proud Mary"* was more laid back and had more of that Riverboat-lazy cruisin' down the river thing, but this beat had to be forceful and had to have a different feel. It shows you how notes can be deceiving: you can look at that song on sheet music and they're totally different songs but there's components that are exactly the same. The main difference in *"Fortunate Son"* is just that it had to be powerful, that song was a driving thing, because we were talking about the Man, the Machine, the War, the World and it was a very heavy-weight song, and the beat had to be laid down with conviction.
>
> With *"Run Through the Jungle,"* that song was very dark, so the idea was I used the tom toms almost like in the jungle, even though it was the Viet

> Cong at that time, but the jungle was the jungle. The drum was the first instrument and was originally a tool for sending codes or signals across long distances, and at night, because you couldn't send smoke signals at night. So the drum was created as a communication tool, and it had that sort of deep, very primitive, long, scary effect they way I played it. The pattern on that for the foot is very simple, and it goes back and forth between what I'm doing on the tom toms and the snare. I put a little accent in there, and its definitely spooky, it gets my goose bumps up when I hear it, it's a scary song, and the drums have a lot to do with that song.

Roots Rock, another sub-genre that CCR specialized in popularizing among rock fans for its first time, and today one that's widely known as Americana, is one that Cosmo felt was a natural extension of the band's love of country music, describing a creative process that reflected the country songwriting principles of "keeping things simple, less-is-more, that was our credence certainly as a band, and it fit perfectly with the style of music that we hung our hat on, which was really was American Roots-Blues and Urban Blues, it was a combination of REAL R&B and REAL Country." Echoing his former bandmate, lead singer/songwriter John Fogerty told Country Music Television in 2009 that "about the time my band, Creedence Clearwater Revival, was about to jump off the cliff and become big time, I was kind of musing about writing songs and the whole kind of gumbo that was brewing in my head. I loved country. I loved folk. I loved bluegrass, blues, shoutin', country and city blues and, of course, rock 'n' roll."

The band's 2nd LP, Bayou Country, best reflects this musical melting pot of influences perfected, on display in every player's performances throughout an album that – upon release in January, 1969, as the Rock & Roll Hall of Fame recalled, "elevated Creedence to the most popular rock band in America." Beginning with the # 2 hit that became one of the band's – and Rock & Roll's – most popular hits of all time, *"Proud Mary,"* Clifford divulged of his own musical motives as the band began plotting the song's arrangement together, that

> it could have been a lot more country, and I didn't want it to go there, so my foot pattern – as simple as it is: 1, 2, 3 and 4, so it sets up that backbeat, instead of 1, 2, and 3, 4, 1, 2, and 3, 4. I hear a lot of bands play the song that play it with the 1, 2, and 3, 4, but that was done with a real conscious effort. As little as it might seem, just moving a beat so it doesn't get into a sweet mode, it sets up the 4, and it conveys your pattern, and its kind of laid back. I'm doing some left-hand things that you hear in the solo part especially, but my left hand was active throughout the song in a very supportive, rhythmic role. That was another part of it too: I wanted it to be more than a modified country song. I wanted it to have its own thing.

The hit's B-Side would become another radio staple for the band in the 50 years that followed, and when he reflects back on the impact *"Born on the Bayou"* had at radio, the drummer chuckles at one common mistake fans and fellow drummers alike have made over the years when listening to the song in thinking that "I'm playing on a ride cymbal on that song, which a lot of people do, but I'm not, its all on the hi-hat. Tom-toms were not part of that, the idea was if you have the guitars carry from the beginning to the end that mood, any other breaks – other than what I did, parts of which were cymbal crashes, a lot of them on the 2 and the 4. The foot parts were all very well thought out and practiced, and each note was like that. That's how that one went, just ride it out, keep it true to the actual building blocks, if you will, of the song." Picking it out years later as still among his most prized beats, Cosmo volunteers that

> its still my favorite CCR song, in terms of the record, is *"Born on the Bayou."* When I hear that, its like I'm listening to somebody else, because it just rips ass! I try sometimes to realize, "Yeah, I remember the session, and I played every one of those breaks, and played that groove," and wow, its just so powerful. That's that quarter-note thing, that open feel, that's what gives it its power: by taking notes away, it gives it its power. The accents are played pretty hard and heavy, and you can hear the dynamics of the bass

> drum, when I'm hitting those accents on the cymbals, I mean it! That part of its pretty fun.

Pulling the curtain back on another little-known variation in his instrumental set-up from the traditional drummers of the band's time that helped give Cosmo his unique rhythmic sound, he revealed that "I use 18-inch cymbals on my hi-hat, I created that little thing in 1969 when we put out all those albums, and it really helped the drum sound be defined. I did a lot of work on the ride cymbal, I used to use the ride cymbal as a crash cymbal alot, and so for instance, if you go on Youtube and watch *'Born on the Bayou'* at Woodstock, or at Royal Albert Hall, you'll see I was using that cymbal because I was playing up on the bell and coming down on to that cymbal. On my kit, I only had one crash cymbal and one ride cymbal, and then switched to the 18-inch hi-hats which I still play today, and that really gives you a whole other level of things you can do between the tip and the shank of the drum stick. Depending on how open the cymbals are, you have just a multiplicity of sounds you could do with that, and you really hear it on that song." Needing a drum set capable of handling his pocket, Doug switched from Ludwigs on the bands first two albums to the famed Campco kit fans know from the Woodstock film, explaining that

> I use GWs now, but the Campo back then was a better-made kit: better wood, better craftsmanship, more plies, it was thought out a little bitter, and was ahead of its time. I remember at the time, a friend of mine had taken me down to a drum shop in San Francisco and said "There's a new drum set you need to come down and try out," and so I did, and said "Order me 3 of them," one for my house, one for the rehearsal hall and one for the road, and then we took the one from the factory out on the road as a spare. But they were just a better drum, they projected, and had better tone, so I was like a kid in a candy store with that.

"Green River," another of the band's definitive Americana hits, and the title of an album where Rolling Stone Magazine declared that "they are now creating

the most *vivid* American rock" out there, was an example where Cosmo remembered he had to fight for what he knew was the right feel song, in opposition to the one bandmate John Fogerty had initially heard for the hit. A moment every drummer will run into in a band situation at one point or another in their career, Clifford remembered that

> we were going back and forth, and at one point John said it should have a shuffle feel, and I was thinking to myself, "I don't know about that... We've been playing it a certain way," and when that conversation came up, it was the first we'd ever heard of it, and I said "I don't know what that means, but I know what a shuffle is, and this is definitely not a shuffle song." So I just sort of stuck with it, and wound up playing a rock and roll pattern to it. Its got a little bit different foot pattern, a 2 measure pattern, and just chugs along.

The album would produce two more of CCR's most rotated radio hits, the aforementioned *"Lodi"* and *"Bad Moon Rising,"* the latter of which Cosmo still regards as "a great one, that's that country 2-step groove," while dialing ahead to the group's fifth studio LP, *Cosmo's Factory*, to touch on the story behind the beat that drove the record's biggest hit, *"Lookin' Out My Back Door."* To accompany the song's easy-going feel texturally, the drummer began by recalling that

> I played that with brushes, so that was a little bit of a different take on things, and the bass drum was a marching bass drum that at the time, I had had refinished and was using as a coffee table in my house. I remember John had said, "I sure would like to have something different bass drum sound," and I said "I think I got the answer," brought that thing down, hooked it up, and that's the only song it was ever on. It looked kind of funny in the studio, because I just had a snare drum and that, and a hi-hat and crash cymbal, but it worked.

"Travelin' Band," another of the band's most celebrated and covered anthems from their catalog, raced up the charts to # 2 in the spring of 1970 and captured one

of the best examples of the energy Cosmo was capable of making rocket off the kit, and a song that he remembered was a tribute of sorts where

> I did the beat for that song thinking about Little Richard's band, and that was really a tribute to Little Richard, and we ended up getting sued by Little Richard (laughs) and lost. On that song, the tempo was probably the fastest song we ever recorded. I just wanted to kind of keep up with what might have been played by Little Richard's band.

Touching on a couple other of the band's faster-paced hits, including the frenzied *"Commotion"* – a song that though it never charted still appeared on the band's 8 million-selling *"Chronicle"* Greatest Hits LP - and one of the band's final hits before disbanding, *"Sweet Hitchhiker,"* which appeared on the band's final studio album. In a nod of loyalty to the band's golden era where Tom Fogerty was still a member of the fold, Cosmo began by sharing that "we doesn't play anything from the Trio album *'Mardi Gras'* that came out after Tom left, we only play the quartet stuff, so we don't play *'Sweet Hitchhiker.'* John Fogerty wrote some brilliant songs, of that there is no doubt, but this was not one of them. I liked it because it was up-tempo and was a fun song with no deep meaning." Feeling a bit more affection toward *"Commotion,"* Clifford remains proud of his playing on the track for the unusual fact that

> I led with my left hand on that, and I remember it was one of those ones I had to take home and break down and really spend time on to make it work. It had some R&B in it, but sped up a little bit, and it's a pretty quick time. The bass drum pattern is pretty simple, but I doubled it in the choruses, and on the beat, its all 8 notes in those sections. So it's a mover.

One of the final shining moments in CCR's prolific marathon run of 7 albums in the 4 years came with the release of 1970 Top 10 smash *"Have You Ever Seen the Rain."* Among the most beloved and moving songs within the band's catalog of Greatest Hits, Cosmo remembered the song as a reflection of the true level of stress pulling and pushing within the band at this point in the studio due to the fact that

> there was a lot of tension in the band at that time. You could walk into the band room and feel it. Tom was getting ready to leave and the brothers were at it and the business was in total shambles, and the song was about that. That's why it was written by John, and I understood it certainly because I was in the middle of that forest too, and it happened that it wasn't a rock song. The beat for that one really had to be strong but supportive of that acoustic-guitar type thing, which to me was the foundation of the chord-playing instruments, which in our case meant all stringed-instruments, all guitars. So in order to make it work, it had to be powerful, but it couldn't overpower that acoustic feeling. I had to make sure that I didn't overpower that song, but at the same time, it was emotionally powerful because I had seen the rain, and it was all around me, all of us. *"Long As I Can See the Light"* was another one like that that took 22 takes to record. There was just something going on with that one, there was a lot going on in the studio and so on and so forth.

Though Creedence Clearwater Revival would break up in 1971 at the height of their popularity, his role in helping to keep the band's catalog of classics alive for newer generations of fans along with the band's longtime listeners – many of whom now bring their kids to shows – is still the greatest thrill for Clifford, who has toured the world for the past 20 years alongside bassist Stu Cook with Creedence Clearwater Revisited. Still one of Rock & Roll's greatest rhythm sections, for Cosmo, the magic of the duo's pocket has always been an extension of

> where I started and where he started. Its where we were learning to play, and I did a lot of things – especially coming from the instrumental band – I did a lot of things off the guitar in our first Junior High incarnation of the band. There was no bass at that time: Stu's left hand was his bass, on the piano. So I would work on a song with the perspective of what the guitar

was doing and try to accent that since it was the only instrument. When Stu switched over to the bass, it made a huge difference in what we were doing and now we were rock & roll, so it was a lift for me because I had the support on the low end.

We don't think about it, its like a hand and glove, we're two parts of this formula and its very comfortable. Once and a while I'll throw that little snappy break, just for him, and he turns around and claps. You have to do that too, you can't take it all too seriously, so we have fun. That's the whole idea of what we do, and the whole idea of rock & roll music is to have fun, and let the pressure cooker go down a little bit in life. That's what I tell the audience when I'm introduced, is "Hey, the idea is to have as much fun as we can while we're taking up space on the planet," and rock & roll is all of that, that's why it was invented.

With our older fans, we get people that tell us "This song got me through Viet Nam," we get a lot of that, and then of course, there's the back of the 57 Chevy with his girlfriend, I hear a lot of those (laughs). We take the music seriously but we don't take ourselves seriously, which is a nice way to do this. The idea is to have fun, and some people sometimes forget that, but we don't. For me, I'm an adrenaline junkie, and I love relating with our fans. That's always been the real connection between what we do and people. The recording side of its more the scientific side, while I've always felt the live side's more the artistic side. You're coming out and people are anticipating a certain song or songs, and when that song comes around you can feel the energy to it.

With so much time spent with the songs on the road, Cosmo confesses that "I don't listen too often to the original music," and when pressed to pick a favorite, like so many of his peers, the pressure proves nearly impossible for the simple truth that "they're all our children. I have 3 children and 5 grandchildren, and they're all different, but you love them the same, and that's just how it works.

So I'm just proud of the work, of all of us, not just what I did. We had a dream when we were 13 years old, and however it turned out, we still have the legacy of music, which is the dream." When passing advice on to the Millennial generation of drummers with the same dream he had at that same age, Clifford begins by offering some brick-and-mortar pointers, starting first and foremost with a heavy emphasis on the age-old adage that

> practice makes permanent, that's another thing, make sure you're practicing the right things, because its twice as hard to undo something as it is to go in the right way. I don't know that my way is the right way, I'm a self-taught guy, but I always had the feel in there, and that's always been my bottom line. Practice puts you in a certain comfort zone, and then once you get to a certain point, then you get out of that comfort zone and challenge yourself and try and move up the latter. Its your latter, and you take whatever speed you want, its really up to you where you want to go and how fast you want to do it, but always look back and remember the basics. Staying in shape, that's key too. I'm at less than 10% body fat, and I'm 69 years old but have the stats of a professional athlete. Never got into the cocaine, and stay away from drugs like that for sure.
>
> If you're in band situation, work together and share your ideas and try things out and if they work they work, if they don't they don't, but you've grown, and that one that doesn't work on a particular song may work on another one. So you don't discard something just because it doesn't fit into one specific idea. Just try and understand musicality of what it is you're working on. From the business side, I always tell people: don't sign anything, (laughs), unless you have a good lawyer, and finding a good lawyer is pretty hard, one that you can trust. So don't sign anything, that's all I can tell you on that.

Above all the accolades the band has received throughout the past 50 years as their legacy has been further realized and acknowledged - including such milestones as induction into the Rock & Roll Hall of Fame, making the cover of Rolling Stone Magazine and a ranking on their coveted list of the 100 Greatest Artists of All Time, playing Woodstock, induction into the 2014 Grammy Hall of Fame, and the ready relevance of being one of the most-rotated classic rock radio catalogs of the past 40 years - for Cosmo, nothing ever quite beats hearing that his playing inspired someone else to pick up the sticks and learn to keep their own behind the kit, confirming in closing that

> that means the world to me, especially guys that are in bands that have had success and just the guy who plays on the weekends. I call it "passing the baton." I remember when I met Al Jackson Jr. in Stax Records, who was my idol, and he mentored me as we did a lot of shows with Booker T and the MGs, not by showing me how to hold a stick, but he told me things, things that made huge, huge sense to me and really helped me in my direction as a player. There was a reason for that baton, and now at this point in my career, I'm handing it out.
>
> I see a lot of these younger guys that are around, we recently did a festival where there were 25 bands on the bill, and I remember while we were playing our set there were 12 of the drummers standing on the side of the stage watching me play, and each one of them wanted a picture, and told me I was one of their influences. And man, that's as good as it gets! That's better than the Rock & Roll Hall of Fame or any of that!

"I'm still just beginning to scratch the surface as far as what's possible on the drums. I hear stuff every day that gets me excited. So I think for me musically, its still the tip of the iceberg." – Jimmy Chamberlin, 2016

Chapter 11: Jimmy Chamberlin of Smashing Pumpkins - The Jazz Drummer

Most Smashing Pumpkins fans agree *"I Am One"* is among the coolest Rock & Roll drum beats of all time, and most drummers agree, one of the hardest to play. As album openers go, its equally celebrated as one of the catchiest, and its genius operator, Jimmy Chamberlin – ranked #60 on Rolling Stone Magazine's 100 Greatest Drummers list – the driver behind the song's supersonic speed, reveals at the top of our conversation that it "was really begat out of a drum machine beat that Billy had come up with that was really almost impossible to play on a drum kit. Its just one of those things where somebody writes something on a drum machine with absolutely no idea of kind of hand-and-foot proximity, and then 'Hey, what do you think about this?' 'Oh, it sounds great,' 'Well, can you play it?', 'Well, I can come back in a week and play it, but in order to play it faithfully, I've gotta do a single paradiddle on my floor tom and then bring my left hand…' Often times, we would look to each other, because drummers after a while, they kind of exhaust their repertoire, so its good to go to somebody who has no idea what drums mechanically can be, and have them offer up ideas. There's a pedagogical component to learning that stuff, so with 'I Am One,' that was really the genesis of kind of moving my big tom over to the left was just trying to assimilate that beat."

"One of modern rock's most potent forces" in the opinion of their hometown paper, The Chicago Tribune, the Smashing Pumpkins took alternative rock by thundering storm in 1991 when they roared onto the scene with their debut LP, *Gish*, and while frontman/songwriter Billy Corgan's genius was obvious throughout the album, so too was Chamberlin as the Mitch Mitchell to Corgan's Jimi Hendrix. Validating this playing parallel, Drummer World Magazine pointed out that while "it certainly helped to have a singer/songwriter of Billy Corgan's caliber fronting the group, the importance of Chamberlin's drumming on the Pumpkins' music cannot be understated…(He was) a glove-like fit for the wide range of material the Pumpkins produced in their existence."

In that spirit, as pockets go, Chamberlin and frontman/mastermind Billy Corgan have one of Rock & Roll's tightest, an intuitive synergy that producer Butch Vig remembered as central to the band's sound because "in terms of playing, a lot of that sort of feel in his guitar playing came from his playing with Jimmy Chamberlin. They had a real sort-of unconscious feel for how they grooved together, it was sort of a push-pull thing." That musical Ying-Yang, for the legendary drummer, has always centered first and foremost in Chamberlin's feeling that

> Billy's a great barometer for my playing, he knows what I'm capable of and he challenges me to move beyond what I think I'm capable of, and I hope he'd say the same thing about me. We both have a great admiration and respect for each other's talents, and I've heard him do things on the guitar

> that are literally like Coltrain-level lead runs, and just stream of consciousness stuff that I've never heard anther guitar player do.

Chamberlain's ability to listen and respond delicately as he did powerfully to Corgan's mercurial songwriting was executed with an orchestral grace on the drum set that Modern Drummer Magazine argued was ground-breaking for its infusion of "an unmistakable flavor of jazz and an embracing of drumming technique: grace notes, ferocious fills, cutting rimshots, and sizzling single-stroke rolls – signature Chamberlin licks…(that) weren't all that common with the 'modern' rock drummers…when the Smashing Pumpkins debuted with *Gish*." Proudly crediting his native genre during the album's writing and arranging as "our secret weapon," Jimmy confirmed that

> I listened to a ton of Jazz and I love to play quiet and loud in the same song, and bring stuff way, way down so you'd have these super-impact moments, and a lot of guys that I work with, they don't understand that. You're getting gated or compressed out of those situations, and Butch is one of the best facilitators of that stuff. So you could say, "Oh, he gets a great drum sound," but Butch knows that the drums sound great anyway, he's just getting the sound.

Tracing his lineage as a Jazz drummer back through the childhood filter of his Rock & Roll heroes behind the kit as he was first inspired to pick up the sticks by the same 70s rock and metal influences his bandmate Billy Corgan was, from Deep Purple to The Who, Led Zeppelin, and Jimi Hendrix. Discovering almost as quickly as he did his unique talent as a drummer that he had more in common with his hero's heroes from the Jazz golden age, a young Jimmy soon began raiding both his brother and sister's record collections for equal input:

> My family is kind of an interesting place: I was the youngest of six kids, and I had a brother who was a drummer and was very into Rock, so Ian Pace obviously is a huge influence for me, and Bobby Caldwell, who played with

> Captain Beyond, is huge, and the usual suspects like Keith Moon, John Bohnam, and Ginger Baker.
>
> But then as my playing evolved, which is quickly did when I was a kid, my sister Laura was really into Jazz, and I absorbed guys like Elvin Jones, Tony Williams, Weather Report, Peter Erstein, Billy Cobham, Phil Collins, Brand X – just all of those guys. Any of that fusion stuff that was going on in the late 70s, early 80s I was listening to, because at least for me, all of us good drummers – if I can include myself in that group – we're all just trying to find our inner Tony Williams. At some point, that's the kind of goal of all drumming, as far as I'm concerned.

By the time he'd hooked up with Billy Corgan and company and begun introducing his unique Jazz-Rock influence into Alternative Rock, Chamberlain's playing proved the perfect rhythmic compliment to what the BBC praised as "arrangements swerving rather than stomping in typical hard-rock fashion, yielding surprises with each turn," adding that "for all its sensitivity to flow, the group could crush your skull when you least expected it, going from near-silence to a thunderclap." Tracing the source of that power within his sound not to the tuning of his drums, the size of the room he recorded in or the amazing ears of drummer/producer Butch Vig, Jimmy shared his feeling first and foremost that

> I know that my sound just comes out of my hands and comes out of my feet, and that's the good news and the bad news, because all drummers bring their tone and their habits with them, and you can't tune that out. So, for me, I found fortunately or unfortunately, it kind of sounds like me no matter what kit I'm playing on, and that's where Butch is such a genius because he knows, within reason, that his job is to just capture what's there – and I think better than anybody. He records drums with so little coloration and so much accuracy as far as like, there's not a ton of difference between where I'm sitting listening to my drum kit, and what I hear coming out of the speakers with Butch.

> That's like a drummer's wet dream, because then I know my bass line dynamics are gonna be where they need to be, I'm not overcompensating for anything and I can pull and push where I want, and volumes and velocities can be done without having to think about compression and other things that are going on. So recording with somebody like Butch – being a drummer – he understands that probably better than anybody, and the Pumpkins especially were all about dynamics.

The influence of *Gish* would be felt as "the first shot of the alternative revolution that transformed the rock & roll landscape of the '90s," as Billboard attested, and Chamberlin's artillery of choice for delivering that historic bang was a Pearl BLX set, one the drummer felt was reliable to handle his attack because

> it was a Birch kit, which was super-focused, a lot of attack, and then the snare on that kit Butch Vig's old Yamaha recording series steel shell, which is like a late 80s Yamaha steel drum that you got if you bought the mid-80s recording series. Just really a great drum, and that sound went on to kind of launch a thousand snares later on, including my own signature snare.

Chamberlin's signatures would be written all over the album's wholly original beatscapes, many of which contained complexities Jimmy had composed prior to joining the band, such that "as far as Gish goes, a lot of that stuff – like *'Tristessa'* – I had in my back pocket. I had been exploring intros like that, and had a perfect vehicle for it." That conveyance of creative ideas back and forth between the Pumpkins' members would provide just as powerful a muse as the band's natural musical brainstorm rained down moment after moment of inspired genius:

> Alot of it – like *"Suffer"* – was just stream of consciousness. When he would play a riff, I would just react, and generally because him and I were most of the time on the same musical wave length, the first thing we each played was kind of what ended up being on the record. I don't know if that's usually the way things happen with other bands, but we had very few disagreements.

> I can't pinpoint any specific times where, other than kind of turning the beat around, where we would stop and go "Oh, that doesn't work." We were very intuitive, and we'd listened to a lot of the same stuff, so our idea of where the destination was both rhythmically and harmonically was often times very similar.

Hailed as "without a doubt the debut album of the year" by SPIN Magazine, by the time the band was preparing to release their highly-anticipated sophomore LP, *Siamese Dream*, Drummer World reported that "Chamberlin's playing had begun to turn many a drummer on their ear," setting up expectations just as high among fans for what he would deliver in the way of new innovations rhythmically as they were fired up to hear what new musical revelations Billy Corgan would lay down overtop that foundation. A band always about discovery and expansion within their musical travels, as a co-pilot on that creative journey, the drummer was grateful that

> again, I think Corgan created a great vehicle in which I could express myself to my fullest capabilities and that just got pushed even further on Siamese, because I think Gish was a very youthful and exuberant record, but with Siamese, we went swinging and we knew we had the goods. We had gotten enough validation from our contemporaries and the market place around Gish to know that we could go in and push it even further, so when you can walk into a studio like that, that's when you can really write those songs like Silver Fuck and even the solos, we had not so much a swagger but a confidence that really elevates the music. Those were great vehicles for me to express the very peak of my ability, so when you get those chances and the universe opens up like that, you're going for it, right?!

Highlighting the dazzling tom aerobatics that open *"Silver Fuck"* as one of his favorite examples of the reactive inspiration that tumbled out of he and Corgan's back and forth pushing each other creatively to the peak of their respective bests, crediting Corgan as much as he does himself for coming up with

> an incredibly crazy drum beat, but you've got to find somebody who can write a song to where you can fit that drum beat in, and the open roll between the right foot and the left hand going around the toms and the off-beat snare thing, just having a partner that can feed you that type of stuff automatically puts you in a whole other arena as far as drumming because there's a lot of guys who can play that stuff, but I was so fortunate to have been able to evolve my playing within the context of those songs. I mean, a lot of guys can go and play that stuff in their practice room, but how many guys are showing up to band practice and go back and forth with their guitar player over riffs like that.

Chamberlin's tirelessly imaginative talent for conjuring up instantly catchy, memorable introductions that made the start of any Pumpkins song that much more exciting heading into the Rock & Roll roller coasters that always followed were on full display at the top of both of the album's smash singles, *"Cherub Rock"* and *"Today,"* which Blender later noted was so infectious that it "achieved a remarkable status as one of the defining songs of its generation." Knowing he needed to bring the fire to what he recognized instantly as a smoking hot hit, Jimmy recalled the day

> I remember Corgan walking in and just driving himself nuts with the fact that we had this obviously bust-out hit but no way to get into the song other than "1, 2, 3…", and we were like "We can't! That's not the start of the song," and then said "God, it needs kind of this twinkley guitar…" and he just played the damn thing, and we were like "Ah, that's it!" I think for us, it was always just kind of a product of knowing what we needed and not being satisfied until it all clicked.
>
> With *"Cherub Rock,"* I remember we were always talking about intros, because we always had songs. The song part was easy, but how the hell do you start that thing? "So with the snare roll, I want the thing to be announced, so let's do like a Military drum roll," those are just ideas you talk about, and

> then somebody plays the thing and you go "Oh, that's it." You have to understand, it was just natural, none of that stuff was really contrived. It was discussed, but it was really like "Okay, this sounds good, do we agree it sounds good? Okay, let's move on…"

Entrusting those executive production decisions almost entirely to Billy when he lays down takes in the studio, Chamberlin has always been grateful for Corgan's instincts as a producer in his own right, specifically in knowing when the drummer has delivered the perfect performance to match what the frontman's hearing in his own head as the band's songwriter. A power of projection that has allowed the frontman to push Jimmy time and again into new territory ahead of where the he – let alone his fans – necessarily knew a drummer could go beforehand, its an understanding he clearly considers visionary on Corgan's part:

> He's got an understanding of my ability that I don't have, so he knows what that intangible is in my playing. If I listen to two takes, and I think one may be marginally better than another, and he picks the one I think is probably not as good, he's probably got better reasons that I do. He's just more objective when it comes to my playing, and he's got the holistic picture of the song in mind: he's listening to all the components that are going to go over the top of it, so he's a great barometer for a great drum performance. He can say, "That's it, we don't need to go any further," where I'll be ready to do more takes, and he'll say "No, its not going to get any better than that, that's the take, that's exactly what I need." So he's a great facilitator.
>
> As a player, when he's oiled up and practiced, I mean not a lot of guys can touch him, even including like Holdsworth and those guys. Technically, maybe yes, but from a song and a melodic and a harmonic sense, at least for me and for my taste, that's really like the best guitar can be. So I think knowing that and knowing that he's got that in his tool belt, I really trust him when it comes to his opinion of what I'm doing.

Siamese Dream took over the Generation X airwaves as a phenomenon upon release in the summer of 1993, selling 6 million copies worldwide as the Pumpkins' influence washed like a tsunami over the direction of Alternative Rock. "One of the era's cornerstones," the band's hometown paper The Chicago Tribune would declare, Rolling Stone Magazine would congratulate Siamese as "a strong, multidimensional extension of Gish that confirms that Smashing Pumpkins are neither sellouts nor one-offs. Now the band can get on with worrying about its third album." With the ambitious plans they already had in mind for the double-album *Mellon Collie and the Infinite Sadness,* there was plenty to juggle musically for the band's drummer, who – in his constant quest for musical growth – was eager to take advantage of the input the band's new producer, Flood, had to offer in the way of suggestion. Underscoring the importance of a drummer's being a great listener first and foremost, not just to the song they're reacting to but also to being constantly open to new approaches one might be encouraged to try at the behest of more-experienced creative collaborators:

> Flood just opened my eyes to all the things that drums could be or could not be, and to this day, the way that I think about drum parts and the necessity of components in drum parts has everything to do with my relationship with Flood, because he was the ultimate questioner, like "Why are you doing that? Explain to me why that needs to be there?", and you would have to really validate everything you did. Everything had to have value, and it really taught me that once you really dig into a part, there's things that are necessary and things that aren't, and Flood would just ask you to do different versions of songs, just trying to get to your answer for what the song really needed.
>
> Songs like *"Blue Skies Bring Cheers,"* we would do a number of different permutations of that song just to arrive where we needed to arrive on the version that was going on the record. And some days we would show up and Flood would have removed all my cymbals, and moved my drums around, and I'd say "What are we doing?", and he'd say "I want you to play

> the song," and I'd laugh and reply, "Well, I can't play the song without any cymbals," and he said "I want you to try and play the song with just these components and let's see foundationally what it is that really matters about what you're doing." So Flood brought a ton of wisdom to the table.

Breaking a rule where the drummer revealed "no Pumpkin record was ever recorded with a click," Chamberlin agreed to apply the approach at Flood's suggestion on " *'1979'* and *'Try, Try, Try'* because we sped the drums up, but I think that's it. We didn't use a click on anything else." Delving into some of the other focal points of experimentation with rhythm that went on within the album's production, Jimmy recalled that

> sonically, obviously, we were doing tons of crazy stuff where, I would play to a click sped up and then I would slow the drums down, or we would play the drums really slow at like 60 BPM and then speed it up. Songs like *"Try, Try, Try"* for instance, I think we recorded at half-speed and then sped the drums up, so you got that super-crisp kind of compressed sound, tons of stuff like that, and working with delay settings.
>
> With *"1979,"* that was "Hey, let's figure out how to make this pop in a Pumpkins context, where its your sound but still have it sound very drum-machiney," that was a great example of that.

When putting together the tumbling avalanche of tom work that charged through the opening build of Billy Corgan's riff as *"Bullet with Butterfly Wings"* takes flight, Jimmy remembered wanting to create an almost volcanic eruption within the energy of the pocket driving what became the album's biggest hit, winning the Grammy for Best Hard Rock Performance and becoming their first Top 40 hit on the Billboard Hot 100 Singles Chart. Knowing instantly that he was listening to a hit as soon as

> Billy brought that to the table, and at first, he just had the chorus and had the lyric "Despite all my rage I am still just a rat in a cage." I remember he

> busted out that lyric while we were playing a gig in Frankfurt one day, and I remember because Earl from Bad Brains was there, and I remember being really nervous about playing that night. So I remember the gig specifically and he didn't have the guitar riff yet at that point, so that song was pretty much written by him. Back then, we could play stuff like that and just kind of reel it off, and not really have a lot of discussion around it. I remember we were doing a lot of stuff with toms, and a lot of stuff with heavy, thudding toms, we wanted to get something like that on the record, so if you listen to the B-Sides on that record and a lot of stuff that's reminiscent of that type of groove, so we were kind of zeroing in on that stuff to the point where it culminated in *"Bullet."*

When his attention was turned to the considerably slower-tempo performance on the band's smash hit ballad, *"Tonight, Tonight,"* Jimmy broke out what Billboard argued was another skill as a player "equally important to the band: his tasteful, understated playing on their quieter numbers. This oft-overlooked side of his ability revealed a musician of considerable depth and creativity with a keen ear for nuance." Vs. reacting spontaneously to Billy in the moment, Chamberlin used the opportunity to bust out some new chops he'd been working up on his own:

> That was very organic, the first time I heard that song, I had a lot of those parts in my back pocket that I'd been wanting to break out. Especially the orchestrated snare drum part, I'd been looking for a vehicle to play that type of drumming in, so there's a lot of stuff when you're in a band like the Pumpkins, you know you're going to get an opportunity to play things that are in your wheelhouse, its just a matter of waiting for the vehicle to come around.

Time Magazine would hail the album as "the group's most ambitious and accomplished work yet," and by the end of the 1990s, even though he'd left the band by then, Jimmy's reputation had been cemented "as the propulsive engine driving the Smashing Pumpkins," Billboard noted, adding that in the process,

"Chamberlin earned respect as one of the most popular, influential drummers of the '90s." Following his absence on 1998's *Adore* which favored programmed drum tracks, the drummer would triumphantly return to his place behind the kit on the band's 2000's *Machina/The Machines of God*. His second outing with Flood working behind the boards as producer, their work together marked the apex where Jimmy felt the band finally "got – in my opinion – to where we always wanted to be sonically, I think that record for me, drums-wise with the distortion and the omni-compression on the snare drum, and the crispy-and-crunchiness of those drums and how they interface with the guitar dynamics, I think is really from a production stand point really our crowning achievement."

Following the old-school spontaneous model of tracking that his Jazz heroes had back in their glory day of capturing the live off-the-floor energy of their performance together in the studio, the drummer smiles sharing his memory of what is becoming more and more of a lost art in modern recording:

> We just recorded live to tape, no Protools, nothing, no click, just "Hey, it feels good or it doesn't feel good," and we'd go for good drum takes and then build the song around it, but we never used clicks. Obviously, that gets prohibitive at some point and there's points in a lot of songs where things dip down or speed up, but we always thought that was just the way we played. We never got caught up in gridding or a lot of that other stuff, because it either sounds good or it doesn't. The records we were listening to – Duke Ellington, Thelonious Monk, Cream – there was variance in the songs just because nobody really played to a click back then, and that's the stuff we were really endearing ourselves to, so we just never did it.

Synched back up with Billy Corgan as if no time had passed, impressing Rolling Stone Magazine championed the fact that "Chamberlin's drums stand shoulder to shoulder with the guitars. The band's chemistry demands human muscle, not machine precision, and with Chamberlin back in place, the music surges forward again." Proud of the progression the band pushed themselves once again to make, raising the bar to a new level where

> the songwriting and the production really hit the same point, that was where it all kind of fell in the same basket, so when you listen to *"Untitled"* or *"Real Love,"* arrangementally, sonically, and the way it was written and where the song goes, I think that's as in lock-step as the band's ever been. Then on something like *"The Sacred and Profane,"* Flood had me playing two different drum beats independent of each other and then looping them over the top, stuff like that I had never done before, just playing over myself.
>
> I think on *"Everlasting Gaze"* we used a big 24-inch bass drum, and drums-wise, it was maple customs all around, and then, I had a green kit made that was basically just different sizes of bass drums. I would use anything from a 22", 24-inch bass drum on some of the stuff, just different configurations, nothing crazy, but more sizes, more choices, but really drums for me were all about sonically – with all the guitars that we had going on – it was important to pick the right drum sizes that would fit in sonically, or find some room within the song to be heard. That's where the Maple was a better choice back then than the Birch because it had a wider harmonic range, and wider tonal range, so you could literally insert it into those multi-guitar tracks a little bit more successfully than some of the other kits. Then there were just tons of various different snare drums. Snare drums probably I changed the most, I think there's a different snare on if not every song, almost every song, on *Machina.*

Coming back to the mothership for one more ride in 2005 was initially something of a challenge conceptually for Chamberlin, who by that point had returned his focus as a player full circle back home to his roots as a Jazz drummer, confessed that, as a consequence, he had to dust off the image of himself as a "Rock" hitter to see if it still felt like a fit:

> I think for me personally as a musician, it represented a little bit of going back and discovering kind of what the key components are, or were, in baking that kind of cake. I had evolved my playing pretty considerably when we started working together again in 05. I had done the ZWAN record, which was a bit of a departure from the Pumpkins, but then I'd worked on my own solo stuff, the Jimmy Chamberlin Complex, which is more representative of my fusion type of drumming, and more kind of rooted in the Tony Williams type of playing.
>
> So to go back and do a Pumpkin record kind of post that journey, it really dictated that I go back and listen and learn how to be that drummer again, and its tough when you have to do that, because as a musician, you want to move on, but then the struggle is like, "What is the brand of the Pumpkins? Does it sound like Pumpkins?" And often times, when you go back and listen to yourself play your early records – not so much *Gish*, because *Gish* is a very representative of a time. But *Siamese Dream/Mellon Collie* was representative of like an evolution in drumming, and when things are moving forward, you go back and you listen and say, "Okay, I like that and I like that, but I don't necessarily think I would have made that choice now…" So you've got to go back and make a judgment call as to kind of what has value, and you've got to be objective in doing that.

Solving the conundrum by infusing his Jazz sensibilities much more presently into his playing as a Rock drummer, with the BBC taking impressed note within the results that "Chamberlain is still a drummer not to be trifled with, and there will be moments when listeners may wonder, like on the taut, puncturing *'7 Shades Of Black',* how exactly the former jazz drummer hits his snares that hard without his elbows disintegrating into dust. Top work, fella." Proud to bring his fusion brand of rock drumming current with Pumpkins' fans, Jimmy affirms that

> I would say the drumming on *Zeitgeist* is more representative of my affinity for Tony Williams, Elvin Jones, Art Blakey, Jack Dasionette – when I listen to my playing now, I hear a lot more of that stuff than I probably gave myself credit for back then. Back then, we were all trying to be rock guys, but I think even if I listen to Matt Cameron now, I hear a lot more Elvin than I do anything else at this point.
>
> On the *Zeitgeist* record, I had been with Yamaha since 93 and I had them make me – specifically for that record – a new maple custom Absolute kit to play on that record. My Yamaha kits are kind of different: I would have them do different bearing edges for me, so a lot of times, we would do thicker floor tom shells with 60 degree bearing edges as opposed to 45, so the idea would be that you'd get a little bit more of the shell resonance than you would with a 45 where you get more of a head-attacky sound. With the more slopey bearing edge, you're getting more head than shell interactivity, and that's really the foundation of that sound on *Zeitgeist.* It's a little bit different than a normal Maples kit, but for my ears, its between kind of Maple and Birch.

Even with his stylistic shift in focus, fans felt the drummer's return to the band's fold was a smart play on Corgan's part, one the Riverfront Times complimented as "a good move" where the Pumpkins' classic fundamentals are alive and well on singles like *"Starz"* and *"United States,"* arguing that Chamberlin's "influence on the new songs is clearly a positive one, at least in terms of keeping *Zeitgeist* reigned-in and focused." Jimmy remembered his highlight in creating these drum performances and others coming with the opportunity to record with the legendary Roy Thomas Baker, reflective of the rock side of the drummer's roots, and an encounter that turned him into an instant teenager again:

> Roy will spend 4 days on the bass drum and have the greatest time in the world, which is more in line with what I like to do, and obviously hanging out with Roy every day was literally like going to College. The guy is a tire-

> less worker, he was the first guy there and the last guy to leave every day, and he brought so much knowledge and so much fun and so much joy to the experience, and so many great stories. I can't remember an experience ever in my life musically where I learned so much. I thank God man, I can't even believe we were able to make records before we met that guy, because he's just a walking encyclopedia of just so much great technique.
>
> *"Starz"* was the first song we recorded with Roy, and the drums obviously are massive and super-distorted and sound like they're going to rip your face off. When we got into tracking "Starz," Roy loved that song, and really loved the breakdown, so I wanted to do a drum part where in the chorus there was no snare drum, where it was just kind of bashing, that was the perfect vehicle for it. I'd been looking for a place on a record to just lay out the snare, so when we got to that chorus, it was just a great vehicle in which to do that. Then I wanted to do a drum solo in the middle of the song, and I'm thinking "Man, this is going to be like a pop song, right? How are we gonna do something that's still hooky enough to where the song's not going to run out of gas, and people aren't gonna go, "Oh My Gosh, drum solo..." So we had done some stuff with clicking on the sticks before, and I think it was Billy who was like "Let's do some stuff with playing the rims" and that type of thing, and that's just how that stuff evolved.

With *"United States,"* where the band was in pursuit in the studio of what PopMatters.com would later note they produced "every bit the classic 'big moment' that a Pumpkins album truly needs to succeed on the most visceral of levels" with the song, Chamberlin remembered a marathon push for perfection among everyone involved that was required because

> the song was so complicated and we had just kind of finished writing it that, arrangementally, there was a lot going on, and I think it was take 12 or 13 that ended up being on the record. It was just one of those days where were like, "Man, I know we can get this just a little bit better," and Billy would

> chime in and say "Do you think you got another one in you?", and I was like "Hell yeah man, let's keep going until we can get it that one better," and I think at that point, our manager walked in, and it was just one of those magical takes where we delivered that performance and we were both like "Okay, that's it. It ain't gonna get any better than that." Again, you're talking about a seamless take all the way through for a song that's 9, 10 minutes long and it's a nerve-racking experience. I don't care who you are, if you're going in and recording to a grid and recording to Protools, you're thinking at some point, somebody's got your back: if I make a mistake, somebody can fix it somewhere and they're going to Beat Detective the damn thing anyway. I hear that in drumming so much when I listen to records now. I like to just hit the tape and know you delivered the performance, and that's the take you've gotta live with for the rest of your life, because if you don't get it, then you're screwed, right? But that type of intensity and focus has everything to do with why the Pumpkins records sound like they do. People would say "Man, you guys are playing like your lives depended on it," and my reply is always "Yeah, because our lives did depend on it!" (laughs) We didn't have a net, you know...

After doubling in his role as both drummer and co-producer, when the album was finished and shipped out to fans, Jimmy remembered feeling a sense of satisfaction at the fact he'd helped successfully push the band into the new musical territory where Billy needed to head in to keep the band relevant, convincing critics like Rolling Stone Magazine in the process that "the cumulative effect of his distortion-orchestra guitar and drummer Jimmy Chamberlin's pinpoint thunder is impressive and convincing, a return to the big pop-wise din of 1993's *Siamese Dream...(Zeitgeist)* makes it a strong new start for Corgan and Chamberlin." For the drummer, the latest summit felt like more of a continuation of his broader push to raise the musical conversation with each and every new challenge he and Corgan's unique chemistry conquered on record:

> The thing I hold closest about the Pumpkins catalog is just the evolution. We're great musicians, and really had a cogent understanding of sonic destinations when we started on this journey, and I look at the art between what was *Gish* and the young exuberance in that record, and then the sonic maturity in Machina, and even *Zeitgeist* to some extent, I'm really proud of the evolution. I think that was key to the Pumpkins, that we were always evolving, and always evolving in a context that was not only pleasant to us, but somewhat mainstream as well.
>
> Some people kind of piss on that as being a cop-out or a sell-out, but its extremely difficult to have success in a modern cultural context and satisfy yourself. I don't know – and I can't speak for any other artist – but I never felt like compromising the band, and I know a lot of drummers who never got an opportunity to play in a band that allowed them to stretch out like that, and maybe that's because they didn't want to, or maybe because that's just the way things happen, but when I look at that, I see a moment in universal time and thank God we were there to kind of live it and you guys were all there to hear it.

Today, though he reunited with Corgan in the summer of 2015 for a Smashing Pumpkins arena run, Jimmy outside of his limited Pumpkins' reunions remains steeped deeply in his identity as a Jazz artist, releasing a prolific bevy of new projects in recent years including The Jimmy Chamberlin Project's appropriately-titled *Life Begins Again* in 2005, and 2010's *Great Civilizations* LP with Skysaw. Discussing in detail his recent successes in the Jazz world playing with many of the finest musicians working in the genre today, the drummer begins by revealing his feeling that

> I'm still just beginning to scratch the surface as far as what's possible on the drums. I hear stuff every day that gets me excited. So I think for me musically, its still the tip of the iceberg: I've got a brand new Jimmy Chamberlin Complex record coming out with Billy Mohler that we just recorded

4 songs for, and I've got the great Ben Wendel playing Sax on that, and Adam Benjamin on keys, and Sean Wilson on guitar, and I've released two records with Frank Catalano, the great Sax player from Chicago, and both of them have gone to # 1 on the iTunes Jazz chart, and one's up for a Grammy Nomination right now.

There's another project called "God's Gonna Cut You Down" which is an organ trio record and we just redid some tracks with David Sanborn on them, then there's another one called Love Supreme Collective that we did a couple years ago that is an homage to the great record by John Coltrain that we reconceptualized with the great Percy Jones from Brand X, which was a dream come true for me. I had stolen so many drum parts from that Brand X "Unorthodox Behavior" Phil Collins record that when I finally got to play with Percy, I thought "Maybe he'll call me out for ripping off Phil Collins!" (laughs) because half of my licks were based on those records. So it was just a great joy to play with him.

So that's definitely where I'm at right now, and even Billy was remarking when we did the Pumpkins tour, "Oh man, I've never heard you play so relaxed and so graceful before," and those parts were always at the top of my ability and years later, going back and trying to play those songs, there was a lot of ramp-up time. For this tour, we only rehearsed for 4 days and I was ready to rock, and it had everything to do with the music I'm playing now because the Jazz stuff is so fucking hard to play.

You can't show up and play *"Impressions"* at 160 BPM and phone it in, you've got to be practicing, because most of the audiences are other jazz musicians, so you've got to show up with you're A game. I think that's been great for me, and getting written up in Downbeat and having Jazz records on the charts and working with Frank is really such a joy. Its such a great vehicle to just purely be an instrumentalist, and be representative of your instrument as opposed to the Pumpkins, who represent something that's branded

> and there's a bunch of constraints that go along with playing in that band. It has to be certain things, its gotta be representative of a certain point in time, and I've done so much other stuff musically, and that's been my saving grace is I'm not just the drummer in the Pumpkins, I've got this other Jazz thing going on and am an artist in so many other ways.
>
> I played a gig last night in Detroit with my Jazz combo, my quartet, and I was just thinking about what a great drummer Tony Williams was, and was thinking, "Its just so hard to play that music with power and intensity like Tony did." We were doing impressions, like John Coltrane and some other quick Bop stuff, and learning how to play that stuff with power and accuracy, it's a whole 'nother journey.

For those drummers just beginning their own journeys based on the inspiration Chamberlin might have passed along through his own playing over the years, in dispensing words of wisdom that have guided him throughout his own 25 year career, he returns time and again to his first love of simply sitting down behind his instrument to play. Striving in that process to give his best as a musician back to the universe that has brought him so much success because of that dedication to excellence, he hammers home the old-school importance of

> just practicing in general, which is a labor of love for me. Just last night, I had this gig that I spent a considerable amount of time getting ready for, and then I remember thinking while I was at the gig, how happy I am to be able to practice for stuff like that. To just bring you're a game at all times, and any musician that's practicing – and I say that because I practice still – and I think in order to call yourself a musician, you've got to be practicing. You can be other things that are musical, you can be say a songwriter or an arranger, but to truly be a musician you've got to be picking up your instrument, and that's the thing that continues to give me joy.
>
> I've seen a lot of people fall out of love with their instrument, or feel like they've tapped it out, and I feel like the drums – for whatever reason – is

just such a fucking difficult instrument to play, and there's always so much more to do, that I just never see it ending, which is crazy, to have a gift like that's just continuously giving you back. Its like an endless well…

"I've always said, 'When you play a song, you have to serve the song. It isn't your drumming or bass playing, or how great of a musician you think you are, this is about serving the song,' because that song will remain when you're gone, that song will always be there." – Matt Sorum, 2015

(photo by Rocco Guarino)

Chapter 12: Matt Sorum of Guns N Roses/Velvet Revolver – Locomotive

If you asked the average Rock & Roll fan or critic to list the most memorable drum intros that kick off a song in the past 40 years, you'd come up with a only handful of songs that leap off the tongue. It's a small club that includes *"Rock and Roll"* by Led Zeppelin's John Bonham, *"Walk This Way"* by Aerosmith's Joey Kramer, *"Hurts So Good"* by John Mellencamp hitter Kenny Aronoff, *"Smells Like Teen Spirit"* by Nirvana's Dave Grohl, and *"Paradise City"* and *"You Could Be Mine"* by Guns N Roses' Steven Adler and Matt Sorum respectively. Handed the sticks not by his predecessor, but rather by a band under pressure to follow up the best-selling hard rock debut album of all time, Appetite for

Destruction, Sorum had just that as he stepped up to fill the hottest empty slot behind the drums in Rock:

> I came into Guns N Roses when they were struggling to find a drummer. They had tried 3 or 4 other guys and it just wasn't clicking, and then when Slash and Duff saw me with the Cult, I think they felt the solid, stellar sort of regimented feel throughout the music. They knew that I could walk in and be the guy who was strong enough the music, and so when I walked in, I'd never heard the material before. We just got up on stage and started hashing through the riffs, and we worked and got things done very quickly.

Answering with a resounding thunder any question about whether the band had their man, Matt would establish his signature as a tom-tom acrobat with the lead single from the band's Use Your Illusion double-whammy, and remembered the memorable moment that opened *"You Could Be Mine"* – which became the theme song for Terminator 2 and Popmatters.com later observed "couldn't have been a better teaser: sound-wise, it took advantage of a big budget that only a Diamond-selling album could have bought, but it still contained that guttural menace that brought statements calling the group the next Rolling Stones." Remembering the fill that launched a phenomenon as a happy accident that arrived while working on the song in the studio, Sorum shares his recollection that

> what happened was, on the second or third take, I did that tom fill almost as like a joke and threw it in as an extra. And I counted the song off and I started the fill, and then everyone looked over and I'd never done it before, and were like "That was awesome!" So that became my signature fill, and it was a really great way of capturing people's attention, and what we realized early on was in the songwriting process is what you want to do in the first 10 seconds is capture people's attention. Whether it was the riff, or if that's with a guitar, or if that's with the drums or bass, the thing that we would so is, Slash would say "Do you wan to take the intro to this?" And I'd say "Let me try something," and what we wanted to do was, when

> you turned on the radio all of a sudden, you're not taking 2 minutes to get into the song. We've got to get them from the get-go, and that fill caught everybody's attention.
>
> That drum beat came from Duff's rolling bass line, so I was really sort of listening to the bass when the tom thing started happening. That pattern was played with a single kick and tom. I always say to drummers: I break out my instrument before I play the drum kit. I always tend to listen to the guitar riff and what's happening in the basic riff for whatever I'm going to be playing on the kick drum, and a lot of times, the cymbal work follows the guitar too. But if I'm working a lower register, like if the bass is leading, I tend to want to work in the tom toms to keep things in sort of a lower register, so I'm not going to step on a bass line with a cymbal or a crash or a ride. If anything, I'd play the hi-hat against a bass, so I was always taught "Ride your hi-hat against the bass."

Sorum's riding partner in the pocket, Duff McKagan, would round out one of the tightest in Rock & Roll, a posse whose chugging gallop could be heard leading a charge with the power and groove IQ of John Bonham and John Paul Jones on other early favorites of Sorum's like *"Locomotive,"* where "it was the same thing: we came up with when me and Duff were fucking around one day. Me and Duff had a really good chemistry when it came to communicating and you gotta remember, those are the early stages of me being in the band, so it was almost like this fresh sort of thing coming in, and they'd already done *Appetite* and were trying to branch out. People always go on and on about *Appetite for Destruction*, and the reality is bands grow and bands change, and you want to push the envelope, and so when I kicked into that with Duff, it just sort of felt right, and I remember even going and grabbing the right snare, because I wanted a snare that had kind of a funky pop to it. That was a white Noble and Cooley snare drum, and I remember I cranked it up kind of high and fucked around with shit like that. " In designing the new drum sound he was bringing to Guns N Roses, Sorum began with the foundational notion that

> I wasn't just going to play the whole album with the same snare drum. I always thought "Well, there's a lot of drummers who have signature snare sounds." Like Alex Van Halen's got a certain snare sound on every song, and I started thinking about snare like another instrument, like playing a different guitar or a different bass where you have a different tone or amp, so I've got that sort of sound in my backbeat, I've got a certain way I rim-shot the snare, and I like to dig in and make it crack. But when I got that drum up on that song, that was like, "Okay, this is cool, this is funky, its got a great sound, it fits in the track properly," I remember I even changed my hi-hat. I used 14s and I used to play with 15s, but I wanted tighter on the hat, and I fucked around with shit like that.
>
> Duff is a lead bass player, he's like a Paul McCartney or John Paul Jones, he's a signature guy, you can't listen to *"Sweet Child O'Mine"* without identifying Duff's bass line, its like listening to Led Zeppelin without John Paul Jones. Duff's an integral part of the GnR sound, and when we played, Duff would watch me and I led him and he sat in the seat, if you will, but at the same time, as a drummer or a bass player, there's no sort of fighting it, you just sort of sit in it, it's a real comfortable feeling, and that's what I get with Duff.

Sorum's downbeat to discovering the talent that would take him all the way to the Rock and Roll Hall of Fame first hit him decades earlier when he shared an epiphany with the rest of his generation of inductees watching what is now permanently known as "the night that changed America," when a young Matt remembered receiving

> my first inclination to want to be a drummer. When the Beatles came on Ed Sullivan and everybody in American was watching, John and Paul may have been up front singing, but I basically had tunnel vision for Ringo because he was up on the drum riser and was a character to look at, and it was a bit like a cartoon character to me. Being a young kid and you see someone whose

> animated like that, before you know it, somehow that animation translates to "That's something I wanna do."
>
> It was similar to a kid who might see a fire engine go by and why are they gravitating to that? Well, it's the wild siren, the guys dressed in cool hats, the uniform and the red engine and same thing with a train, so there was something visual to it that stimulated me and I think that's what I saw in Ringo – the whole big picture of that image that he was portraying at the time. It wasn't necessarily his musicianship, but to be that young and be transfixed on something that said to you, "This is something I want to do, I want to be like that guy!"

Lucky to have the leg up of not having to sell his parents on bringing a musical instrument into the house given that "my family was musical," Sorum revealed of his distinguished musical lineage that "my grandfather was a Professor of Music at Rochester, New York and ended up at University of California, Long Beach, Dr. Robert Winslow. His major instrument was Brass, he was a trumpet player, and then that trickled down to my mother who was a classically-trained pianist, and then she was basically a choir teacher and also played the organ in churches when I was a kid and taught piano around the house. Then my older brother was a classically-trained violinist, and very proficient at a young age and always was first chair, and my middle brother didn't have much musical stuff going on except that he was really into Rock & Roll, and bought me my first record at age 6, *A Hard Day's Night,* after the Beatles came to America." Begging his parents for the kind of headache holiday gift that comes with a hyper-excited child asking Santa for his first drum set, Matt's St. Nick wish came true that year

> when it came time for Christmas that year, I said "I would really like to be a drummer," and there used to be drums that were sold in the Sears and Robuck and Montgomery Ward, you could get them in a catalog, and my mother had the catalog and I saw it: there was a little Sears Tigger Tiger

> drum, and it was a drum set with a picture of Tony the Tiger on the front. So that was another way I kind of got roped into wanting to be a drummer at like 5 years old.
>
> When I think about why did I gravitate toward wanting to go and bang on drums, and I always think that people find their destiny in so many different ways, where something catches their attention. That's why I'm so interested in kids, and I work with kids a lot and see the little spark in their eye and am thinking, "That could be the spark that changes their life forever," especially between the ages of 3 and 6 because kids are just these little sponges. We don't really accept their intelligence at that age, but they do what feels right at the time and enjoy shit and its bold, but as we get older, we start to shut those intuitions down and try to say, "Oh, I'm not going to listen to that voice," but I tried to always be true to my intuition, and my intuition at a very young age was that that was sort of it. I remember dreaming about drums, and how big a set of drums I could have – it was all I knew at that point forward, and I'd draw drum sets in this folder I used to keep at school and all that stuff.

Growing up in the golden age of the late 1960s and early 1970s just as Heavy Metal and Hard Rock were still young themselves and their first generation of stars were being born. Their limelight inspired a million kids to pick up instruments, whether it was Eric Clapton with his custom Gibson Fender his Ginger Baker shining behind his Silver Sparkle Ludwig drums, dazzling aspiring drummers like Matt who still looks back on it all as

> the perfect time to grow up, it was based on drummers, because out of The Beatles came Cream and Ginger Baker, and by the time I was in Junior High School it was the early 70s, so bands were coming out that were focused on drummers. So the drum language was very loud in those days, and those guys were identifiable and had names that went with it and were characters, so you were able to gravitate towards a guy like Ginger Baker:

> he had this kooky weird name and he played drums in a very unorthodox way, he was an African-style drummer, he didn't play like a white person, and the fact that he was out front, that was another guy along with Ringo that I gravitated towards.
>
> Then I started getting into early 70s music like Deep Purple, and the first time I ever saw a drummer play backwards, that was Ian Pace. He was a left-handed drummer, and I remember gravitating towards him not only because he could play backwards but also for his speed – he could play real fast, and I remember thinking that was exciting. I think when young kids are listening to heavy metal, or Neal Peart for both his speed and technical ability, so I kind of took the things that spoke to me and that's why later I became the drummer I am: I understood technical ability but I still liked the character in drummers. I liked to know that there was a drummer that was gonna bring something besides just being a good drummer to the picture, and that's why I started getting in bands.

A natural leap forward in his evolution as a journeyman behind the kit, every day when the bell rang and school let out, Sorum rocketed just as quickly out of class and "home from school and practice, because my parents got home around 5:30, 5:00, and I was only allowed to really play when they were gone, so I would hustle home and remember after last period, running down the street to get to my house and get on the drum set, and I did a couple 3 hours in there banging away, and it was just pure joy." A euphoria that continued to lift his ambition higher and higher toward dreams of Rock Stardom, Matt quickly realized that joining his first band was both a vehicle toward getting him more time to practice each day and an important transitional step that would allow him to begin playing in front of an audience:

> After my parents got home, I wasn't allowed to really make noise anymore, so I would play as much as I could, and by the time I was in the 7th grade, I was already putting bands together, and started realizing I was a band guy.

It wasn't about me being a flashy soloist or doing anything crazy like that, I liked playing songs and playing with other guys, and I started practicing with my band. So in the early days of my playing, I used to practice a lot, but I always say that the guys who are really great drummers or great, great technicians, the thing that got me going right away was being in a band.

By the time I was in high school, I had the coolest band in my town: we played all the parties, we played all the dances, and we were the coolest guys in the school. This was my band Prophecy, and I had found this guitarist named Jeff Ferris who was like the premier local guy, I've got to say he was the closest thing to Jimi Hendrix I'd ever heard, and we started this 3-piece band and before we knew it, we were already playing up in Hollywood. So at 14 years of age, I'd tell my mom I was going to go stay at my friend's house for a slumber party and in those days, there were no cell phones, there was no tracking devices, so we'd go up the Freeway, play a show, and I could be back at my friend's house by like 1 in the morning. So I was playing in clubs on the Sunset Strip when I was 15 years old, and they'd sneak me in the back door because I was the youngest guy in the band.

For as far as he'd already traveled by that point, Sorum would soon realize he still had a long way to go toward mastering such important drumming dynamics as swing and feel. Thankfully, Matt possessed the kind of on-steroids enthusiasm to learn that could only be met with an equally expansive opportunity to soak up new knowledge, and he'd meet that mentor stylistically in the discovery of Jazz:

What happened in High School was in the 70s in High School, you were allowed to take what was called 3 electives, meaning you could pick your curricular activities outside of Mathematics and Science and stuff. So in those days, there was a lot of music classes, so I took Marching Band, Wind Ensemble, and Jazz Band. So I had 3 different music classes a day, which is like pretty unbelievable for that era, where other kids were taking Home Economics or Shop. So I started my day taking Marching Band, and then I

> would find myself in Jazz Ensemble in 3rd period, and they were 40 minute classes each, so the Jazz influence came in with Big Band during my Jazz Ensemble class and I had an amazing teacher, Terry Newman, who ended up being the guy who really made me want to be a professional, because he saw something in me that I didn't see in myself.
>
> In those days, we played a lot of charts, like from Maynard Ferguson's *"MacArthur Park"* and *"Chameleon,"* and there were 3 drummers, so it would become about "Who could perform the music best?" So there was a guy who played with a real light feel and was a little bit jazzier to me, and I would try to add a little bit of a wallop and the *"Chameleon"* chart had a little bit of a funk feel to it, it had swing to it, but it had a bit of a funk rock influence, and Terry would always pull me up front for those tracks, and those were the ones that were showstoppers. I was like a Conductor, I always felt like the drummer needed to be like the conductor to the band and really drive the band.
>
> I realized early on that I could lift the band up if I kicked them in the ass with the drums, meaning I wasn't going to let them lead me, I was going to lead them. But when I realized I was a Rock & Roll drummer, is when I started dabbling in fusion and Jazz music toward the end of High School, and I was listening to Lenny White and Billy Cobham and Return to Forever with Stanley Clarke and Tony Williams and Weather Report, and I started thinking I was going to be a Jazz fusion musician.

Bringing that acceleration full circle back into his Rock & Roll roots would not come without the growing pains that come with being a teenager feeling so impassioned about one's love for something that it can begin to take on pompous proportions. Sorum admitted struggling with this symptom a bit first-hand as he felt the difference in demand between the music he was being challenged to play in class and what he was banging out with his Highschool band after school:

> My friend and I had a band, and we were playing more like hard rock, Black Sabbath and Deep Purple, and I started becoming a little bit of a Jazz snob, like "Those guys aren't real musicians, listen to this shit!", and they'd kind of laugh at me. Then at one point, a couple of them sat me down and tough-loved me, and said basically what needed to be said to me: "You know what Matt, you're a great Rock drummer but you're not a great Jazz drummer," and I said "Well, what do you mean? I can be," so they replied, "Look, you need to go with what you do best, and you're a really great rock drummer." That's when it all of a sudden dawned on me, that I needed to focus on being a rock drummer, and that's when I decided "I am a Rock Drummer, that's what I do."

Still, by then, the Jazz/Big Band influence over Sorum's swing and feel had been permanently impressed into his sensibilities as a player, especially within its live performance side where – in the grand tradition of pioneers like Krupa and Moon – "when we'd go do an event, I'd get up on the kit and I realized pretty early on that people were looking at me and that I could do stuff to capture everyone's attention when there was 25 other guys on stage in a Big Band. All of a sudden, I became like referred to as a showy kind of drummer, and I actually tamed myself down quite a bit when I joined The Cult and Guns N Roses years later, but back then, I'd spin my sticks and was pretty showy, like Gene Krupa and in my rock band as well because I loved Keith Moon." Knowing his future lied in making the type of full-time commitment he'd already had locked in for years to becoming a professional player, for Matt, that duty to his dream meant moving onto the Sunset Strip fulltime:

> As soon as I saw what was going on in the clubs, that's when I caught the Hollywood bug, once I saw the energy of that, that's what said to me, "As soon as I get out of High School, this is where I'm headed." I felt the energy of the city, and you gotta remember, this is the late 70s, so Rock & Roll was on fire in those days, and that's what I did: as soon as I graduated, I packed my bags and threw my drums in my car, and it was only 60 miles

North from Orange County where I grew up, and I actually left Prophecy after 4 years of playing together because I'd told them, "Guys, if we want to make it in Rock & Roll, we gotta get out of here, we have to go to where the action is! We can play dances and parties for the rest of our lives, but if we're not going to be putting this on a record, we're never gonna get seen."

My parents weren't around at that point. My mother bought a sail boat and she and my stepfather decided they were going to sail around the world, and my two older brothers had already moved out and gone. So I was kind of solo, and I was always taught that. It was always instilled in me as a kid, and I was never a spoon-fed kid, like "You can live here as long as you want…" I don't want to say I was kicked out, but my parents basically gave me an ultimatum like "We're selling the house, you can either come on the boat with us, or you can venture off on your own," and I said "Well, my destiny is music so I'm going to head up to Hollywood and give it a shot," and

The rest of the guys in my band said, "Well, I can't leave, I've got my girlfriend that doesn't want me to move," and another guy had a job at a bank he said he couldn't leave, so I took off on my own, and didn't have any money in my pocket and didn't really know where I was going, except for I saw in the Recycler there was this drummer guy looking for a roommate. So I moved in with this other drummer and a bass player guy, and it wasn't like I really got any financial support, but my Stepfather was very strict, and was like "If you're gonna be a man, go out there and make it on your own." So in a way, as hard as it was, in the early days that I called my "Starving Years," I paid my dues, and those dues that you pay as a musician, if you have the wherewithal to stick with it, knowing you have something – regardless of what happens or what people say to you – it's a reason to drive on, and at the same time, I didn't really think I had much else to offer as my talent. I was like, "I'm a really good drummer, and people like that about me, and that's who I am."

Those starving years were spent racking up miles and miles of experience behind the kit, learning a thousand songs and earning a degree of expertise in Top 40, Hard and Classic Rock, and Metal that would serve him well in staying steadily employed around the L.A. club circuit. Practicing the tried-and-true adage of "taking any gig you can get" when just starting out in the world of the professional playing circuit, Matt was a industrious networker, maintaining a work-a-holic schedule where

> for a while there, I was just trying to make a living and not have to work a day job, and I never did work a day job, to my benefit, I could always say to myself, "I never had to do a regular 9-5," I always worked as a drummer from the minute I moved to Hollywood. I always found things to do, whether it was going and rehearsing with a band for $20 or playing a show for $50, I did it, and at one point in my early career, I would be in 7, 8, 9, 10 bands at a time.
>
> So I would do Top 40 four or five nights a week, I would play 5 sets a night, and one early player I met out on that circuit was Josh Freese, when he was a kid he saw me, and I saw him when he was 15 and already playing the clubs, and it was pretty much I was on one stage, Gregg Bissonnette was on another, Josh on a different one, and this is back when we were playing every Top 40 gig in town. So if I had a gig and had to go play with my regular band, of which I had quite a few, I could call a guy like Gregg Bissonnette or a bunch of other drummers who would sub for me. So we would switch off gigs, and al of these guys were such great musicians, they could walk in and 5 sets of music in a night, 45 minute sets. We'd start at 8 and get the dinner set, 15 minute break, and you'd play 8, 9, 10, 11, 12 1 o'clock, 5 or 6 sets a night of Top 40, 5 nights a week.
>
> That's when I really got my chops together because I was playing every night, and I had to learn all these songs, because the reason they called it Top 40, these were the days when clubs were run by musicians, not DJs, and you'd

> go in and play the latest charts, so it could be Loverboy into Tears for Fears into Prince, and you'd play all these styles of music. And I'd have to learn all these songs, basically by listening to them on cassette on the way to the gig, and I started being able to figure out how to listen and learn quickly, and I'm still good at that. I can listen to a song and play it almost instantaneously, like I went out with Motorhead and didn't rehearse once. They called me and said "Can you do this?", and I had no problem saying "Yes," because I wasn't scared. I've seen other guys who have to transcribe it all out, but I do it differently: I always try to take the music inside me and not have to read it off a piece of paper, even though I can read.

Even against that diverse backdrop of stylistic specialties, at heart, Sorum throughout remained "a Rock & Roll drummer when I woke up in the morning," revealing a deeper metamorphosis taking place where he and his dream truly became one and the same: "When you encapsulate that into who you are as a human being, you feel it kind of in a deeper sense, and so when I first moved to Hollywood, I dabbled in other stuff, like playing briefly for Gladys Knight and the Pips, and Solomon Burke, and did a couple of R&B things, and did some Blues sessions and played in a band with this guitar player, Greg Wright, we were more of a Texas blues 3-piece, and always got an opportunity to push it and try other styles, even when I got into Tori Amos's band, which was more of a new wave/experimental. But what I realized in my early 20s when I started doing more sessions, and made kind of a little bit of a niche for myself in the studio world, before I became a more well-known rock drummer, was that it wasn't until I got into The Cult that I was solidified as a Rock Drummer." The kind of proverbial "big break" moment Matt had been beating his way towards for the better part of 10 years professionally and all his life as a Rock & Roll dreamer would finally come true in 1989 when Ian Astbury and Billy Duffy shown the world one of Hollywood's true diamonds in the rough, giving Sorum his first chance to shine on a national stage as the band's live drummer on the "Sonic Temple" tour.

As one of the hottest guns for hire in the business, Matt in the process established his specialty of, "if you look at my career, always being a guy to come in and replace someone," and with The Cult, the drummer was stepping into the considerable shoes of veteran session/live hitter Mickey Curry, who had logged hits with Alice Cooper, David Bowie, Tom Waits, Elvis Costello, Tina Turner, Bryan Adams, and The Cult before Sorum stepped into the stirrups. Tapping into the years of training he'd racked up playing across the entire spectrum of styles and genres to learn the band's back catalog in the short time he had to before hitting the road, the drummer proudly affirms that to this day,

> I listen to the records, play along with them, and then walk in and had it nailed, so when I came into the Cult, I had a large catalog of music that I had to walk in knowing, and I always say, "If you're going to walk into an audition and play with a band, you better have your bases covered." You better know how to dress, how to act, be on time, and a lot of what goes into being a musician and the reason I've got a career is my ability to be open minded and willing to try anything with any other band that I've been in, and as a drummer, knowing your position in the band and giving it your all as the foundation of the band, and being something that lifts the band up. I've met kids that are really great but who are walking around with way too much attitude for their own good, but at that point in my career, I was feeling pretty good about things. I was in a really cool band, I'd found my stride. I fit really well, my groove was right for them, and my style – which was meat and potatoes Rock & Roll drumming – was right for The Cult.

The position would give Sorum enough credibility and visibility within the Rock & Roll stratasphere to quickly shine as one of its brightest rising stars behind the kit, soon catching the attention of the wandering eyes and ears of Slash and Duff McKagan as Guns N Roses was on the quick hunt for a new drummer to replace the recently-fired Steven Adler. Matt would shoot up enough flair within his flashy, powerhouse style and substance to make his suitors feel he might be their needed new ingredient:

> When I joined Guns, it was a little different thing. Steven Adler had a little bit different feel than I did, he was a little bit more Street-Garage style, there was no technical ability in it at all, where I dabbled in technical ability and what I would call finesse. I always prided myself on having a little bit of that thing where, if you look at drummers connected with a band who have a unique style or sound, ala The Who, where drummers really set the mark. In Guns N Roses, I was the guy who kind of added the backbone to it to hold it all together.

Hitting the road on a stadium tour shortly after joining the band that would spread into 197 shows across 27 countries, the drummer credits his training camp playing live with The Cult right as the band was beginning to blow up on Radio and MTV, launching Matt right into the arenas the band soon graduated out of after starting out in Theatres. For Sorum, the elevation was huge for both his confidence and professional experience in working large audiences while at the same time keeping the beat for both the band and its fans live, and a transition he credits with preparing him for the sea-of-people crowds he'd soon be facing drumming for Guns N' Roses:

> I don't think I could have walked into Guns N Roses had I not had the arena experience I got with The Cult. So by the time I got to GnR, playing on a stage in front of 25,000 people was just another day at the office, like when I took the stage at Rock in Rio, we were playing in front of 500,000 people, and it was the most comfortable feeling I've had in a long time. I said, "This is exactly what I'm supposed to be," and when I sat down and kicked into the first song, *"Pretty Tied Up,"* all of a sudden I felt the energy of the audience and the whole atmosphere that was out there around me sort of took over my body. I can't really explain it, except for the fact that I was knowledgeable enough to know that feeling, and I've been in that position many times in my career. Now, any other drummer might have gotten up there and shit his pants, but I didn't feel that way at all, and I've always said,

> at the beginning, playing stadiums with Guns N Roses, that was an everyday occurrence for us, and so going back to play arenas was sort of intimate.
>
> What I try to do more than anything now is keep myself calm before I go on stage. I try to be relaxed because I don't want to overcompensate and play way too fast. Most of the bands I've been in, I don't play to a click, I don't do any of that, what I want to do is make sure I'm playing the songs as close to the right tempo, I want to lock in, I want to get the best groove possible. And still to this day at my age, being on stage, the more mature I get, the more mature my playing gets. So like, in Hollywood Vampires, I felt like all those years of experience paid off, because here we were at The Hollywood Bowl and that was our first show, and everybody else was like "Oh my God!", and I was like "We'll be alright…" (laughs)

Even before he hit the road with his new bandmates, Matt would get a warm-up session learning the material and composing his drum parts he'd be playing out on tour in real time with their recording over the spread of two albums and thirty songs in three short weeks. Revealing that behind the scenes of the band's badboy Rolling Stones Rock & Roll partying lifestyle laid a real work ethic that set the tone from the first time he ever hooked up with the band, as he got down to it in the studio writing with his new bandmates, Sorum remembered the band grinding at a grueling pace from day one:

> This was a worker band. Everyone has this sort of mystified idea of what we did, like everybody was fucked up all the time, and it was just not the truth at all. Slash, Duff and Izzy Stradlin were premier songwriters, and really deeply cared about the craft and crafting the songs, so we'd start at noon and work throughout the night, and we'd play. We would play together until we were the place where we felt we could put it down on a piece of tape, and then we'd record it onto a Dat.
>
> Then at the end of the day, we'd mark this big board we had with all the songs listed, and we'd say "That one's ready," and we'd go through 2 or 3 songs a

> day, and we would, at the end of each day, have some sort of arrangement or idea of what it was, and we wouldn't stop until we had it right. Then we'd take a little break, get a couple beers, and we'd get back to work, and we'd do that 5-6 days a week, and it wasn't fun and games. Once I stepped in, they were like "Let's get this going, let's start the record."

Racing out of the gate for a test-drive with the band recording their now-legendary re-invention a certain Bob Dylan classic for the soundtrack to the Tom Cruise racecar movie *Days of Thunder,* Sorum divulges of his very first recording session ever with the band that "the first track I ever cut for Guns N Roses was *'Knockin' On Heaven's Door!'* That was sort of a precursor to Use Your Illusions, and it actually became a song included on the album. I think I'd heard Steven Adler's live version in passing but didn't want it to reflect on what I was going to do, and I didn't overthink it in those days. It was a pretty simple song, and I ended up just playing what I felt like at the time. We went into Studio A at the Record Plant, and we were actually trying out the room as a band to see if it would be a good place to record, so we all went in the big room so we could set up live, and Duff and Slash had their spots to stand, and I set up the kit in the middle of the room. At the time, I used Jeff Porcaro's drum tech, who set up a Gretch kit in there for me."

The momentum he'd drummed up with the band quickly became contagious around the band's inner circle, spinning enough buzz to eventually catch the curious ear of the band's frontman, lead singer Axl Rose, who's seal the drummer revealed would make his place in the band permanent. The coup to steal Sorum away from his on-loan homebase with The Cult began shortly after Rose walked in to the first rehearsal where he and Matt ever came face to face, with the drummer cracking a smile as he remembers seeing the singer's own upon hearing him play:

> When we went in to start the record, the first couple weeks that we were working on that material, there was no sign of Axl, and then he showed

> up about 2 weeks in because Slash and Duff had called me and said "Axl's coming in today." At that point, I was only going to do the record and then go back to The Cult, but then Axl walked in and saw me playing with the band, and he pulled Slash aside and then Slash took me up to his house and asked me to join. I think they felt something different about me, # 1) I was showing up and was together – sure I drank a few beers and would have a couple shots – but we were just a bunch of regular guys being in a band, being together, being dudes and # 2) Axl had told Slash, "I really like what's going on," and the music was coming together.

As Rose began communicating with Matt on a musical and compositional level, they quickly got started to work plotting what would become a trilogy of stories connected by a now-legendary tom fill that the drummer reveals here was in fact so fitting to each of the pieces it accompanied that he used identically throughout all three as a signature. Pulling the curtain back on the myth that drumming on a slow song is easy because its simple as a part, Sorum shared that as he went about listening to Rose's narrative, in his mind, he began weaving three of the album's biggest hits – *"Don't Cry,"* a smash that cracked the Top 10 on the Billboard Hot 100 Album Chart, *"November Rain,"* which remains the band's highest-charting hit to date at # 3, and *"Estranged,"* which cost $4 million to shoot a music video for and became one of the band's biggest MTV-rotated hits – together through the recurrence of

> that drum fill that everybody knows me for, "Bom, bom, bom bom bom," because I use the same drum fill in all three songs! That's the correlation between those songs – *"Don't Cry," "November Rain"* and *"Estranged"* – was that they were a trilogy and was actually sewn together and connected, that's a complete series of music. Nobody can really understand what that means except for the fact that those 3 songs are inner-connected. Axl Rose came to me and said, "Matt, these three songs are connected lyrically, they all represent part of a trilogy, it's a story line, but it basically starts with *"November Rain"* and goes into *"Don't Cry,"* and comes out with *"Estranged."*

> So Axl asked me to find some more of representative thing that could tie the songs together, and I came up with the idea of the drum fill. People would razz me about it, and I said to a couple drummers, "Look, the signature of that fill, as simple as it was, became part of the song." Its like, it wasn't the most brainiac drum fill in the world, but the idea was to bring a melodic part that was sewn throughout, almost like a hook. In fact, I believe I played that fill 23 times through those 3 songs, and that was on purpose, and I didn't think I couldn't come up with something different, but I wanted to be part of the musical passage. When Axl heard it throughout all 3 songs, he said "Awesome, that's what I want!"

In designing the sonic atmosphere of the album's drum sound, Matt found true teammates in producer Mike Clink and drum tech Jimmy Doyle, who helped him match the right drums to the right songs. Taking fans inside a look at the dynamic knowledge a drummer needs to have in the studio world, and an education Sorum got courtesy of his extensive resume hustling as a session drummer during his journeyman years chasing his dream around L.A., he recalled that

> when we went in to do Illusions, I brought in Jimmy Doyle, my drum tech from The Cult, and we set up my Rock Tour Custom kit, which I'd picked up when I first started playing for the Cult and endorsed Yamaha. At the time, I was playing a Birch kit, and it was lower line but a good-sounding kit, and I used to play 3 rack toms across the front, and I had 4 cymbals, and quite a bit bigger set-up. Then towards the end of the Cult, I went to a single rack tom and decided I wanted to be seen a little bit more, and then when I went in to record *Use Your Illusions 1* and *2*, I went back to playing a full 3 racks across the top, I believe I went 12", 13", 14", 16", 18," so I had 3 big rack toms. In those days, the Rock Tour Custom drums were pretty deep, and so I had the drums up quite a bit higher than I have them now. I had a pretty good set of cymbals, and a lot of shit going on.

> So I had quite a few drums around, and then I had a really good buddy of mine, Mike Gazzano, who has gone on to be become a big tech for Green Day and all the Rick Rubin records, and he brought in what became a pretty legendary snare on that record, Big Red, which was an old Tom Birch drum, and I started using that for all the ballads, including *"November Rain"* and *"Don't Cry."* Mike had started collecting drums as a tech, so we had 20, 30 snare drums sitting around the room to pull from, and then when it came time to cut the ballads, I grabbed the big 8 inch 14 x 8 tom because I thought I want to go for something real deep and thumpy and something that's going to have more of a low-end character to it. I didn't want to have some higher cracking kind of snare in a ballad. In Guns N Roses, I always had a side snare, and would either use it for a piccolo kind of thing or I would switch off the snare for Timbali.

Sorum's sound turned out to be just the shot in the arms critics felt the band needed to get the engines freshly fired up for their Stadium era, with Rolling Stone Magazine spotlighting their observation that "during the seventy-five and a half minutes of *Use Your Illusion II*…the drums slam…at the hands of new band member Matt Sorum," while years later, iTunes would celebrate "Sorum's lashing drum work" throughout the 150 majestic minutes of music. Diving into the story behind some of his other favorite performances from the album, he digs out one of the Illusion I's hidden treasures, *"Double Talkin' Jive,"* recalling in a reflection of the group's prodigal pace as songwriters, "that song was recorded in one take, we never even rehearsed it! Izzy Stradlin came in and had this riff which was based on sort of like Spanish Flaminco music, and I remember he came into the studio and started playing that lead electric riff, and I kicked in with sort of like this floor-tom/kick drum double bass drum kind of pattern." Sharing another secret from the session, Sorum – in a demonstration of just how talented a trick he's been playing on all the ears admiring and trying to imitate his double-bass technique – exposes the truth that

that was actually a *single kick,* I didn't play that beat with a double bass drum! My right hand was on the lower floor tom and I was playing the kick drum against it, so its basically creating like a rolling thing, but the trick of all that sort of power is to play your floor tom as hard as you play your kick drum. So my thing was, if I'm going to play this sort of rumbling double-bass drum kind of pattern, I'm going to play this on a floor tom, because I wasn't really doing double bass drum with Guns N Roses. I never any on the albums!

Inspired by what the Village Voice would later distinguish as "perhaps the best bassline on the *UYI* albums," Sorum's reaction to Duff and Izzy in *"Pretty Tied Up"* remains one of his favorites for sentimental reasons: "That was the first song I played at Rock in Rio, we opened the show with that! The reason I started the song with a hi-hat was the bass line, so it was a nice subtle opening, a nice subtle intro, what am I going to do to lend to the ambience? I'm going to use my cymbals in sort of an atmospheric way, and when I heard that, something in my head said "Go to the hi-hat, and make it kind of pop out," then when the band kicks in, give it a good wallop and then "Boom!", your in and all of a sudden the chorus lifts."

Guns N' Roses would dominate the first half of the 1990s, competing on every level of success and credibility commercially and creatively with the biggest Grunge acts of the day, holding down Rock & Roll's relevance at a time where it otherwise would have disappeared entirely. Exhausted from a 28-month trek around the globe, by the mid-1990s, once it was clear the band was breaking up for good in 1997, Matt decided to take a gamble on the reunion circuit when the call conveniently came from The Cult in 1999 to record a reunion record and tour the world at a time when fan fever for the band was starting to heat up in a major way, Sorum decided to take the dive, and though critics like Billboard would celebrate his "frenetic drumming" in rave reviews of the album like Uncut's, which proudly declared of the band's comeback that "it's loud, powerful and tight. Guitars scream as the drums imitate the bombing of Dresden....The return of a national institution." Sorum's rating of the results personally was lower than his fans' or critics, recalling that at the outset, his hopes were set far higher given the opportunity he felt The Cult had to ride the buzz their comeback was generating back into Millennium relevance:

> You gotta remember, times were changing, so as a musician, I would try to listen to what was going on in the universe and what was happening with music, so now we were coming into an album with a band who hadn't really had a hit record since basically when I'd left. After *Sonic Temple*, the *Ceremony* did okay, but it had been a good 10 years since they'd really had a solid record that was resonating on the air waves. They still had a good life career, and had a great live audience and great *cult* following, if you will, but when we went to do that record, there was a lot of Nu Metal and bands like Stained and Incubus. All these weird bands were at the top of the charts, and I like Incubus, but it was interesting with the beats what the drummers were doing, because they were dabbling in drum and bass, and there were interesting, weird things happening in the music that came from Hip Hop.
>
> So when we sat down to talk about it, me and Bob Rock, and Bob would say "What can you do on this to make this a little cooler?", and I kind of fought him a little him a little bit, because I wanted the Cult to remain true to its core sound, and I was thinking more AC/DC with the Cult, like "Let's go back to the early days and try to re-create the *Love* album," and was like "Let's draw upon that and move that into record we're making now." Instead, we kind of listened outside of the band, and I wasn't really a fan of some of the music that was going on, and I wanted to keep the music more true to the Cult, but instead, the guitar started getting tuned lower, full step/half step, and my beats needed to be heavier, with the exception of a song like *"Ride"* where I play pretty straight forward. But when we did *"War,"* there were like these drum breaks and shit, and I wasn't doing James Brown-type drum breaks, I was doing them in more of a Hard Rock way. So if you listen to the beginning of that song, I was doing this kind of drum and bass thing, so I set up two snare drums, and had two snare drums on

> one song, so I'd play the main beat on the regular snare, but would go over to the left to play the break-beat on the side snare.
>
> So that was a difficult album to make, a hard record, we were experimenting, and there were actually a couple songs on that album that were cut at two different studios and actually have two different drum tracks on one song, because I started fucking around with crazy different sounds for the verses and choruses.

Velvet Revolver packed the kind of sexual energy Rock & Roll fans were clamouring for by 2004 when word hit the street that the musical core of Guns N Roses – Slash, Duff and Matt – would be teaming up with Stone Temple Pilots frontman Scott Weiland to smuggle a little *Contraband* onto radio. With the band's debut album, that's precisely what they would with hit singles including *"Slither,"* which shot to # 1 on the Billboard Hot Mainstream Rock and Modern Rock Tracks charts and won a Grammy for Best Hard Rock Performance, and the ballad *"Fall To Pieces,"* which stayed at # 1 for a record 11 weeks on the Billboard Hot Mainstream Rock Tracks chart.

Succeeding in preserving "its beloved roots: Glam meeting punk with a touch of grunge," the New York Times praised the band for maintaining "the impact of guitar riffs and power chords backed by mighty drumbeats." Wanting to walk the fine line between playing to the band's classic fans while still building relevance with the Millennial generation of Rock & Roll kids in the same time, Matt remembered that

> when we got into the *Contraband* album, we were coming out funky, coming out banging, we'd lived through the Guns experience, and when we went in to make the *Contraband* it was very apparent that the music needed to come out youthful. Obviously we were in our early 40s in that period, so here we are coming out with a new band competing with the younger audience and younger bands, but knowing that we still had a lot of Rock & Roll to give.

> So what happened on *"Contraband"* was we were coming out banging with *"Suckertrain Blues,"* which is a barn burner, and I remember I'm a little bit older, going "Maybe that's too fast, maybe we should slow it down?", but then Duff was like "No man, its fucking Punk Rock!" So I was like "Okay, cool," and then we did *"Dirty Little Thing,"* which is another barn burner, and Weiland was saying "Maybe we should slow it down more like STP?", and I was the one going "Naw, its punk rock." So we kind of put the energy in it in a youthful way.

Upon release, Rolling Stone Magazine would celebrate the return of "the tumbling growl of McKagan's bass and Sorum's hammering pulse," and it's a pocket Matt was happy to be back in with Duff, reflecting a respect built over 15 years playing together that while it had become intuitive by that point, still kept both of them on their toes as they'd become more mature musicians in the intervening years between bands:

> He listens, and I've even seen him stand next to me when he can't hear my bass drum and then watch my bass drum, if we're in a room where we don't have a good P.A. or something. He's very aware of what's going on with my kick drum, and even after Velvet Revolver, me and him have gotten tighter, and we have a thing that is really special. I've played with a lot of guys, and a bass player for a drummer is so important, I know a lot of drummers haven't been able to have a lifetime bass player like I have with Duff, but he's a drummer too, so he get's what I'm doing, and will always suggest things: "Try this or try that." So we have that rapport, and we've had maybe a couple arguments in the 25 years we've known each other, but not many, and one of the only arguments I've had with him was in Velvet Revolver when I wanted to slow *"Slither"* down and he didn't think so, and we kind of argued about it a little bit, but in a brotherly way. The song was almost screaming for attention.

Debuting at # 1 on the Billboard Top 200 Album Chart, by 2005, Goldmine Magazine would report that – back in Arenas again – "Velvet Revolver was one of the hottest bands around. Loaded with rock gods…(who) truly deserved its 'supergroup' status." The band would aim even higher with their sophomore studio album, 2006's aptly Libertad given the freedom the band was feeling creatively having proven themselves as a modern mover and shaker on the charts, a move Rolling Stone in their review of the band's eclectic sophomore outing would compliment as an "impressive act of defiance: a bandof old-school bad boys from twentieth-century megagroups who make a rocket-guitar racket that is more compelling than most current woe-is-me punk and emo." While some in the band understandably wanted to take some new chances on the band's new album, Matt remembered feeling it was equally as important to maintain their hard rock edge:

> When we went to do the second record, we were doing pretty well: we had a multi-platinum album, we'd done a sold-out arena tour, now were successful, and now we wanted to say some different stuff, especially Scott was wanting to make an album that had a little bit more subtlety, and I got worried at first because that had happened to STP, where they had started going pretty arty after the first two albums, and I just wanted to make another Rock & Roll record. I just wanted it to rock, and I thought that we needed to represent that. We needed to make a Rock & Roll album with sheer attitude and just let it blaze through.

What the band did pull was a more sophisticated brand of their hybrid stylistic sensibilities on display within both the songwriting and performance excellence like the hit single, *"The Last Fight,"* which the BBC distinguished as "one of the highlights of the album is the ballad. While it feels odd to use the adjective 'exquisite' to describe any of this band's type of full-on rock, with its haunting melody and subtle guitar line it wouldn't feel out of place on a classic Pink Floyd album." A triumphant tribute to lead singer Scott Weiland's fallen brother, Matt remembered pulling from his High School band days for inspiration

> when he brought *"The Last Fight"* in. When they started playing it, I went back to my Marching days and all the way back to what I'd learned playing rudiments and press rolls, because I was in drum core and I said "Well I can do something that would maybe be something like Steve Gadd would play?" So all those things were in my head.
>
> *"American Man"* was another single where I went back to when I played in all those Top 40 bands and learned all of these different different styles of music that I could take and put into Rock & Roll. I wasn't just playing a straight-up regular groove like every other Rock drummer would play, "Boom, whack, Boom Boom whack," its like "What can I do differently?" So I think I came up with a Motown beat on that, when it goes double-time, which is basically 4 on the floor kick and snare and then you turn it around, so its really a sped-up Motown beat.

Going solo, so to speak, in 2003 and again in 2014 when he released *Hollywood Zen* and *"Stratosphere"* respectively, Sorum seized the chance to display the multi-instrumental sides of his talented musical personality, with Billboard latest studio album for daring to explore "earthy, Americana singer-songwriter styles… bluesy ambience… Middle Eastern textures…(and) noir, orchestrated pieces," the last of which fulfilled a lifetime dream of Matt's:

> I always loved strings, and always wanted to make a record with an orchestra, so I did 3 tracks with orchestration. Then there are songs on the album that don't even have drums, that are mostly all percussion. I played all the drums on *Hollywood Zen,* but on my second solo album *Stratasphere*, I handed that off to someone else, and it was a relief to me because I wanted to make a different record. I didn't want to make a rock album, and at that point in my life I wanted to make a smart album, and I'm the "rock guy," but wanted to make a record to show people that I had something to say, and not even to show people, I just wanted to prove it to myself, that I could go out and make a work that was all me.

So on *Stratasphere,* what I did is I collected all of my favorite guys for that particular style, and I didn't call Duff or Slash – the obvious guys – I called all these other guys, and I went way out of the box. For me, it was very freeing to do it because I didn't care about the radio, I didn't care about selling records… It was probably one of the most magical times of my life as a musician because I was purely making music for music's sake. No agenda, no record company, I just wanted to say some shit, and I started becoming an activist and a philanthropist, and that was the first time I ever made a record purely based on myself.

Today, with his name routinely synonymous in press mentions with the rightfully-earned stature of *legendary*, Matt sits comfortably and confidently in the knowledge that "I don't feel I have to prove anything to anybody, because I really feel like I've done everything that there is to do in Rock & Roll, I've done it." Reaching the professional pinnacle of induction into the Rock & Roll Hall of Fame in 2012 as a member of Guns N' Roses, while the band's induction was shrouded in some controversy surrounding band members who didn't attend, Sorum was proud of the acknowledgment:

I'm very grateful for that tribute, and yes, was that a nice moment, of course, I mean that gives you a reason to have fought through all this stuff, and to have fought the good fight. When someone gives you an accolade, you want to be grateful. I fall into the ideology of Rock and Roll and what it means, which is a celebration of that.

I think my career as a musician has given me a life education, on so many things about myself, and I've taken a lot of things that have happened in my life and its actually turned me around as a human being. I can't say I was ever a bad guy, but I would say the life lessons I've learned all through my career – for someone who never went to college, I graduated High School – but all my education in life has come from my music career. I feel like I'm a pretty intelligent guy these days, and that's all from lessons learned through my music.

> I have a lot of knowledge and wisdom from it, but at the same time, when it comes to the Rock & Roll Hall of Fame and Awards and Accolades and all that kind of stuff, when you're a young musician, you're always trying to prove yourself, and especially living in Hollywood, its very easy to get caught up in "I gotta stay on top, I gotta keep moving," but I'm not like that anymore.

For those drummers who are still chasing the dream, or for those who have just picked up the sticks and sat down behind their first drum set, Sorum offers an honest lay of the modern-day landscape, beginning with the caution that "I would say anybody that's gonna just take on the idea of getting in the music business, and be a drummer and have a career, I would say fasten your seatbelt! You're gonna have to have more tenacity than any other person you know, and that you're gonna have to have a fuckin' suit of armor to be able to withstand the amount of stuff that you take on. Its not just some nice little ride through some mystical idea of what you might have, because it doesn't go down like that." From The Cult to Guns N' Roses to Velvet Revolver to his newest All-star project co-starring legends like Alice Cooper, Aerosmith lead guitarist Joe Perry, actor Johnny Depp as well as the permanent rhythm section of Duff McKagan and Slash, Matt maintains they same steady beat he's always kept as one of Rock & Roll's most durable drummers:

> Going up on stage and playing in a Rock & Roll band – and I don't want to say it because I've never been into battle – but probably the closest similarity would be going into battle, and its like, if you can take it, if you can take all the highs and lows of the music business, I'll guarantee, only the strong survive, and the ones that don't survive either quit or they die, and that's the truth. Its not like "Okay, we've lost a lot of great musicians along the way, and a lot of people just quit," and there's a reason for that, because if it was fuckin' easy, everybody would be doing it. At our first Hollywood Vampires show this year, I felt like all those years of experience paid off, because here we were at The Hollywood Bowl and that was our first show, and everybody else was like "Oh my God!", and I was like "We'll be alright…" (laughs)

Author Bio:

Award-winning Music biographer Jake Brown has written 44 published books since 2001, featuring many authorized collaborations with some of rock's biggest artists, including 2013 Rock & Roll Hall of Fame inductees Heart (with Ann and Nancy Wilson), living guitar legend Joe Satriani, country music legends Merle Haggard/Freddy Powers, heavy metal pioneers Motorhead (with Lemmy Kilmister), country rap superstar Big Smo, late hip hop icon Tupac Shakur (with the estate), celebrated Rock drummer Kenny Aronoff, legendary R&B/Hip Hop Producer Teddy Riley, late Funk pioneer Rick James, superstar country music anthology 'Nashville Songwriter,' and the all-star rock producers anthology 'Behind the Boards,' Rock & Roll drummers' anthology 'Beyond the Beats,' and the 'Hip Hop Hits' producers' series among many others. Brown recently released his first 20-chapter audiobook DOCTORS OF RHYTHM under a long-term deal with Blackstone Audio, and has also appeared as the featured biographer of record on Fuse TV's Live Through This series and Bloomberg TV's Game Changers series, in 2018 will appear in the BET "The Death Row Chronicles" series, and has received national press in CBS News, The Hollywood Reporter, Rolling Stone Magazine, USA Today, MTV.com, Guitar World Magazine, Billboard, Parade Magazine, Country Weekly, Fox News, Yahoo News, etc and writes for regularly for Tape Op Magazine (including the 2015 cover story feature with Smashing Pumpkins frontman Billy Corgan). In 2012, Brown won the Association for Recorded Sound Collections Awards in the category of Excellence in Historical Recorded Sound Research.

Look out in 2018 for the following
New Books In Stores From Jake Brown:

BEYOND THE BEATS:
Rock & Roll's Greatest Drummers Speak! Vol 1. Audiobook
(Due in Stores from Blackstone Audio March, 2018)

NASHVILLE SONGWRITER II:
The Inside Stories Behind Country Music's Greatest Hits
(Due in Stores August, 2018)

NASHVILLE SONGWRITER II Audiobook
Due in Stores from Blackstone Audio, August, 2018

MY LIFE IN A JAR:
The Book of SMO
(Due in Stores Fall, 2018)

SCIENTISTS OF SOUND:
Rock & Roll's Most Legendary Record Producers Speak!
(Due in Stores from Blackstone Audio, November, 2018)